Lloyd Kaufman: Interviews

Conversations with Filmmakers Series

Edited by Mathew Klickstein

University Press of Mississippi / Jackson

The University Press of Mississippi is the scholarly publishing agency of
the Mississippi Institutions of Higher Learning: Alcorn State University,
Delta State University, Jackson State University, Mississippi State University,
Mississippi University for Women, Mississippi Valley State University,
University of Mississippi, and University of Southern Mississippi.

www.upress.state.ms.us

The University Press of Mississippi is a member
of the Association of University Presses.

Cover photograph by Jan Willem Steenmeijer.

Copyright © 2025 by University Press of Mississippi
All rights reserved
Manufactured in the United States of America
∞

Library of Congress Cataloging-in-Publication Data

Names: Klickstein, Mathew, editor.
Title: Lloyd Kaufman : interviews / Mathew Klickstein.
Other titles: Conversations with filmmakers series.
Description: Jackson : University Press of Mississippi, 2025. | Series: Conversations with
 filmmakers series | Includes bibliographical references and index.
Identifiers: LCCN 2024043159 (print) | LCCN 2024043160 (ebook) | ISBN 9781496855206
 (hardback) | ISBN 9781496855213 (trade paperback) | ISBN 9781496855220 (epub) |
 ISBN 9781496855237 (epub) | ISBN 9781496855244 (pdf) | ISBN 9781496855251 (pdf)
Subjects: LCSH: Kaufman, Lloyd, 1945—Interviews. | Kaufman, Lloyd, 1945—Criticism and
 interpretation. | Motion picture producers and directors—United States—Interviews. |
 Motion pictures—Production and direction.
Classification: LCC PN1998.3.K3827 A5 2025 (print) | LCC PN1998.3.K3827 (ebook) |
 DDC 791.4302/33092 [B]—dc23/eng/20241030
LC record available at https://lccn.loc.gov/2024043159
LC ebook record available at https://lccn.loc.gov/2024043160

British Library Cataloging-in-Publication Data available

Contents

Introduction   ix

Chronology   xxvii

Filmography   xli

Filmmakers: Cecil B. in a West Side Walk Up   3
    N. R. Kleinfield / 1981

TROMA Films: They're Not Art, but They Make Money   6
    Jill J. Lanford / 1983

Savage Movies Don't Bloody Investors in Troma's Schlock   10
    Patrick Reilly / 1986

Cannes 87: Mayhem, Toxic Waste—The Fun Side of Cannes   14
    Jack Mathews / 1987

Green on the Screen   17
    Andrew Smith / 1992

Holy Shit! What Is All This Green Stuff?   20
    David Carroll / 1994

Lloyd Kaufman Chides AFMA on Press Freedom   30
    Lloyd Kaufman / 1994

Kaufman Brings His Mutants to Life in Tromaville   32
    Aaron Bell / 1997

Troma Entertainment: Movies of the Future!   35
    Doug Sakmann / 1999

Anything I So Desire   41
    Roel Haanen / 2001

A Tale of Two Toxies!   51
    Neil Dowling / 2001

Lloyd Kaufman Interview   55
    Vitorrio Carli / 2004

The Art of Trash: Evaluating Troma Entertainment as Paracinema   59
    James W. MacDonald / 2006

The Den of Geek Interview: Lloyd Kaufman   66
    Sarah Dobbs / 2008

Lloyd Kaufman   74
    Sean O'Neal / 2008

Lloyd Kaufman's San Diego Comic-Con 2009 Roast Retort   82
    Lloyd Kaufman / 2009

Produce Your Own Damn Movie!   86
    Beth Accomando / 2009

Lloyd Kaufman Interview   95
    Robert Ziegler / 2011

Lloyd Kaufman Interview with James Rolfe   100
    James "The Angry Video Game Nerd" Rolfe / 2013

Lloyd Kaufman on *Squeeze Play!*   113
    Lloyd Kaufman / 2013

Troma's Lloyd Kaufman: "I Hope the MPAA Burns in Hell"   115
    Simon Abrams / 2014

Getting Tromatized with Lloyd Kaufman, an Interview   120
    Ed Sum / 2015

Deep in the Bowels of Tromaville with Lloyd Kaufman   126
    Drew Fortune / 2017

I'm Lloyd Kaufman, President of Troma Entertainment and Creator of *The Toxic Avenger*!   130
    Lloyd Kaufman / 2017

Troma: A Love Story   146
    Leslie Pariseau / 2018

Lloyd Kaufman's Top Five Troma Films of All Time   160
    Chris Gore / 2020

Troma Cofounder Lloyd Kaufman Tells Us What Disgusts Him in Movies   173
    Danny Gallagher / 2022

The Clown and the Auteur   175
    Mathew Klickstein / 2023

Index   185

Introduction

Insulting art (like insulting the audience) is an attempt to head off the corruption of art, the banalization of suffering.
—SUSAN SONTAG, INTRODUCTION TO *ANTONIN ARTAUD: SELECTED WRITINGS* (1973)

The trouble with interviews is that you say the same things so often, you end up believing them.
—EDWARD GOREY

Lloyd Kaufman (b. 1945) is first and foremost one of the last great peppermint-stripe-suited, bow-tied showmen and entertainers in the Jewish American vaudevillian badchen style. He is a pioneering (if not *the* pioneering) force in contemporary filmmaking's postmodern paradigm of "schlock,"[1] a stridently DIY-based genre-bending mélange of over-the-top graphic violence/horror and engagingly fourth wall–busting Brechtian metahumor in the vein of "camp,"[2] typically infused with a prole-ish punk rock ethos.

Kaufman is also cofounder and president of fifty-year-old B to Z movie studio (quite possibly the longest-running independent studio in cinema history) Troma, and writer-director of more than fifty feature-length films of his own.

And he will likely be dead by the time this book is at long last published.

We have to face the brutal, pragmatic realities here twofold.

1) As poet Robertson Jeffers's stoical "Be Angry at the Sun" (1941) would nudgingly remind us, it's simply not worth investing any energy into frustrations stemming from the long-acknowledged snail's pace of book publishers these days (at least those not in the panicked throes of flailingly rushing out some extremely topical newsy tome, trending "influencer" and/or celebrity and/or media/political pundit's memoir/autobio/bio, or yet another sequel to some latest lusty YA novel/fantasy/graphic novel). This is especially true viz. those released in the academic/scholastic/university marketplace.

2) Despite having become a vegetarian in the early 2000s with daughter Charlotte after reading Eric Schlosser's impactful j'accuse *Fast Food Nation*

(2001), which also inspired Kaufman's own *Poultrygeist: Night of the Chicken Dead* (2006), American independent cinema's most irrepressible renegade takes notoriously terrible care of himself.

Exhibit, regardless his lifelong claims toward Eastern inspiration from Taoism and Zen, Kaufman's easily observable and well-documented neurotically compulsive driving of himself (and many of those around him) unrelentingly up the wall with all manner of stress about his place in the cinematic pantheon, the dozens of live-event and multimedia projects forever swirling around his general proscenium, and just about every possible global conflict happening all at once.

Meanwhile—at nearly eighty at the time of this writing—consider Kaufman's miraculously and perhaps dangerously jet-setting to anywhere and everywhere he can go to pitch, produce, support, and promote both his own ever-growing slate of filmic concoctions and those of his hundreds of acolytes who are only too aware that Kaufman, like some demented cross between an ejaculative birthday clown and "Crazy Eddie"–esque used car salesman, will appear to huckster when asked for the mere cost of even the lowest-grade travel accommodations, lodgings (air mattress/couch accepted), and Del Taco/Pizza Hut fare (just ask *South Park* [1997–] creators and filmmakers behind Troma's own *Cannibal! The Musical* [1993] Trey Parker and Matt Stone).

While wrapping up the final trappings of this omnibus of interviews, feature articles, Q&As, commentaries by Kaufman himself, etc., I was texting with the man probably best known for his thrusting upon the world stage the iconic *The Toxic Avenger* (1984) about this unfortunate revelation.

"We'll probably have the book launch during your eulogy, Lloyd," I (tongue somewhat firmly in cheek) explained to him. Which in turn led—as is so often the case with Kaufman both in actual "real-life" discussions with him and those you'll see presented in this very collection of articles—from the cartoonishly jokey to (*ahem*) deadly serious.

Kaufman's noted admiration for the works of Shakespeare (having "adapted" two major works to date—*Tromeo & Juliet* [1996] and *#ShakespearesShitstorm* [2020] based on *The Tempest*—and his constant touting of *Hamlet* as "101 Moneymaking Screenplay Ideas" as well as his repeated incantation of that play's "To thine own self be true") makes it ever the more potently apropos to recall, "Many a true word hath been spoken in jest," from the Bard of Avon's *King Lear*.

Despite the fact that you will read Kaufman's constant parroting of "To thine own self be true" no less than four times throughout the pieces ahead, it's this latter Shakespearean adage that may far better articulate if not encapsulate both Kaufman's consistently contradictory and nuanced weltanschauung and his similarly dualistic decades-in-the-making gesamtkunstwerk comprised of the most outrageously taboo-demolishing goofiness (inspired as he is by *Tom and*

Jerry [1940–]) and the most disruptively agenda-pushing agitprop (equally inspired as he is by 1960s counterculture godhead sociologist C. Wright Mills's *The Power Elite* [1956]). Well, all of that and the singular agenda expressed through his obstreperous declaration on the set of his *Tales from the Crapper* (2004): "I don't want dialogue! I want head squishing! And killing people!"

I can think of no better example of Kaufman's astonishing adeptness at conflating outlandish absurdity with devastatingly incisive (if not stunningly prescient) polemics than that of a particularly fractious fragment from his 1992 profile in the British sociopolitical magazine the *New Statesman* (with the subhead inquiring if "Troma films can save the world with an old-fashioned watch"):

> The profligacy of film-makers spending US$100 million on special effects seems slightly disgusting at this time. We're moving away from the form-over-substance ideas of recent years. It's for this reason we made the manufacturer put a traditional, circular face in the Toxie[3] watches [the US is awash with "Toxibelia"], rather than the usual digital ones. We wanted to encourage kids to grow up, viewing time as a circular continuum, rather than as a linear construct. If it's linear, you want instant everything, and you grow up to be a grasping, greedy, thoughtless person, a big fat slob with bushy eyebrows and a tendency to fall off boats—that's where that leads to. With the Toxie watch, indicating time as a continuum, kids learn to take a long-term view; they work hard, they save their money, they have a full and fruitful life, and Troma eventually becomes a major studio, strictly on its own terms.

And there we are. *Is Kaufman kidding here?* Is he vaunting some kind of pre-established, prepackaged, "marketable" "loose cannon" persona[4] for the purpose of breaking through the "white noise" of today's blaring media maelstrom? Or . . . do we need to "read between the lines" of what Kaufman is "actually" saying, and the very valid points he's making about the utter *obscenity* of how the mainstream movie scene operates and of the general Western societal sensibility writ large?

After all, what "reading between the lines" do we need to execute here? The man *says* exactly what he means, right up front and without any suppression of his typically splenetic umbrage at, as he himself would say, how "fucked up" "everything" is these days (even down to, say, how children are taught to understand the very system of Time Itself) . . . before going on to say that some tiny underground film company like his can invest the resources properly into ensuring wristwatches they merchandise from a popular film franchise in such a way as to perhaps, yes, "save the world." Truly, then, what's so funny about *that*?

It's long been my feeling that the best way to insert pertinent and impactful sociopolitical rhetoric into the zeitgeist is first through those cultural realms that are not much taken seriously (and thus left alone to their own devices, unexpurgated). We saw this in early punk rock and hip-hop music, for example. Nobody in the mainstream media took these idioms seriously (if they even knew about them, to begin with), and hence these prophetic outliers could "sneak in" much that could not be said elsewhere.

Was there any more apt and nuanced analysis of the outlandishly contentious 2016 presidential election season than that which was broadcast through the twentieth season of the long-running continuing story of *South Park* (1997–)? Show creators/runners (who, as mentioned, achieved their start under the Troma aegis) were able to "get away" with what they were saying (including a relentless fusillade of "truth bombs") in those provocative episodes because, well, "It's just *South Park*."

So too can we witness the same exacted by science fiction[5] godhead and the man responsible for such vibrantly prescient works as *Fahrenheit 451* (1953)[6] thunderingly railing at an audience of young fanboys (and a small smattering of fangirls) at the inaugural San Diego Comic-Con in 1970 that the *only* national publication worth reading is not anything from the "conservative press" nor the "liberal press" but rather—"*Goddamn it!*" he proclaimed—the cartoon-based humor magazine (and one of many early influences on Kaufman and Troma) *MAD*. To Ray Bradbury, *MAD* was more than a jokey underground rag of sorts. No, it was NEWS. And the *only* News worth reading during one of the United States' most volatile periods in contemporary times, at that.

As Southern Gothic writer and vehemently contrarian moralist Flannery O'Connor used to say, people are not seeing and listening to what they need to see and listen to these days, and thus they must be awakened through an electrifying and stimulating jolt that some may find uncomfortable to experience. How otherwise to awaken them from their befogged torpor?

In Troma terms, this translates to—as *Film Threat*'s Chris Gore opines in his COVID-time (2020) Zoom interview with Kaufman transcribed in this volume— "[W]hat I've always loved about the Troma films is, while there is an environmental thread through the Toxic Avenger's movies, there's also, you know, it's also just a super-fun movie. . . . It's kind of a parody of a superhero movie. It also has that messaging. But the way that you weave in messaging is: there will be blood, guts, um, comedy, nudity—all, to me, healthy ingredients—along with a little political messaging. But not so much that if you're not, you know. . . . You can just enjoy the movie. It's entertaining first."

Furthermore, we must acknowledge the vital essentialism of Kaufman's rather ascetic filmmaking style (some, including frequently Kaufman himself, may dysphemistically use the word "crappy"). This goes to the point, which he makes *very* often, that to best represent *authentically* the rather (let's use it again here) "crappy" state of affairs of the Kafkaesque modern-day world in which we all are consigned to exist, so too should Kaufman's stylistic expressions be, well, at times *crappy* too.

Think here of Marshall McLuhan's aphoristic "medium is the message" structuralism that encompasses the creation (and promotion) of such early postmodern and extremely brutalizing aesthetic systems as Brazilian scribe Augusto Boal's Theatre of the Oppressed;[7] Cuba's Imperfect Cinema; underground comix a la Gilbert Shelton's *Fabulous Furry Freak Brothers*, Frank Stack's *The New Adventures of Jesus*, and Robert Crumb's *Zap Comix*; the French Nouvelle Vague (along with "new wave" cinema of Iran, Germany, Britain, Czechoslovakia, etc.—all of which was portended and galvanized by the raw, cinema verité sensibilities of postwar Italian neorealism, of course); Detroit-based punk rock as exemplified in the very machine/industrial (think of the ubiquitous car manufacturing of the time and place) music of the MC5[8] and the Stooges; and the first novels of manically irascible author Hubert Selby Jr. who would refer to his body of work as "a scream looking for a mouth."[9]

It's worth noting that *all* of these creative movements first burbled up out of the mucky ground water of the same tempestuous times that Kaufman first got going with his feature film productions. All soon leading to such next-generation creative endeavors as hip-hop, the New York "No Wave" arts/music/film scene (buttressed by the deeper underground Cinema of Transgression), and eventually so-called "grunge" rock (with exemplar Nirvana front man Kurt Cobain referring explicitly to the "scream looking for a mouth" notion every time he spat his shrieking lyrics into a microphone).

Pretensions aside, it's all playing into the legacy brought on by such modern Western culture metaliterary works as Thomas De Quincey's *Confessions of an English Opium Eater* (1821), Walt Whitman's *Leaves of Grass* (1855), Fyodor Dostoevsky's *Notes from Underground* (1864), Arthur Rimbaud's *A Season in Hell* (1873), Knut Hamsun's *Hunger* (1890), Kate Chopin's *The Awakening* (1899), Upton Sinclair's *The Brass Check* (1919), Franz Kafka's "The Hunger Artist" (1922), John Dos Passos's *Manhattan Transfer* (1925), B. Traven's *The Death Ship* (1926), Herman Hesse's *Steppenwolf* (1927), George Orwell's *The Road to Wigan Pier* (1936), James Joyce's *Finnegans Wake* (1939), Ralph Ellison's *Invisible Man* (1952), Aldous Huxley's *The Devils of Loudun* (1952), J. P. Donleavy's *The Ginger Man* (1955), Allen Ginsberg's "Howl" (1956), Hannah Arendt's *Eichmann in Jerusalem* (1963), James Baldwin's *The Fire Next Time* (1963), Iceberg Slim's *Pimp* (1967), Joe McGinniss's *The Selling of the President* (1968), Hunter S. Thompson's *Fear and Loathing in Las Vegas* (1971), Thomas Pynchon's *Gravity's Rainbow* (1973), John Kennedy Toole's *A Confederacy of Dunces* (1980), and most tellingly: Aleksandr Solzhenitsyn's *The Gulag Archipelago* (1973), the early works of William Burroughs and Henry Miller, and August Strindberg's *The Occult Diary* (1896–1908). Perhaps, for some, works by David Foster Wallace, at least when it comes to his posthumous *The Pale King* (2011).

All of them, as with cartoonist Edward Gorey's debut book *The Unstrung Harp* (1953), are as much about the *making* of the work and the *environs* (both external and internal as regards the author) in which that work was developed as they are about what the work itself encapsulates in the tone, style, voice, and aesthetic formality of their background context/subtext.

"It seems to me that the modern painter cannot express this age—the airplane, the atom bomb, the radio—in the old forms of the Renaissance or any other past culture," abstract painter paragon Jackson Pollock pronounced during a 1951 radio interview. "Each age finds its own technique."

We are here expanding on the oft-repeated modality of midcentury jazz and blues music (and its somewhat unlikely inheritors in bebop-influenced Beat poets and standup comedy progenitors Lenny Bruce and Mort Sahl, et al.) being not only products of their environments but also, to harken back to McLuhan, a message *of* those environments.

"Do you think that one can allow less literary authenticity and effectiveness to a poem which is imperfect but filled with powerful and beautiful things than to a poem which is perfect but without much internal reverberation?" asked actor, writer, and theater theorist Antonin Artaud in a letter to publisher/editor Jacques Rivière in 1923.

It is the drive and *passion for expression*—the scream searching (in vain?) for a mouth—that Artaud is ranting about here. Hence Cobain's own explanation of what drove *him* to the idiom of punk rock as a young seeker: the grime and grit of its impressions bursting with an implacable vitality so eruptive (and perhaps orgiastic) that any sense of formalistic propriety was rendered irrelevant. It didn't matter how "good" something was, only how impassioned its creator, how brutally raw and "real" his or her passion could be relayed through the creative process.

As Kaufman will elucidate in more than one article ahead, Troma and he so often traffic in viscera-splattered horror because, well, our collective society is pretty gorily horrific (and often grotesquely *horrible*). Or, to cadge a phrase from Alfred Hitchcock, "A glimpse into the world proves that horror is nothing other than reality."

To be honest about this—which the frenetically impulsive/compulsive Kaufman can't possibly avoid in his thoughts, expressions, interviews, and certainly filmmaking—he has to maintain that horror/horribleness in everything he does. Or as he much more eloquently puts it:

> I thought it was important to start *Terror Firmer* with some brutal moments, because to a certain extent that is what American society is: brutal. The reality of American life is constant racial and sexual violence. My movies are a reflection of that. From

The Toxic Avenger on, we have been involved in fighting hatred and violence and the puritanical dictatorship in America. It's always been there in our movies and these important buttons have to be pushed.

For further explicit explanation of Kaufman's fervent take on "horror as savage reality," see the maestro's own direct-to-camera introduction to Episode 15 of *Troma's Edge TV* (2000–2001).

On a more personal and introspective bent, Kaufman's seeing the world through the eyes of someone who grew up in the realm of the very "elite" that he's forever railing against, referring to his youthful background in upper-crust Manhattan as "the ultimate bourgeois. I went to Trinity School in New York and Yale University."

His parents would throw lavish parties that were often populated by the likes of Broadway star Elaine Stritch. Montgomery Clift came by at one point. Oliver Stone, who too would have a rather intimate view of the "elite" world while spending his entire career deconstructing and disrupting it with profound apoplexy, was a nearby boyhood friend.

This intimate connection with the bourgeois society Kaufman grew up with and within was then short-circuited by the "Red diaper baby" worldview endowed by his grandmother, who was a kind of "eat the rich" pseudo rabble-rouser in the mold of an Emma Goldman, pushing her pubescent grandson early on to despise his upper-crust/jet-set society for its hypocrisy, venality, cupidity, and sociopathic cruelty.

And, by god, Kaufman did despise that society and says his grandmother still to this day remains one of his most potent influences on both his filmmaking and the way he leads his "damn the man" lifestyle.

However, this apoplexy at bourgeois duplicity (manifested by what he sees as the twin marplots of pharisaic "limousine liberals" and puritanical Reaganites—two sides of the same *very* expensive, multinational conglomerate-forged coin) is tempered in *both* his filmmaking and worldview by the other major influences with which he grew up—aspirational Broadway musicals, buoyant animated cartoons, and idealistic comic books.

Hence the visceral colorfulness (both literally and figuratively) in his work. Hence the playfulness. Hence the hope and optimism that still exists under the surface of the muck and mire. Hence the "geeks shall inherit the earth" agenda of virtually every one of Kaufman's directed pictures and stories.

The freaky weirdo misfits and underdogs in his movies may be (sometimes literally) shat upon by the bullies and villains and society itself. But they can still have some uproarious good times, find friends, find love, and ultimately succeed in defeating that same vile villainy nearly every time by picture's end. Doing so through a world that may be odious, but also infused with an effulgent,

Mondrianesque brightness (and *boldness* that at once states: "*We are here, TOO!*" and "*Look at THIS!*").

Charlie Chaplin and Mel Brooks—both, particularly the former, having profound influence on Kaufman—always said (and promulgated in their respective works) that one of the best ways of dealing with society's horrors and hypocrisy was through irreverent, nose-thumbing ridicule. So it is with Kaufman's Troma.

It was in fact the aforementioned "Toxie clock saves the world" interview segment that I sent to Kaufman over text that kicked off what may, on the onset to the uninitiated, appear an exceedingly morbid conversation about how Kaufman may very well not be around to see the publication of this very book whose production he's been supportively aware (hence his granting me of an interview as coda exclusively for it). Read onward, though, and you'll notice—if you can't already tell from his films (both those he's made himself and those by Troma's scads of cultish congregants)—"morbidity" is but one more bourgeois, elitist, and—most sinful of all in the mode of Oscar Wilde—*boring* taboo that downright *requires* exploding.

Regard how, once again as almost pious incantation, throughout these interviews Kaufman proclaims he's prepared to "blow [his] fucking brains out" with a pearl-handled derringer he allegedly keeps at all times stowed away in his desk.

And yet, even if his thinly veiled blind independent filmmaking doppelganger "Larry Benjamin" (played, for those who still think there's any need to "read between the lines" with any of Kaufman's output, by himself) in *Terror Firmer* (1999) *also* pronounces that he'll shoot himself in the head if things keep not adhering to his needful sense of *how things are done properly* (on the set of, here we go again, Troma's upcoming fourth installment of *The Toxic Avenger*), there's inherent here that customary Kaufmanesque dualism of "is he kidding/insane? Or is he frighteningly serious? Is he trying to get attention? Or should we be calling the cops/mental care facilities?"

The joke may be on us here, though—because, as long as I've known Kaufman (more than half my life first as a young, peripheral Troma-ite and later as a longtime chronicler of the film maven's life and work for a variety of previous publications)—he's always been calm, collected, sweet, gentle, generous, and absolutely, positively in love with his fans (even if some of them scare the hell out of him), his staff (even if some of them piss him the hell off), his films (even if, as you'll read ahead, he denounces them as candidly as he may praise them), and, most profoundly, his three now-grown daughters and lovely and always-in-his-corner wife of fifty years (whom he married, in what Jews such as we may refer to as rather *bashert*, the same year he started Troma with his *other* much-loved, five-decades partner, Michael Herz).

"I might scream about the big issues, like war or Hillary Clinton or Pathé-is-the-Devil and all that," Kaufman explains in a 2001 Q&A for the Dutch fanzine

Schokkend Nieuws.[10] "But the reality is that my family is much more important. I'm more proud of the fact that I'm still married to my wife after twenty-five years, that my kids are reasonably normal and happy, and that I'm still working with the same business partner after all these years, than getting awards from festivals."

This is *also* something that Kaufman repeats, almost as though reading a script word-for-word, in various other profiles and interviews curated here, including the recent 2017 piece for *Paste* in which he updates the "twenty-five years" milestone with "forty-three years."

Now, does this sound like someone who is truly so explosively upset at *everything* and *everyone* around him that he's ready to end it all in one final grand exhibition of just how "crazy" he may be? Kaufman seems to be having way too much fun for all of that rot.

Granted, in that same *Schokkend Nieuws/Flashback Files* piece, there's a close-up of a freakishly manic-looking Kaufman holding a gun to his temple. But, still, I've known and worked with Kaufman and been close enough with his ever-changing lineup of Troma Team members (and those who have clung on to the Tromatic rollercoaster ride by the fingernails as long as I, if not longer) to know that Kaufman's much-repeated "I'll blow my fucking brains out!" mantra is as much a quirky catchphrase as, say, his continuous (and, certainly, *life-affirming*) proclamation: "LET'S MAKE SOME ART!"

Because, you see, Kaufman is incredibly consistent *and* he's incredibly affected by James Joyce's "ineluctable modality of the visible" at the same time. His life may seemingly not change as per Too Much Coffee Man creator and *New Yorker* cartoonist Shannon Wheeler's "same crap, different flies" assertion a la the Stoics' (to some, nightmarish in the Sisyphean sense) concept of "eternal recurrence" (popularized centuries later by no less than Friedrich Nietzsche).

But his *perception* of what's going on around him may nevertheless vacillate according to whom he's speaking with, how he's feeling, or (as we see in the Reddit AMA included here or in a particularly embarrassing moment from one of Troma's many behind-the-scenes feature docs, *Poultry in Motion: Truth Is Stranger Than Chicken* [2008]) whether or not a bad burrito is causing him to dash to the washroom.

This is how Kaufman can stay intransigently unmoved in the macrocosmic way he proceeds and speaks of himself, his work, and society at large, while at the same time, on a microcosmic level, can seem all over the place in his thoughts and emotions. Truly, it's chaos theory's "scaling" component in motion: On the outset, everything remains the same; but zoom in a few thousand clicks, and it's utter madness. (Or vice versa.)

This, of course, harkens back to Kaufman's professed Taoist leanings based on his having been a Chinese major in college at Yale and his influence—again, constantly referenced in the articles ahead—of living via the inviolable mechanism of "yin and yang."

Let's set aside his "blow my fucking brains out!" catchphrase for now and focus on "LET'S MAKE SOME ART!" (the tagline, incidentally, to the as-mentioned-meta feature film *Terror Firmer* [1999]).

In Jill J. Lanford's 1983 piece appropriately titled "TROMA Films: They're Not Art, but They Make Money," Kaufman professes: "Going to a TROMA film is not an art experience, and it's not supposed to be. We make movies that appeal to a young audience that is looking for a few laughs, a thrill or two and some mild sex. That's it. We don't even try to appeal to your mind—just your raunchier senses."

True, this was back in the earliest days of Kaufman's (and, by proxy, longtime partner Herz's) oeuvre being known as being built upon soi-disant "sex comedies."[11] But, still, how *serious* is Kaufman *really* being when he's not only bandying around the rather pedomorphically idiomatic "LET'S MAKE SOME ART!" but also proclaiming something like this: "Look, when van Gogh made his paintings, nobody understood it. He had to cut his ear off. I don't know about a more influential artist than van Gogh. Troma is like van Gogh. But the difference is that Troma has been lucky enough to find an audience while we're alive. We can support ourselves by our movies. Van Gogh did not have that luck."

To make matters more confusing to the investigative mind, Kaufman follows up a seemingly uberpretentious statement of how he would put Troma's work in the same ring as van Gogh's with: "On the other hand, [van Gogh] didn't have to worry about distribution. He had a rich brother to support him, so.... If I had a rich brother, I probably wouldn't have bothered doing anything. But I didn't have a rich brother when I started. Now I do. My brother is very rich. He's made a big business of bread."[12]

Har har? But, wait... fifteen years later, in (what would become an incredibly viral) James "The Angry Video Game Nerd" Rolfe's interview with Kaufman, we see the maverick filmmaker *once again* speaking of his work in the same breath as that of van Gogh's (not to mention—are you *serious?!*—Stanley Kubrick):

> Well, it's an art form, and in the same way that Picasso painted or van Gogh painted, you want to give something in your soul to express it. You know, Kubrick spent ten years on [the unproduced] *Napoleon*. He had a project called Napoleon, and he had a file card.... There's a Kubrick show somewhere, and it's in LA, I think, and he had file cards for every day of Napoleon's life. He spent ... obviously obsessed about it.

Oh, and guess what? Kaufman also completely invalidates his repetitive pronouncement that what he is most proud of in his life is his family by disclosing in the same interview later, "I mean, again, I think you have to be a bit eccentric.

I know that in my own personal life, I put filmmaking way ahead of my wife and family, and I regret doing it. But there was no other way to make the movie."

Yes, Kaufman may repeat himself (often word-for-word, even when it comes to a groaningly Henny Youngman/Milton Berle–esque joke-telling style). And then cross out what he's said in some kind of (often very self-aware) Dadaist *découpe* style a la Brion Gysin and Jean-Michel Basquiat. And then repeat again (in all fairness, he *does* right after that last statement in Rolfe's interview add, once again, how proud he is of maintaining the same wife, business partner, and even childhood friends he's had for decades).

Yes, Kaufman has been (knowingly?) playing this randy game of dialectics for so long that it does become virtually impossible to recognize when Kaufman is being serious, when he's being facetious, when he's being a bloviating showman, and when he is being a forward-thinking prophet.

The impishly diminutive Kaufman would likely grant us a Mel Brooksian *nisht getoygen* shrug and remind us that, as a spiritual protégé of Charlie Chaplin (both in artistic sensibility of combining the serious with the live-action cartoon *and* in the financial savvy of keeping his own film negatives to own the distribution/exhibition rights to his pictures), he'll put it to the Tramp who (as became one of *Chaplin*'s repeated catchphrases) famously responded to the same question, "If you want to know me, watch my movies."

Beyond sitting through (and sometimes, as he himself would suggest, *suffering* through) his fifty flicks, we can maybe best discern the intersection between who Kaufman really is and what he projects himself to be in the many interviews of this compendium via Patricia Kaufman's speaking to Leslie Pariseau for *The Ringer* as recently as 2018.

Really, who would know better than Kaufman's decades-long wife and occasional business and creative partner, the woman he refers to—reverently—as "The Commissioner"?:[13]

> Here's this character who loves his mother, is loyal to his wife. He cares about the underdog and supports the little people. He's enraged by evil and must stop evil wherever it is. Who do you think that character is? It's Lloyd! Lloyd was the ninety-pound weakling. Lloyd is like the superhero fighting for the rights of little people. I have always contended that Toxie is Lloyd.

For further punctuation of all of this still, in the same piece as per Pariseau herself:

> Known to his fans as "Uncle Lloyd," Kaufman is an unlikely hero, beloved by hundreds of thousands of followers who call themselves the Troma Army. When he's

not in drag, he's usually dressed neatly in a blazer with a pocket square and a bowtie. And though he has a penchant for euphemisms and winking, naughty humor, his manners are impeccable. With a flexible, stretchy face that often lifts into an expression of wide-eyed surprise, mouth slightly agape, as if someone had just goosed him or pinched his nipple, Kaufman is the Mister Rogers of the punk-nerd film underground. He's been making movies for fifty years, and is best known for raising a middle finger to Hollywood while specializing in a genre so specific—a combination of comedy-satire and surrealist shock-horror—it's simply called "Troma" . . .

Like a demented, upside-down Marvel Cinematic Universe, Troma will hold on by the skin of its teeth, championing its horrifying heroes, its social pariahs, loser rejects, and hopelessly pathetic, pure-hearted nerds. As long as Lloyd Kaufman is around, the good guys will always be avenged, and the little people of Tromaville will always live happily ever after.

A Note on the Text and Acknowledgments

One of Kaufman's other much-repeated tropes throughout the articles and interviews laid out in this collection is the continually staunch belief that filmmaking has become in the past few years far more "democratized," in that "anyone" can grab a cheap video camera (or, perhaps these days, a phone) and make their own movie with cheap-to-free software easily downloadable online.

I respectfully disagree (and, with more nuance and further discussion, Kaufman would likely similarly revise), being that though the means of *production* have in many ways been "democratized," distribution/exhibition/promotion is still as plutocratic and exclusionary as ever, if not more so. Though it's true that "anyone" can make a movie today, that doesn't mean "anyone else" will ever see or know about it. And we do indeed see in the articles ahead that Kaufman begins to adapt his thoughts on the digital realm's potential for "democratization" as more corporate (and political) interests infiltrate that arena (the way they had with previous outlets for exhibition Kaufman also intimately tracks over the course of this book, such as cable television, the video market, art house cinemas, and film festivals).

This all said, we do see here (and in both the work onscreen and BTS in his various "making-of" docs) that Kaufman nevertheless remains unflappable about his sense of independent film being one of the last, if not the only bastion of true "democracy" today. Though he never uses the word himself, I'd go so far as to say he's a true *egalitarian*, particularly on his film sets, as best exemplified in his conversation with *Tabula Rasa*: "[A]nyone else who's around, anyone on the set, is a director. Everybody is a director—it's the 'Troma Team'—anyone who's got a joke, anyone who's got an idea. Until the film actually goes in front of the lens, until it's exposed, anything goes. The Troma truck driver, the pizza delivery man, we let them all direct if they have something to say!"

As such, I wanted to be particularly egalitarian with the curation of the articles herein. Aside from some silent "polishing" of a few needful areas of the pieces ahead—some fact-checking, spell-checking, etc.—the articles have for the most part been left as is. The recorded interviews we've transcribed are typically left as is, as well, including most visibly the one involving James "The Angry Video Game Nerd" Rolfe, which does maintain wholly Kaufman's signature style of being the kind of hyperactive visionary who speaks faster than he thinks (think fellow impassioned filmmakers such as Quentin Tarantino, Paul Thomas Anderson, Martin Scorsese, et al.)—hence the stammering, repeating himself (while also somehow concurrently contradicting himself), tendency toward aposiopesis (hence the many ellipses), and rather colorful (sometimes humorously intentional) solecisms and malapropisms.

The point being that, like Kaufman and Troma, I wanted all voices to be heard and represented here, and wanted to show too that no matter if it's some unknown punk rocker's Xeroxed zine from the midnineties or fan boy blog or the *New York Times* or the *Village Voice*, Kaufman treats all outlets quite similarly. Whether he's speaking with an Australian college student for his thesis or renowned film critic Jack Mathews at the *Los Angeles Times*, Kaufman treats them all with the same aforementioned combination of seriousness and levity.

You'll see here that serious side of Kaufman little glimpsed elsewhere as he castigates the American Film Market Association for not properly promoting themselves press-wise in a commentary/letter written to same.

On the opposite end of the spectrum, you'll see (for the first time in the illustrious twenty-five-year history of the Conversations with Filmmakers Series) (an excerpt of) a Reddit AMA (Ask Me Anything), as well. Here you can experience firsthand Kaufman at his animated carnival barker best, speaking directly with and interacting with his fans (in documented real time), including those moronic goofballs who may be heckling him or goading him on.

We've also done what we could to keep consistency with certain words, phrases, titles of films, etc. However, it's clear Kaufman himself enjoys the playfulness of such inconsistency over the years, as per hero Andy Warhol (whose very last name itself is a typo and lifelong inside joke), James Joyce, P. T. Barnum, et al. who famously would purposely make alterations to their works, biographies, interviews, etc. both out of spite and humor, but also to showcase—as does Kaufman and Troma itself—the "cracks in the system," so to speak, of the larger media machine today.

Is "Troma" spelled thusly, or is it "TROMA"? Is it *simply* "Troma," or is it "Troma Team"... or "Troma Entertainment"... or "Troma Studios"? Is their latest film *#ShakespearesShitstorm* or *Shakespeare's Shitstorm* or *ShakespeareShitstorm*? There again, we leave it to Kaufman's Brooksian *nisht getoygen* shrug and say, as he would, just go with the flow and follow the Tao.

Lastly, I want to be as forthright and honest about myself as Kaufman is (yet again, for the most part) here in the pages ahead.

During the entirety of this book's production—from first laboring to convince University Press of Mississippi to allow there to be an installment of the series on Kaufman in the first place (spoiler alert: it took a *lot* of convincing!), through completing the final edits (spoiler alert: that hasn't been done yet, but just go with me here)—I've gone through an unending series of seismic, often woefully traumatic sea changes and paradigm shifts in my life.

The one car we owned broke down on us (don't buy Fords anymore, folks), rendering us stranded for weeks without viable transportation. My wife and I amicably divorced after eight years of marriage. I moved out of my home in Dayton, Ohio, to stay with an old friend in Boulder, Colorado, jobless and living for a stint off of dwindling savings. Frantically job-hunting, including for positions that would render me ignominiously underemployed.

And then—the good stuff—being invited *back* to the Dayton, Ohio, area for an apropos job in the marketing department of a private college that would allow me to buy a used car, move back to the area, get a small place of my own, and ultimately underwrite the rest of the process of finishing this book.[14] All while, on *this* side of the "yin and yang," gaining much-needed emotional support from a new girlfriend (along with being back in proximity to my ex-wife, who remains one of my best friends . . . and in need of the occasional ride around town to run errands).

Get it? It's been a *long* six months. Has felt much, much more like six *years*. Or *lifetimes*.

But talking with Lloyd Kaufman throughout this maddening period, immersing myself fully in his world and the Troma scene, revisiting old films of his I hadn't seen since my late-night viewing on the USA Network or "Skinemax"[15] at sleepover parties when I was much too young to be watching them, and just generally being lifted up by his and Troma's insuperable sense of optimism about the future even when everything may seem absolutely chaotic around you . . . kept me going and strong. Even when, as with myself and in the classic DIY Troma vein, you have a laptop you're working with whose "i" key doesn't really work anymore, Paul Sheldon style (though his typewriter had no "n").

So, I want to thank Kaufman for that, the Troma folks for same, and his dedicated assistant Garrett Sullivan for his help keeping the always-harried and busied Kaufman connected and engaged to this labor of love project.

I want to thank my editor at UPM, Emily Bandy, for agreeing (at last!) to go with me on this journey into the inner sanctum of Troma and Lloyd Kaufman's rather unique mind and worldview. And the rest of the UPM gang (whomever is still there by the time this finally comes out).[16]

Of course, thank you graciously to the many publishers and writers of the articles herein who granted their permission for use, and to the handful of others whose works were not included but who also granted permission (as these few pieces were also very helpful with background research, context, etc.). Particular gratitude to Tania Visosevic who helped us well beyond the call of duty to track down James MacDonald for his fantastic Q&A for his university thesis. Special thanks too to Jan Willem Steenmeijer for allowing us to use his fantastic photo of Lloyd Kaufman for the cover of this book.

And I want to acknowledge here too Drew Todd, whose installment in the Conversations with Filmmakers Series on Jafar Panahi made this longtime reader of these installments realize that I both wanted to and *could* contribute with my own subject, my longtime friend and semimentor Lloyd Kaufman.

It was Todd too who mentioned in *his* acknowledgments longtime Conversations former editor Gerald Peary (who Todd says inspired *him* with Peary's own John Ford installment), which led me to reaching out to Peary cold-call style. Peary was warm, welcoming, and generous in his connecting me to the UPM team, particularly Bandy. It is because of his early consultation, support, and encouragement that this book exists. It simply would not otherwise.

Thank you, Gerry.

Assistance in seeking out articles and in transcription came from my good friends and regular collaborators Jon Niccum and Joseph Griffin, as well as Niccum's daughter Lola, who was able to get into her university's archival system when I myself would not have been able to. (Good lord, those subscriptions are prohibitively expensive! RIP Aaron Swartz!).

Much appreciation, too, to the ever-so-lovely living doll that is my longtime good friend Erin O'Brien, who swooped in last-minute (quite literally) to generate and finalize our index for us. I honestly don't know how else I would've been able to do that, and certainly not at a rock-bottom price that I could actually kind-of afford. Thanks, Erin!

I would have never gotten involved in the realm of Troma on a personal level had it not been for the graciousness of not only Lloyd but also lifelong friends such as Doug Sakmann and, in his own way somewhat later, Tim Seeley. Both opened up many doors for me into Troma and beyond, and prove that whatever faults the Troma Team may have, there is a real sense of camaraderie and friendship there that lasts and keeps the world's longest-running independent studio going strong.

Kaufman is right: It's the fans and the people behind the scenes that make all the difference.

Finally, as mentioned earlier, this has been a *very* strange trip to take in many regards over the past half year, and I could *not* have made it through mentally, physically, nor financially without the love and support of Howard Zaremba, Becky Clark, Michael Monagan, Mike Kenneally, Scott Shaw!, Wendy All, Jim Cornelius, Rick Geary, Gary Groth, Joseph Trinh, Patrick Mallek (and Kim and Alice!), Kathleen Lees, Chelsie Reed, Shaun and Jess Oshman, Niccum and Griffin, Michael Cavender, Heather and Frank Bailey, Doug Meyers, Jill Woodhouse, Zach White, Mike Restaino, Adam Rehmeier, Andy Slade, Aaron Sheley, Mike and Denise Reiss, Jesse Alba, Rob Kutner, Michael Hirschorn, Adam Nayman, Nick Mullendore, Jim Fagan, Ryan Stack, Tore Knos, Aron Flasher, Devon Yeider, Caseen Gaines, Jonathan Friedmann, Jesse Cilio, Jon Weinman, Janet Rosen, Rob Schulte, Rick Castañeda, Judd Apatow, Andrea Comparato, Rob Salkowitz, Scott Hiller, Patrick Reed, Sam Gallant, Ryan Brook, Paul M. Sammon, Mike Anderson, Jonathan Barli, Roy Schwartz, Danny Fingeroth, Richard Fleming, the Kids of Widney High, Kenneth Wajda, Steve Leonard, Jake Friedman, Whitney Grace, Lou Perez, Nadir Maraschin, Scott Hull, Peter Beckendorf, Mark Osborne, Chris Arrant, Michael Lehmann, Libby Ballengee, Mark Yarm, Miriam Mora, Andrew Bujalski, Daniel Rolnick, Rodney Veal, Rich Johnson, Rich Johnston (yup, one with a "t" and one without), Jonathan "Dr." Katz, Tom Snyder, Loren Bouchard, Al Jean, Mike Price, Steve Rotterdam, Matt Bayman, David Isen, Tej Joshi, Dave Keith, Christopher Tyler, Dr. Erin Hanna, Carly Schwartz, Philippe DeNeree, Jim Borgman, Joey DiFranco, Matt Dunford, John Siuntres, Steve Coard, Ken Reid, Jim "Mr. Skin" McBride, Robert Gordon, Eileen Grubba, Johnny Ryan, Andy Mangels, Richie Kern, Ellis Henican, Kyle and Jenn, Justin Hall, Miles Francis, Allen Salkin, Adam Kirshner, John Fleming, Jonathan McNeal, Mark Askwith, Vincent Haddad, Eric Cupps, Josh Yawn, Phil Moore, Sara Driver, Alex Cox, Tod Davies, Danny Wolf, Daniel Weisinger, Jonathan Dortch, Guinevere Turner, Shannon Wheeler, Chris Hanley, Mark Habegger, Mary Harron, Pablo Kjolseth, Marc Summers, Steve Balderson, Seraphin, Fally Afani, Josh Karp, Dr. F. Erik Brooks, Nick Hrkman, Tricia Romano, Julie Seabaugh, Jon B. Cooke, Anthony Sturmas, Ed Catto, Chad Painter, Dustin Marquel, John Cierpial, Ann Rotolante, Andrea Szwarko, Anthony Musco, Julie Kliegman, Maggie Thompson, Bill Wendel and family, Angela Perrone, Oscar Boyson, David Permut, Alex Astrachan, the rest of the SDCC kids, the Fuzzy Door folks, the rest of the Dayton gang, the rest of the Boulder gang, the rest of the Lawrence gang, the rest of the Baltimore gang, my folks at Central State University's Department of Institutional Advancement (particularly the world's best boss, Debbie Alberico), Dominique Tingley (the Sara to my Melvin), and of course, my ever-loving family.

While finishing the final stages of this project, we experienced the loss of one of the great heroes and inspirations of the overall story here: Roger Corman

(1970–2024), as well as the passing of a dear friend and additional multihyphenate inspiration, Trina Robbins (1938–2024). Our best to their legacies, families, and fans of their own, too (some of whom overlap with Kaufman's and Troma's—though likely *far* more in the Corman camp than in Trina's!).

On an even more direct note of sadness, at the very last-minute, we learned of the untimely passing of forty-three-year-old Doug Sakmann. My editors generously allowed me to add in this note thanking Doug once again for his longtime (nearly half our lives) friendship, his originally helping me get introduced on a personal level to the Troma-verse, and all the fun and good times we had together over the years all over the country.

Doug was funny, brash, bold, and completely embodied balls-out pure artistic energy, innovation, and independence. He could get arrested at Cannes for fighting with authority figures screwing with a Troma production and he could be a crackshot artistic director on a top-rated Netflix show. He could do it all.

Right before his death (which, at the time of this writing, remains a mystery as to cause), we were talking about his upcoming traveling Troma museum he'd been trying to get off the ground and his long-dreamt-of sequel to Troma's own *Sgt. Kabukiman N.Y.P.D.* (1990). He was someone who had a massive influence on me and I'm sorry he won't be around to see this book (which includes an interview he did with Lloyd himself). My final text message to him on the day we later learned he was gone was, "Finally saw *Tales from the Crapper*. What the HELL is this?!"

Last note: For those who wonder, as I would imagine it will come up often, my favorite Troma movie is *Mother's Day* (1980).

In no particular order, the others I could most recommend are (TRIGGER WARNING: IF YOU NEED A TRIGGER WARNING, YOU MAY WANT TO WATCH SOMETHING ELSE!): *The Toxic Avenger* (1984), *Citizen Toxie: The Toxic Avenger IV* (2000), *Combat Shock* (1984), *The Wedding Party* (1969), *Poultrygeist: Night of the Chicken Dead* (2006), *#ShakespearesShitstorm* (2020), *The Battle of Love's Return* (1971), *Doggie Tails* (2003), *Blood Sucking Freaks* (1976), and *Poultry in Motion: Truth Is Stranger Than Chicken* (2008).

MK

Notes

1. From the Yiddish *shlak* (German provenance: *Schlake*), essentially meaning "trash"; hence "schlock" often also being referred to (rather endearingly) as "trash cinema," in a manner that seems to make Kaufman himself at times proud. From scholar James W. MacDonald's 2006 thesis interview—Kaufman: "I don't know what trash means. I assume it's something that's out of the mainstream, but

I've never really investigated it. I know that the French do refer to Troma as trash films, and it has a good connotation."

2. Importantly, in no-budget mise en scène only; as tempting as it may be to compare schlock with camp, as per Susan Sontag's authoritative "Notes on 'Camp'" (1964), philosophically "camp" is imbued with an ebullient, often kitschy (and as often swishy) naïveté in the art brut style, while schlock and the bulk of Kaufman's canon is sardonically self-aware or even snarky in tone; this explains why Ed Wood, whom Kaufman despises for making independent cinema look bad, is "camp," while Troma and Kaufman are decidedly not . . . except, again, in similarly (needful) DIY aesthetical stylistics.
3. Nickname for the Toxic Avenger.
4. Remember that the provenance of "persona" descends from the Greek word used to describe the *masks* worn by *actors*, after all.
5. A genre, it should be remembered, that was not "taken seriously," even within the literary and academic communities, well into the 1980s, more than one hundred years after it was first birthed from the minds of the likes of Mary Shelley and H. G. Wells.
6. Which first made its way to its larger audience less than a year after its initial run by being serialized in none other than soft-core porn publication *Playboy*.
7. Complemented by Brazilian contemporary Paulo Freire's *Pedagogy of the Oppressed* (1968).
8. "Motor City," a nickname for Detroit.
9. Quite possibly a reference to similarly vitriolic science fiction writer Harlan Ellison's short story "I Have No Mouth, and I Must Scream" (1967), which was published right around the same time as Selby's first novel *Last Exit to Brooklyn* (1964).
10. Reprinted in this compendium as translated in English for Roel Haanen's online archive *Flashback Files*.
11. A genre they more or less invented if not popularized years before the mainstream took notice and began overstuffing the 1980s with everything from *Porky's* (1981) to *Hamburger: The Motion Picture* (1986), leading Troma to move on to a genre everyone in the industry had thought was dead: horror . . . with that uniquely comedic twist they fashioned as the aforementioned "schlock."
12. Kaufman is not using a punning colloquialism for "money" here; his brother, Charles, after making a few movies for Troma himself, did indeed quit the business to found and run what remains today a very successful bakery in San Diego.
13. As she was indeed the longtime NYC Film Commissioner.
14. Par for the course, by the time we completed the final stages of the book, I had been laid off from the aforementioned job due to budget cuts . . . right in time for the holidays, launching a whole *other* series of tumultuous misadventures thereafter that only "mostly" resolved by the time this project was to be sent off to the printers.
15. A jokey sobriquet for the early cable movie channel Cinemax, particularly in reference to its notorious late-night softcore porn-themed programming.
16. Closer to prepping final manuscript for publication, that would turn out to be Corley Longmire, Kerri Jordan, Joey Brown, Courtney McCreary, and Amy Atwood.

Chronology

1945   Stanley Lloyd Kaufman Jr. is born on December 30 in New York City to Ruth (née Fried) and prominent attorney Stanley Lloyd Kaufman Sr.

1964   Attends Yale University, majoring in Chinese studies with the intention of learning more about the world outside his upper-class NYC upbringing; this includes taking a gap year in 1966 in which he works as a Pathfinder for the Peace Corps and teacher in the Republic of Chad; it is during this year-long African adventure that Kaufman makes his first film, a short 16mm (Bolex) b&w cinema verité piece in which he films a pig's slaughter by neighboring villagers; in showing the film back home in the States, Kaufman is inspired not only by the run-and-gun filmmaking style but the fact the film clearly disturbs its viewers and shows a side of society normally not seen onscreen or in mainstream media.

1967   Befriends fellow Yalie, the younger freshman Michael Herz, who had years earlier gone to summer camp with Kaufman's brother, Charles, who gave Herz Lloyd's contact information; Kaufman claims Herz was less interested in talking with him and more in the b&w TV Kaufman happened to have (a rarity at the time) in his dorm room; Herz later becomes Kaufman's lifelong business partner and cofounder of Troma, working with Kaufman while still in college on numerous film projects, including Kaufman's first feature, the silent,[1] b&w, avant-garde, Warholesque *The Girl Who Returned* (1969), which also includes production assistance from Herz's future wife Maris.

1967   On a trip to Japan to learn even more about culture outside his Western enclave, Kaufman is influenced not only by Eastern business, filmmaking aesthetics, and lifestyle but also office architecture and design; he will prefer in his offices of the future to set up spaces where everyone can see and talk to one another, similar to setups in many Silicon Valley startups (more collaborative, less isolated).

1968   Produces Robert Edelstein's eighty-minute sophomore cinematic effort, a 16mm adaptation of Nathaniel Hawthorne's "Rappaccini's

Daughter" (1844), which stars Perry King of future *The Lords of Flatbush* (1974) and Andy Warhol's *Bad* (1979) fame; the film is, in Kaufman's words, "fairly well reviewed by the college newspapers and audiences."

1969   Graduates from Yale after his regular interactions with film fanatics and Yale Film Society cochairs Edelstein and Eric Sherman introduce him to the vast realm of cinema that before, as a self-avowed theater/musical/Broadway devotee, he previously dismissed; Kaufman: "I needed to see every movie ever made. I wanted to eat them, dream them, put them in an eyedropper and let them seep into my optic nerve." It is when he sees Ernst Lubitsch's *To Be or Not to Be* (1942) through the film society that Kaufman decides to become a filmmaker. Upon graduation, Kaufman takes an assistant editor job at Cannon and meets soon-to-be lifelong mentor and future Academy Award–winning filmmaker John G. Avildsen (*Rocky* [1976], *The Karate Kid* [1984], *Lean On Me* [1989]).

1969   Kaufman becomes lifelong friends and occasional collaborators with soon-to-be legendary Marvel head honcho Stan Lee[2] after they develop and write multiple screenplays together, none of which are produced, including one for French filmmaking maven Alain Resnais.

1971   Release of Kaufman's first nonexperimental, feature-length film, *The Battle of Love's Return*, which stars Kaufman himself and is additionally notable for being the film debut of actor-cum-director (and childhood friend/Yale classmate) Oliver Stone.

1972   Avildsen's X-rated[3] *Cry Uncle* opens after Kaufman had been brought on during shooting by his mentor personally to work as production manager; Kaufman had smartly invested some of his money in the project, which becomes financially successful and continues to bolster his slowly growing economic portfolio he will use to support his own independent filmmaking aspirations; he later purchases the rights to *Cry Uncle* outright for Troma to distribute.

1972   Kaufman and partners Theodore Gershuny and Ami Artzi found Armor Films, ultimately a failed venture presaging Troma; Kaufman executive produces and cowrites Gershuny's soft-core erotic *Sugar Cookies* (1973; though premieres at Cannes in 1971[4]), which is also noteworthy for being an early entry in Queer Cinema and for crewing associate producer and first-time feature filmmaker Oliver Stone; it is during the production of *Sugar Cookies* that Kaufman realizes he needs to have total control over all future rights, as confirmed by the massive catastrophe of Armor Films' 1973 entry *Big Gus, What's the*

	Fuss?, which Kaufman (who is credited as codirector and cowriter with Artzi) deems his biggest life regret and which nearly ends his film career.
1974	After the collapse of Armor, Herz and Kaufman found Troma; Kaufman will act as president and focus on being both the face and creative visionary of the company, while publicity-shy Herz will remain more behind-the-scenes as CEO and handle business/operational concerns.
1974	Kaufman marries future NYC Film Commissioner (as of 1995) Patricia Swinney,[5] with whom he'll have three daughters (Lily Hayes [1980], Lisbeth [1986], Charlotte [1987]).
1976	Herz and Kaufman acquire Joel M. Reed's mordantly Grand Guignol–esque splatter-fest *The Incredible Torture Show* for distribution, renaming the picture as the memorable *Bloodsucking Freaks*, which becomes the first "official" Troma film (being that all others in the catalogue were produced/distributed before Troma was formed); "[T]he film is sadistic and has no redeeming social values," Kaufman says. "*Bloodsucking Freaks* is the single film in the Troma library . . . that I feel queasy about distributing. I may have possibly secured my place in Hell just by watching it. It's one of those rare films that is actually *more* offensive now than it was twenty-five years ago"; the film is nevertheless a commercial success that allows Troma to continue to rapidly expand.
1976	Avildsen's career-making *Rocky* is released after Kaufman is crewed in various production management capacities, including as location manager, locking down the famed Philadelphia staircase up which the film's titular character triumphantly runs in one of cinema's most celebrated sequences; the film's vaunting of the forthcoming "fitness craze" sweeping America inspires Kaufman to consider a horror film that could take place in a gym, some of the earliest germs for what eventually becomes *The Toxic Avenger* (1984), which was originally to be called *Health Club Horror*.
1977	Initially to be directed by Avildsen (who leaves the picture partway through), *Saturday Night Fever* is released, having been crewed in multiple production management capacities by Kaufman, who locks down John Travolta's protagonist's house and the iconic discotheque in which much of the film takes place.
1977	Due to a peculiarly bureaucratic technicality, so that he can receive his credit as producer on Avildsen's Paul Sorvino–starrer *Slow Dancing in the Big City*, Kaufman joins the Director's Guild of America

(DGA), meaning he will not be allowed to take official credit on any future (all nonunion) Troma projects (using pseudonyms instead, particularly that borrowed from his great-grandfather, "Samuel Weil"); this will last for decades, including on some of Kaufman's most notable films, well until the 1996 release of *Tromeo & Juliet*.

1979   Lifelong friend and mentor Kirk Douglas brings Kaufman aboard the production of *The Final Countdown* as associate producer/unit production manager (and in the onscreen role of "LCdr. Kaufman"[6]); Kaufman decides once and for all that "I never wanted anything to do with a major studio film again. And besides small favors for friends, I never have."

1979   Release of *Squeeze Play!*, Troma's first in-house production, at a budget of $115,000; after nearly being a total failure in its first theatrical run attempts, a single screening as part of a double-bill with Peter Falk/Alan Arkin comedy *The In-Laws* at a small theater in Norfolk, Virginia, miraculously explodes the film's popularity single-handedly, leading to what will become the company's first major success, including rhapsodizing write-ups in such publications as the *New York Times*, a continuous run on *Variety*'s "Top 50" theatrical winners for the year, and a $1 million deal for a sale to cable television distribution; "It was *Squeeze Play!* that let me know I was on this world to be making movies after all," Kaufman says. "It was *Squeeze Play!* where I saw, for the first time ever, someone laughing hysterically at a movie Michael and I had made."

1979   Buys first Troma building in NYC's Hell's Kitchen at 9th Avenue and 49th Street (after working out of a so-called "broom closet" rented for eighty-seven dollars a month in the *McCall's* magazine building where Herz and he were allegedly forced to keep cleaning supplies and allow janitors to come and go as they pleased, followed by a penthouse at the Actor's Equity building at 165 West 45th Street); Troma will reside here until 2002 when Herz "wanted to take some money off the table," according to Kaufman; "then we bought a shittier building in Long Island City."

1981   Kaufman works as production manager on Louis Malle's *My Dinner with Andre*, which includes a credit for Troma itself as having granted "production support"; Kaufman works in similar production management capacities on projects with *Friday the 13th* (1980) creator Sean Cunningham, Academy Award–winning documentarian Barbara Koppel, and highly regarded producer Sidney Beckerman

	of *Marathon Man* (1976), *Kelly's Heroes* (1970), *Cabaret* (1972), and *Buckaroo Bonzai* (1984) fame.
1982	Internal company newsletter *Troma Times* kicks off as a jokey but pertinent news outlet for Troma affairs, becoming something of a vintage item in later years and transitioning to a brief online-only run in 2012.
1983	Kaufman later regrets Troma's turning down of a young Madonna for *The First Turn-On!*; the film does end up featuring a very young Vincent D'Onofrio.
1984	For Troma's tenth anniversary, the American Film Institute (AFI) puts on a retrospective of the studio's library and Kaufman's work to date.
1984	At the behest of wife Pat, the husband-and-wife team launches 50th Street Films, the "family-friendly" wing of Troma, acquiring their first film to be distributed—John Hanson's recently completed *Wildrose*—and following up with such projects as the 1993 English-language version of Japanese master anime filmmaker Hayao Miyazaki's soon-to-be classic *My Neighbor Totoro* (1989); the venture collapses in part due to Disney's 1996 purchase of Miyazaki's catalogue (including *Totoro*, despite its still having a year under 50th Street's contract), infuriating Kaufman particularly when the *New Yorker* shortly thereafter writes a glowing profile of Harvey Weinstein that claims Weinstein's Disney-owned Miramax had been the one in the States to first discover *Totoro*.[7]
1984	Release of *The Toxic Avenger*, which will become Troma's most recognizable and iconic film, leading to the character of the Toxic Avenger himself becoming as much of a public face for the brand as Kaufman; the film will spawn three sequels, a big-budget reboot produced by megastudio Legendary Pictures in 2023 starring Peter Dinklage as the Toxic Avenger, comic book series, video games, a globally touring live-action musical, a novelization by Kaufman, and more, across every conceivable spectrum of media, entertainment, merchandise, and even politics (becoming leveraged as an endorser for both the Green Party and Ralph Nader's presidential run campaigns, as well as a variety of environmental groups such as the Environmental Protection Agency [EPA]).
1986	An article in the *New York Daily News* refers to "Lloyd Kaufman" as opposed to his nonunion alias Samuel Weil directing a scene on the set of *Troma's War* (1988), which leads to Kaufman's being brought before the DGA board for violating compliance rules about a union

	member working on a nonunion set; Kaufman is able to dissuade the board from expelling him due to the sheer ridiculousness of the scene being "directed"; Kaufman nevertheless resigns shortly thereafter.
1986	First meets inspirational filmmaker Roger Corman while the two are being honored at the Tokyo International Film Festival.
1986	Troma readies twenty-four of its films for exhibition via syndicated television but must first significantly recut and rework them for said programming, which precludes any "X" or "R"-rated material;[8] the films—purchased at a reported $150,000 to $700,000 each—will be packaged in two groups of twelve and sold off starting in August.
1987	Troma acquires *Redneck Zombies*, which becomes the first-ever movie shot entirely on video to be distributed worldwide.
1987	Fervently loyal to his old (prep) high school Trinity, Kaufman becomes president of the Alumni Board and member of the school's Board of Trustees.
1990	*The Toxic Crusaders* cartoon airs globally through 1993, penetrating 96 percent of the US television market and often is as the top-rated show in its "Saturday morning cartoons" time period; action figures are released through Playmates as well as a board game—Battle for Tromaville—through Mattel, playing cards through Topps, videogames from Nintendo and Sega, and more; Kaufman is involved in all aspects of the show and merchandising,[9] and is joined on the writing staff by famed television scribe Jack Mendelsohn (*The Carol Burnett Show* [1967–1978], *Rowan & Martin's Laugh-In* [1968–1973], cowriter of *Yellow Submarine* [1968]), and future titan of TV Chuck Lorre (who also wrote the series's theme song); the *Toxic Crusaders* animated film is released in 1996, with its sequel, *Toxic Crusaders 2: The Revenge of Dr. Killemoff*, released one year later in 1997.[10]
1990	Kaufman-directed *Sgt. Kabukiman N.Y.P.D.* is released and includes an indelibly cinematic car-flipping scene (emulating, Kaufman later asserts, a similar sequence from Brian De Palma's *Carrie* [1976]) that will become a meta in-joke for future Troma films into which (despite causing continuity errors) the exact same clip is edited.
1991	Troma West (LA office) is formed in partnership with producer Marty Sokol and run by writer-director David Schultz; offices are closed in 2002, as immortalized by staff tearing down the sign and other elements of the building in Troma omnibus production *Tales from the Crapper* (2004).
1992	Early cable channel Cinemax telecasts a series of Troma films including *Class of Nuke 'Em High* (1986) and *Chopper Chicks in Zombietown*

(1989), kicking off a spate of such showings and partnerships with cable channels including HBO (parent company of Cinemax), the USA Network, and TNT, which will help to spread Troma's brand to audiences who don't have a chance to see or even hear about the films during their more limited theatrical runs; "These films are kind of like sushi," says HBO programming vice president Dave Baldwin at the time. "Once you've got the taste, they're a hell of a lot of fun."

1993   Wife Pat undergoes needful care and surgery for breast cancer in the same year that Kaufman's father—who had previously handled the lion's share of Troma's legal dealings—passes away from melanoma of the liver; Kaufman indefinitely halts preproduction on the next Troma film, *The Troma Western*; he will some years later survive his own battle with melanoma (skin cancer).

1993   Columbia TriStar Home Video (CTHV) and Troma sign a distribution agreement in which CTHV will release Troma movies in Australia and New Zealand theatrically and on home video under the banner of Troma 2000; the first two films so distributed are *Sgt. Kabukiman N.Y.P.D.* (1990) and *Class of Nuke 'Em High Part 3: The Good, the Bad and the Subhumanoid* (1994).

1993   Two years before the internet is privatized, Troma becomes one of the first (if not *the* first) film studios to create its own website, Troma.com; Roger Ebert (longtime distant frenemy of both Troma and Kaufman) claims at the time that Troma is indeed the first.

1993   Troma acquires its first film written, produced, and directed by a woman: Margot Hope's *Femme Fontaine: Killer Babe for the C.I.A.* (1994), starring both Hope and James Hong (*Wayne's World 2* [1993] and *Blade Runner* [1992]).

1994   Los Angeles's American Cinematheque puts on a twentieth-anniversary Troma respective in June; others that follow include those via the National Film Theatre in London, the San Sebastian Film Festival, and (previously, in 1992) the British Film Institute (BFI).

1994   Future *South Park* (1997) creators Trey Parker's and Matt Stone's feature-film debut *Cannibal! The Musical*[11] (originally called *Alfred Packer: The Musical*) is rejected from the Sundance Film Festival, leading Parker and Stone to book a counterprogramming screening of their own during that year's festival in Park City, Utah, in a conference room at the Yarrow Hotel; Kaufman eventually picks up the rights for the film, releases it after Parker and Stone make a few "Tromaesque" additions and needful cuts, and essentially helps launch the duo's career; Kaufman is inspired enough by the Sundance

	counterprogramming concept that, five years later in 1999, the Troma-Dance Film Festival launches and runs for years thereafter during each Sundance at Park City's Phat Tire Saloon.
1995	Desperate for a screenwriter to complete the multiple false starts and drafts of his dream project, a Tromaesque remake of *Romeo and Juliet*, Kaufman receives a fax from Jill Champtaloup, a friend and supervising programmer at HBO/Cinemax: a resume of a young student in the Columbia University masters program named James Gunn with the note "HE'S YOUR MAN"; Gunn is paid $150 for the rewrite of the script that he will have to turn around for a tight week-long deadline.
1995	Troma Team Video is created as Troma's video distribution/exhibition wing, allowing the company to control everything—from how films are marketed, to spreading of the brand—while keeping all profits for itself; sadly, this happens right as the independent video market begins its precipitous decline, especially with the influx of large megachains such as Blockbuster Video that will either not carry Troma films (and those like them by other filmmakers) or will require massive edits to the versions they design to stock (anathema to Troma and Kaufman).
1996	Kaufman acts for the first time in twenty-five years in his directed[12] and cowritten (with James Gunn) production of *Tromeo & Juliet*, a film whose commercial and critical success proves to be so substantial that it singlehandedly reignites the brand power of Troma and introduces the studio and its films to a new generation of fans.
1996	Troma's first-ever computer-generated effect plays at the end of *Bugged*, a sexy comedy horror film about monster-sized insects, directed by Ronald K. Armstrong and acquired by the company for distribution.
1996	Takes New Line Cinema to court after years of contentious contractual and legal battles stemming from New Line's alleged breach of a lucrative deal[13] made in 1991 that had guaranteed a big-budget *Toxic Crusaders* live-action film[14] to be released by spring 1993; Kaufman demands $50 million in damages due to loss of earnings from not only the film but merchandising and other ancillary possibilities; Kaufman and Troma ultimately acquire through the proceedings only slightly less than their legal fees.
1997	*The Tromaville Café* is created by Kaufman and protégé James Gunn as a late-night television program broadcast by the BBC throughout the United Kingdom until 2000, showcasing a variety of classic Troma films with interstitials featuring a cast of regulars (and Kaufman himself), such as five-hundred-pound Troma mainstay Joe

Fleishaker as Michael Herz (a running gag in the Troma community about which Herz himself was delighted); similar programming would be produced under the banner of *Troma's Edge TV* for both UK/European television and DVD releases such as *TromaTV* and *Troma's Basement*, with such distribution partners as Bravo and Channel 4.

1998 Kaufman cowrites *All I Need to Know about Filmmaking I Learned from the Toxic Avenger* with James Gunn for Berkley Boulevard (an imprint of Penguin Putnam); five more books (all with cowriters) are subsequently released, all about Kaufman's personal experiences in filmmaking and brimming with practical, educational, and inspirational tips on DIY filmmaking, with the consequence of becoming the basis for Kaufman's long-running *Make Your Own Damn Movie!* lecture and seminar tours: *Make Your Own Damn Movie!* (2003), *The Toxic Avenger: The Novel* (2006), *Direct Your Own Damn Movie!* (2008), *Produce Your Own Damn Movie!* (2009), *Sell Your Own Damn Movie!* (2011).

1999 CNN stops by Troma Studios to produce and air a piece on the twenty-fifth anniversary of the company.

1999 For its thirtieth anniversary, Kaufman's feature-length directorial debut, *The Girl Who Returned* (1969), is transferred to video for the first time.

1999 Controversial, iconic filmmaker Elia Kazan receives an honorary Oscar at the seventy-first Academy Awards, causing many in the audience and film community—upset at Kazan for having "named names" during the regrettable Army–McCarthy Hearings of 1954—to resist, not applaud the presentation, and to speak out; this includes Kaufman who uses the Troma website as a platform to do just that, in addition to calling for more than fifty of his LA-based staff to create picket signs to protest the Oscars in person; the protest (including a staff member dressed as the Toxic Avenger) is covered by *Good Morning America* and Canal+; two months later, Kaufman again pickets at that year's Cannes Film Festival.

1999 Directs and cowrites *Terror Firmer*, which is the first Troma film to be cut on a nonlinear editing system (AVID); the postproduction process requires the cutting of the entire first half of the film before all footage is dumped, so that the second half of the film can be edited and added to the first.

2001 With a focus on internet-related issues, particularly "net neutrality," Kaufman is both elected as vice chairman of the American Film

	Marketing Association and becomes the chairman of AFMA's newly created New Technology Opportunities Committee.
2001	Receives Lifetime Achievement Award at Rome's Cinecittà Film Festival for his "services to independent film."
2002	While at the Cannes Film Festival, Troma and Kaufman announce their Dogpile 95 Doctrine of Digital Filmmaking, both emulating and somewhat mocking Lars von Trier's Dogme 95 Vow of Chastity—a new movement in independent film promising the rawest and most authentic digital video strategies and aesthetics; anyone who so wishes can incorporate a Dogpile 95 logo on their film for free;[15] proclaims Kaufman: "Long before Dogme 95 was born, Troma was making movies with poor lighting, amateur acting and crappy sound. However, we just haven't been able to rise to the level of boredom that the Dogme 95 films have attained. This is one of the reasons that Dogpile 95 has been founded."
2004	*Tales From the Crapper* becomes Troma's first in-house DV (digital video) feature.
2006	After reading Eric Schlosser's *Fast Food Nation* and making *Poultrygeist: Night of the Chicken Dead* (2006), becomes a lifelong vegetarian along with daughter Charlotte.
2006	TromaPalooza concerts first kick off as fan-based fundraising concert events for future TromaDance Film Festivals.
2007	Chicago-based Devil's Due Publishing releases *Lloyd Kaufman Presents: The Toxic Avenger and Other Tromatic Tales*, a graphic novel collection of Troma-based characters and stories drawn and written by Tim Seeley, Sean McKeever, Ivan Brandon, and Brendan Hay.
2008	Becomes chairman of the IFTA (Independent Film & Television Alliance), running on a platform of lobbying Washington to educate lawmakers and the FCC that independent art is under assault in the United States.
2008	The critically acclaimed *Toxic Avenger* live musical—with music by Bon Jovi keyboardist David Bryan and book by Tony Award–winning playwright Joe DiPietro—successfully opens at the George Street Playhouse in New Brunswick, New Jersey, before touring Off-Broadway and around the world, with its New York City premiere held at the New World Stages on April 6, 2009; a film version of the musical is released in 2018 by BroadwayHD.
2008	Dresses as a chicken (specifically film character "Colonel Cluck") to picket the Tribeca Film Festival outside the Village East Cinema after Tribeca demands that, during its own screenings at said venue,

all posters for Troma's new *Poultrygeist: Night of the Chicken Dead* (2006) be taken down and all trailers for the film be halted from screening; the protest, which includes other Troma staff and fans as well, is covered by local press including the *New York Post*; "The Tri-Beak-a Film Festival has consistently ignored Troma's thirty-five-year history and has never shown a Troma film," claims Kaufman; *Poultrygeist* sells out that Friday's showings.

2010   TromaDance relocates from its regular location in Park City to Asbury Park, New Jersey, and will remain nomadic for its ongoing duration.

2011   Always being bellwethers and early adopters of new tech, Troma becomes one of the first film studios/distributors to embrace Microsoft's videogame system Xbox as means of offering its catalogue to fans.

2013   New York City's Museum of Modern Art (MoMA) books an early release of *Return to Nuke 'Em High Volume 1* (2013)[16] in its prestigious "Contenders" series alongside Woody Allen's *Blue Jasmine* (2013) and Palme d'Or award winner *Blue Is the Warmest Colour* (2013).

2014   While presenting a Lifetime Achievement Award onstage at the Chinese American Film Festival in Pasadena, Kaufman takes the opportunity to make an impromptu speech—in Chinese[17]—about what he feels is China's ill treatment of American independent filmmakers. "Though I assumed I had pissed off everyone involved," Kaufman later said, "I was surprised to be invited back the following year, which [gave] me hope that this conversation [was] not a lost cause."

2015   Troma releases its streaming service Troma NOW via the recently established VHX digital distribution platform, which is acquired by Vimeo in 2016; by 2021, Troma NOW is additionally distributed through new partner Roku, followed in 2023 by Amazon's Freevee; also starting up in 2015 is Troma Movies—Troma's YouTube page, offering two hundred and fifty free Troma projects, as well as a variety of DIY how-to videos for independent/low-budget filmmakers.

2015   Completion of *Toxic Avenger 5* script; there's (as per usual in the Troma realm) no money to fund it; film would have taken place in (and perhaps filmed in) Chernobyl; a daughter of a Ukrainian billionaire who is a Troma fan and wants to break into the film industry tries to cajole father to give Troma half the budget for the film, but the two disappear completely after the 2014 Russo–Ukrainian War breaks out.

2016   The Troma NOW podcast launches.

2016   MoMA screens *Tromeo & Juliet* (1996) on October 15 as part of its "Breaking Bard" Shakespeare film series, with assistant film curator Anne Morra referring to the Kaufman-directed Troma picture as "dreamscapes which remind me of surrealism. This is *Romeo and Juliet* as if Salvador Dalí had a hand in it."

2018 — Lloyd Kaufman is the first major voice/celebrity to publicly defend longtime friend and protégé James Gunn[18] after Gunn is fired by Disney from his role as director on the much-anticipated *Guardians of the Galaxy Vol. 3* (2023) due to the unearthing of tweets between Kaufman and Gunn from the earlier, more "Wild Wild West" days of Twitter that Gunn had already apologized for in the past and which, despite being cheekily Tromaesque in dark humor, were deemed offensive and vulgar enough by online outrage driven by conservative pundit Mike Cernovich to summarily "cancel" Gunn; Gunn is quickly picked up by Sony and DC Comics to helm its *Suicide Squad* reboot (2021), and is thereafter brought on to run the DC film multiverse (as both cochairman and co-CEO of DC Studios) and, due to massive outpouring of support from fans and the film community writ large, is brought back on by Disney to ultimately direct *Guardians Vol. 3*.

2019 — France's prestigious film archival organization, the Cinémathèque Française, honors Kaufman for his decades of independent filmmaking and for the forty-fifth anniversary of Troma; the organization also screens two Troma films—*The Toxic Avenger* (1984) and *Return to Return to Nuke 'Em High AKA Volume 2* (2017)—at Paris's the Max Linder Panoramo Theater.

2023 — After decades of the project being passed around to a variety of potential producers, directors, writers (including wildly prolific Academy Award winner Akiva Goldsman), lead actors, et al., Legendary Pictures' big-budget *Toxic Avenger* reboot starring Peter Dinklage as the Toxic Avenger and written/directed by Macon Blair (*I Don't Feel at Home in This World Anymore* [2017–]) is completed and opens the year's Fantastic Fest at the Alamo Drafthouse South in Austin, Texas, on September 21; Kaufman is flown out first class by Legendary and also promotes the latest Troma film, *Kill Dolly Kill*; despite mostly positive reviews through the festival and various other limited screenings thereafter, the reboot is indefinitely shelved by Legendary, with star Dinklage demanding that fans should "write to their Congressmen" about the injustice of same.

2024 — Ahoy Comics reboots the Toxic Avenger comic book series in partnership with political cartoonist and multiple Pulitzer-Prize finalist Matt Bors.

Notes

1. With some narration, music, and minor FX.
2. Thirty years later, Lee narrates the introduction and epilogue to Kaufman's *Citizen Toxie: The Toxic Avenger Part IV* (2000).
3. At the time, an "X" rating meant merely that it was a film for "mature" audiences, with such highly acclaimed works as *A Clockwork Orange* (1971) and the multiple Academy Award–winning *Midnight Cowboy* (1969) being so rated during this period, as well.
4. Kaufman's first time going to Cannes with a film.
5. Discloses Kaufman: "By law, my wife has to recuse herself from anything to do with Troma—and I think she would probably like to recuse herself from anything that has to do with me, period. . . . While film commissioner, she was appointed by Republicans and Democrats alike (unheard of in this position) and created the incentive for New York–based film crews, which allowed productions to receive thirty percent of costs back."
6. Kaufman also makes brief appearances in a number of other films on which he's worked, such as "Drunk" in *Rocky* (1976)—a role he reprises in *Rocky V* (1990)—"Second Hippie" in *Cry Uncle* (1971), and "Usher" in *Slow Dancing in the Big City* (1978), in addition to nearly five hundred further acting credits in films for an eclectic array of independent filmmakers whose productions he has supported over the years.
7. If this sounds like a peculiar choice of film to distribute for Team Kaufman, lest we forget that one of the cinematic renegade's many inspirations, Roger Corman, was the one to distribute in the USA the French animated art film *Fantastic Planet* (1973) through his New World Pictures.
8. This is done by having Troma editors substitute "PG"-rated footage shot during production for the raunchy parts.
9. Something Kaufman later regrets for obviating his ability to make any new films during this time, allowing Troma's first two *Class of Nuke 'Em High* sequels to be directed by someone else.
10. A single episode of the *Sgt. Kabukiman N.Y.P.D.* cartoon is also produced at this time by DIC Entertainment's Andy Heywood in prep for the *Toxic Crusaders* release, but ultimately leads to nothing else.
11. Kaufman also discusses with the filmmaking duo the idea of distributing their pre–viral age viral short "The Spirit of Christmas" (1995) and retitling it *A Very Troma Christmas*; the boys reject the concept and soon expand the short into what becomes *South Park* (1997–); this in turn greatly ups the value and interest in *Cannibal!*; "Troma were the first people to believe in us, so we're always behind Troma," Parker later writes in the foreword to Kaufman's *Make Your Own Damn Movie!* (2003).
12. Notable too as Kaufman's first solo directing effort on any Troma feature film to date.
13. Academy Award–winning filmmaker William Friedkin around the same time becomes embroiled in a similar legal battle with New Line over the company's lack of production of his Jack the Ripper project.
14. On the heels of New Line's successful *Teenage Mutant Ninja Turtles* (1990) live-action film.
15. The first of such films being *Wiseguys vs. Zombies* (2003) and *Meat for Satan's Icebox* (2004), released as a double-bill video by Troma.

16. Troma's first in-house production to include CGI.
17. Kaufman also speaks fluent French.
18. Who, during his lengthy tenure of apprenticeship at Troma, acted in such integral capacities as coscreenwriter, associate director, and executive in charge of production on *Tromeo & Juliet* (1996); codirector and cowriter of *Tromaville Café* (1997); original webmaster on the Troma World Wide Web; and Troma's director of production (1995–1997).

Filmography

As director (*selected*)

THE GIRL WHO RETURNED (1969)
Director: **Lloyd Kaufman**
Screenplay: **Lloyd Kaufman**, Robert Schacteland
Producers: **Lloyd Kaufman**, Robert Edelstein (Associate Producer)
Cinematographer: **Lloyd Kaufman**
Editing: **Lloyd Kaufman**
Music: **Lloyd Kaufman**, Jake Thompson
Assistant Director: Jesse Nichols, Robert Yu
Production Coordinator: Bob Kaminski
Cast: Gretchen Herman (Lucy), Beverly Galley (Geneva), Tim McClean (The Mongolian), Judith Dresh (Daisy), Letha Baker (Rose)

THE BATTLE OF LOVE'S RETURN (1971)
Director: **Lloyd Kaufman**
Screenplay: **Lloyd Kaufman**
Executive Producer: Garrard Glenn
Producers: **Lloyd Kaufman**, Frank Vitale
Cinematographer: Frank Vitale
Music: André Golino, **Lloyd Kaufman**
Editing: **Lloyd Kaufman**
Cast: **Lloyd Kaufman** (Abacrombie), Lynn Lowry (Dream Girl), Stanley Kaufman (Mr. Crumb), Andy Kay (The Loafer), Ida Goodcutt (Old Lady), Jim Crispi (Bridge Foreman), Bernard Brown (Detective Glass), Roderick Ghyka (Dr. Finger), Bonnie Sacks (Army Sergeant), Robert S. Walker (Preacher), Oliver Stone (Cliff), Theodore Gershuny (as Ted Gershuny) (Narrator)

BIG GUS, WHAT'S THE FUSS? (also known as HA-BALASH HA'AMITZ SHVARTZ, BRAVE DETECTIVE SHWARTZ, and FAT SPY) (1973)
Director: Ami Artzi, **Lloyd Kaufman**
Screenplay: Ami Artzi, **Lloyd Kaufman**

xlii　　FILMOGRAPHY

Producers: Ami Artzi, **Lloyd Kaufman**
Cinematography: Hassa Wollich
Music: Beni Nagari
Editing: Dov Hoenig
Cast: Ilan Dar, Joseph Shiloach, Dubi Gal, Sassi Keshet, Elisheva Michaeli

SQUEEZE PLAY! (1979)
Director: **Lloyd Kaufman** (as Samuel Weil)
Screenplay: Charles Kaufman, Haim Pekelis
Producers: Michael Herz, **Lloyd Kaufman**
Cinematographer: **Lloyd Kaufman**
Editing: George T. Norris
Costume Design: Karen Galonough
Makeup Department (Special Makeup Effects): Karen Galonough
Art Designer: Sandy Hamilton, Susan Kaufman
Assistant Director: David Alexander
Production Manager: William B. Kegg III
Cast: Jim Harris (Wes), Jennifer Hetrick (as Jenni Hetrick) (Samantha), Richard Gitlin (as Rick Gitlin) (Fred), Helen Campitelli (Jamie), Rick Khan (as Rick Kagn) (Tom), Diana Valentien (Maureen), Al Corley (as Alford Corley) (Buddy), Melissa Michaels (Mary Lou), Michael P. Moran (Bozo), Sonya Jennings (Max), Kaye Bramblett (as Sharon Kyle Bramblett) (Midge)

WAITRESS! (1982)
Director: **Lloyd Kaufman** (as Samuel Weil)
Screenplay: Charles Kaufman, Haim Pekelis
Producers: Michael Herz, **Lloyd Kaufman**
Cinematographer: **Lloyd Kaufman**
Editing: George T. Norris
Costume Design: Karen Galonough
Makeup Department (Special Makeup Effects): Karen Galonough
Art Designer: Sandy Hamilton, Susan Kaufman
Assistant Director: David Alexander
Production Manager: William B. Kegg III
Cast: Jim Harris (Wes), Jennifer Hetrick (as Jenni Hetrick) (Samantha), Richard Gitlin (as Rick Gitlin) (Fred), Helen Campitelli (Jamie), Rick Khan (as Rick Kagn) (Tom), Diana Valentien (Maureen), Al Corley (as Alford Corley) (Buddy), Melissa Michaels (Mary Lou), Michael P. Moran (Bozo), Sonya Jennings (Max), Kaye Bramblett (as Sharon Kyle Bramblett) (Midge)

STUCK ON YOU! (1982)

Director: Michael Herz, **Lloyd Kaufman** (as Samuel Weil)
Screenplay: Jeffrey Delman, John A. Gallagher, Tony Gittelson, Michael Herz, **Lloyd Kaufman**, Darren Kloomok, Warren Leight, Duffy Caesar Magesis, Melanie Mintz, Don Perman, Stuart Strutin
Executive Producer: Spencer A. Tandy
Producers: Michael Herz, **Lloyd Kaufman**, Stuart Strutin (Associate Producer)
Cinematographer: **Lloyd Kaufman**
Editing: Richard W. Haines, Darren Kloomok, Ralph Rosenblum
Costume Design: Rosa Alfaro, Walter Steihl
Special Effects: Leslie Larraine
Art Direction: Barry Shapiro
Assistant Director: David Alexander
Production Manager: Sue Dember, Kate Eisemann
Cast: Irwin Corey (as Professor Irwin Corey) (Judge Gabriel), Virginia Penta (Carol Griffiths), Mark Mikulski (Bill Andrews), Albert Pia (Arie Poulet), Norma Pratt (Bill's Mother), Daniel Harris (Napoleon), Denise Silbert (Cavewoman), Eddie Brill (Caveman), June Martin (Eve), John Bigham (Adam), Robin Burroughs (Isabella), Carl Sturmer (Columbus), Julie Newdow (Pocahontas), Patricia Tallman (as Pat Tallman) (Queen Guenevere), Kent Shelton (as Mr. Kent) (King Arthur), Barbie Kielian (Josephine), Louis Homyak (Lance Griffiths), Ben Kellman (Indian Chief)

THE FIRST TURN-ON! (1983)

Director: Michael Herz, **Lloyd Kaufman** (as Samuel Weil)
Screenplay: Michael Herz, **Lloyd Kaufman**, Georgia Harrell, Stuart Strutin, Mark Torgl
Executive Producers: William Kirksey, Spencer A. Tandy
Producers: Michael Herz, **Lloyd Kaufman**, Stuart Strutin (Associate Producer)
Cinematographer: **Lloyd Kaufman**
Editing: Adam Fredericks, Richard King
Costume Design: Danielle Brunon
Makeup Supervisor: Jennifer Aspinall
Special Effects: Leslie Larraine
Art Direction: Ellen Christiansen
Production Supervisor: Nelson Vaughn
Cast: Georgia Harrell (Michelle Farmer), Michael Sanville (Mitch "Stud"), Googy Gress (Henry Putz), John Flood (Danny Anderson), Heidi Miller (Annie Goldberg), Al Pia (Alfred Zizler), Betty Pia (Mrs. Anderson)

THE TOXIC AVENGER (1984)
Director: Michael Herz, **Lloyd Kaufman** (as Samuel Weil)
Screenplay: **Lloyd Kaufman**, Joe Ritter, Gay Partington Terry, Stuart Strutin
Executive Producers: William Kirksey, Spencer A. Tandy
Producers: Michael Herz, **Lloyd Kaufman**, Stuart Strutin (Associate Producer)
Cinematographer: **Lloyd Kaufman**, James A. Lebovitz (as James London)
Editing: Richard W. Haines (as Richard Haines)
Makeup Department: Jennifer Aspinall, Ralph Cordero, Tom Lauten
Special Effects: Matthew West (Assistant)
Art Direction: Barry Shapiro, Alexandra Mazur
Production Manager: Caroline Baron
Music: Christopher Burke, Mark Hoffman, Dean Summers
Cast: Andree Maranda (Sara), Mitch Cohen (as Mitchell Cohen) (The Toxic Avenger), Jennifer Babtist (as Jennifer Baptist) (Wanda), Cindy Manion (Julie), Robert Prichard (Slug), Gary Schneider (Bozo), Pat Ryan (as Pat Ryan Jr.) (Mayor Peter Belgoody), Mark Torgl (Melvin Junko)

CLASS OF NUKE 'EM HIGH (1986)
Director: Richard W. Haines, **Lloyd Kaufman** (as Samuel Weil)
Screenplay: **Lloyd Kaufman**, Richard W. Haines, Mark Rudnitsky, Stuart Strutin, Graham Flashner
Executive Producer: James Treadwell
Producers: Michael Herz, **Lloyd Kaufman**, Stuart Strutin (Associate Producer)
Cinematographer: Michael Mayers
Editing: Richard W. Haines
Costume Design: Ivy Rosovsky
Special / Makeup Effects: Scott Coulter, Brian Quinn
Art Direction: Arthur Lorenz, Art Skopinsky
Production Manager: Sandra Byrd Curry
Assistant Director: Ann McCabe
Music: David Barreto, David Behennah, Biohazard, Clive Burr, Ray Haleblian
Cast: Janell Brady (Chrissy), Gil Brenton (as Gilbert Brenton) (Warren), Robert Prichard (Spike), Pat Ryan (as R. L. Ryan) (Mr. Paley), James Nugent Vernon (Eddie), Brad Dunker (Gonzo), Gary Schneider (Pete), Théo Cohan (Muffey), Gary Rosenblatt (Greg), Mary Taylor (Judy)

TROMA'S WAR (1988)
Director: Richard W. Haines, **Lloyd Kaufman** (as Samuel Weil)
Screenplay: **Lloyd Kaufman**, Mitchell Dana, Eric Hattler, Tom Martinek, Rick Washburn

Producers: Michael Herz, **Lloyd Kaufman**, Jeffrey W. Sass (Associate Producer), Rick Washburn (as Ryan Richards) (Associate Producer)
Cinematographer: James A. Lebovitz (as James London)
Editing: Brian Sternkopf
Costume Design: Ivy Rosovsky
Makeup Department: Regina Deavers, Alita Griffin, Tom Martinek, Kathleen Richards
Assistant Director: Denis Hahn
Music: Christopher De Marco
Special Effects: David Barrett, Wilfred Caban, Anthony Calandrillo, Lawrence Ferber, Jorge Fernández, George Giordana, William Jennings, Pericles Lewnes, Tom Martinek, Stephen Patrie, Paul Pisoni
Cast: Carolyn Beauchamp (Lydia), Sean Bowen (Taylor), Rick Washburn (as Michael Ryder) (Parker), Patrick Weathers (Kirkland), Jessica Dublin (Dottie), Steven Crossley (Marshall), Lorayn DeLuca (as Lorayn Lane Deluca) (Maria), Charles Kay-Hune (as Charles Kay Hune) (Hardwick), Ara Romanoff (Cooney), Brenda Brock (Kim), Lisbeth Kaufman (Jingoistic Baby), Lisa Petruno (as Lisa Patruno) (Jennifer)

THE TOXIC AVENGER PART II (1989)
Director: Richard W. Haines, **Lloyd Kaufman** (as Samuel Weil)
Screenplay: **Lloyd Kaufman**, Gay Parington Terry, Pericles Lewnes, Fumio Furuya, Yoshiko Miyamoto, Andrew Wolk, Phil Rivo, Joe Ritter
Producers: Michael Herz, **Lloyd Kaufman**, Jeffrey W. Sass (Associate Producer)
Cinematographer: James A. Lebovitz (as James London)
Editing: Michael Schweitzer
Costume Design: Susan Douglas
Makeup Department: Timothy Considine, Yoichi Fukoka, Joel Harlow, Roy Knyrim, Jerry Macaluso, Kathy Mulshine, Mayumi Shōji, Noboru Tamura
Assistant Director: Kazuo Ito, William Jennings
Music: Barry Guard
Special Effects: Dawn Bradford, Wilfred Caban, Timothy Considine, William Decker, George Giordano, Kelly Gleason, Kenny Lee Hamel, Arthur M. Jolly, Pericles Lewnes, Satoshi Narumi
Cast: Ron Fazio (The Toxic Avenger / Apocalypse Inc. Executive), John Altamura (The Toxic Avenger), Phoebe Legere (Claire), Rick Collins (Apocalypse Inc. Chairman), Rikiya Yasuoka (Big Mac Bunko), Tsutomu Sekine (Announcer), Mayoko Katsuragi (Masami), Shinoburyō (as Shinoburyu) (Shōchikuyama), Lisa Gaye (Malfaire), Jessica Dublin (Mrs. Junko)

THE TOXIC AVENGER PART III: THE LAST TEMPTATION OF TOXIE (1989)
Director: Richard W. Haines, **Lloyd Kaufman** (as Samuel Weil)
Screenplay: **Lloyd Kaufman**, Gay Partington Terry, Pericles Lewnes, Andrew Wolk, Phil Rivo, Joe Ritter
Producers: Michael Herz, **Lloyd Kaufman**, Jeffrey W. Sass (Associate Producer)
Cinematographer: James A. Lebovitz (as James London)
Editing: Joseph McGirr
Costume Design: Susan Douglas
Makeup Department: Timothy Considine, William Decker, Kelly Gleason, Vincent J. Guastini, Vincent J. Guastini, Joel Harlow, Arthur M. Jolly, Roy Knyrim, Jerry Macaluso
Production Manager: Jeffrey W. Sass
Assistant Director: William Jennings
Music: Barry Guard
Special Effects: Wilfred Caban, Evan Campbell, George Giordano, David Grasso (as Dave Grasso), Pericles Lewnes, Kenny Myers
Cast: Ron Fazio (The Toxic Avenger / Apocalypse Inc. Executive), John Altamura (The Toxic Avenger), Phoebe Legere (Claire), Rick Collins (Apocalypse Inc. Chairman / The Devil), Lisa Gaye (Malfaire), Jessica Dublin (Mrs. Junko), Tsutomu Sekine (Announcer), Michael J. Kaplan (Little Melvin), Traci Mann (Snake Lady / Apprentice Bad Girl)

SGT. KABUKIMAN N.Y.P.D. (1990)
Director: **Lloyd Kaufman**, Michael Herz
Screenplay: **Lloyd Kaufman**, Andrew Osborne, Jeffrey W. Sass, Robert Coffey, Cliff Hahn
Executive Producers: Tetsu Fujimura, Masaya Nakamura
Producers: Michael Herz, **Lloyd Kaufman**, Jeffrey W. Sass (Line Producer), Andrew Wolk (Associate Producer), David Greenspan (Associate Producer)
Cinematographer: Robert Paone (as Bob Williams)
Editing: Peter Novak, Ian Slater
Costume Design: Cherie Zucker
Makeup Department: Ann-Mari Jacobsen, Steve Ramsey, Josh Turi (as Joshua Turi)
Production Management: John J. Kelly (as John Kelly)
Assistant Director: Andrew Wolk
Music: Bob Mithoff
Art Direction: Michael O'Dell Green (as Michael Odell Green)
Special Effects: J.C. Brotherhood, Timothy Considine, Mr. Dead (as Christopher Davis), Kelly Gleason, Drew Jiritano, Pericles Lewnes, Anthony Mark Viverito

(as Anthony Mark), Stacey L. Mark (as Stacey Mark), Allan Neuwirth, Mike Rios (as Michael Rios), Paul Sciacca, Patricia Stratico, Josh Turi (as Joshua Turi), Adam Weiner
Cast: Rick Gianasi (Harry Griswold / Sgt. Kabukiman), Susan Byun (Lotus), Bill Weeden (Reginald Stuart), Thomas Crnkovich (Rembrandt), Larry Robinson (Rev. Snipes), Noble Lee Lester (Capt. Bender), Brick Bronsky (Jughead), Pamela Alster (Connie), LaRosa Shaler McClure (Felicia), Jeff Wineshmutz (Hernandez), Joe Fleishaker (Josephs), Fumio Furuya (Sato), Masahiro Masahiro (Ichiro)

TROMEO & JULIET (1996)
Director: **Lloyd Kaufman**
Screenplay: **Lloyd Kaufman**, James Gunn, Andrew Deemer, Jason Green, Phil Rivo
Executive Producers: Daniel Laikind, Grant Quasha, Robert Schiller
Producers: Michael Herz, **Lloyd Kaufman**, Franny Baldwin (Line Producer), Jonathan Foster (Coproducer), Robert Hersov (Coproducer), Andrew Weiner (Associate Producer)
Cinematographer: Brendan Flynt
Editing: Frank Reynolds
Costume Design: Kyra Svetlovsky
Makeup Department: Sandee Brockwell, Callie French, Vincent Schicchi
Production Management: Franny Baldwin, James Gunn
Assistant Director: Robert Bauer
Music: Willie Wisely
Art Direction: Hannah Moseley
Special Effects: Joe Macchia, Neil Ruddy, Vincent Schicci, Louie Zakarian
Cast: Jane Jensen(Juliet Capulet), Will Keenan (Tromeo Que), Valentine Miele (Murray Martini), William Beckwith (as Maximillian Shaun) (Cappy Capulet), Steve Gibbons (London Arbuckle), Sean Gunn (Sammy Capulet), Debbie Rochon (Ness), Lemmy (The Narrator), Stephen Blackehart (Benny Que), Flip Brown (Father Lawrence), Patrick Connor (Tyrone Capulet), Earl McKoy (Monty Que), Gene Terinoni (Detective Ernie Scalus), Wendy Adams (Ingrid Capulet), Tamara Marie Watson (as Tamara Craig Thomas) (Georgie Capulet)

TERROR FIRMER (1999)
Director: **Lloyd Kaufman**
Screenplay: Patrick Cassidy, Douglas Buck
Executive Producers: Charles Berry Hill, David Hill (as David Berry Hill), Kenneth B. Squire, Elizabeth van Merkensteijn (Coexecutive Producer), John H. van Merkensteijn (as John H. van Merkensteijn III) (Coexecutive Producer)

Producers: Michael Herz, **Lloyd Kaufman**, Patrick Cassidy (Associate Producer), Zack Coutroulis (Line Producer), Jonathan Foster (Coproducer), Will Keenan (Associate Producer), Stephen Schmidt (Line Producer)
Cinematographer: Brendan Flynt
Editing: Gabriel Friedman
Costume Design: Stefanie Imhoff (as Stephanie Imhoff)
Makeup Department: Timothy Considine, Katherine O'Donnell
Production Management: Yurgi Ganter
Assistant Director: Adam Hammel
Music: Nobuhiko Morino
Art Direction: Marc Turnage
Special Effects: Alex Attimonelli, David Bracci, Brigida Costa, Joseph Dilud, George Giordano, Drew Jiritano, Ruth Pongstaphone-Safer, Mike Shapiro (as Michael Shapiro), Pam Siegel
Cast: Will Keenan (Casey Kaufman), Alyce LaTourelle (Jennifer), **Lloyd Kaufman** (Larry Benjamin), Trent Haaga (Jerry), Sheri Wenden (Mysterious Woman / Waitress), Debbie Rochon (Christine), Yaniv Sharon (Naked P.A.), Charlotte Kaufman (Audrey Benjamin), Gary Hrbek (Toddster), Joe Fleishaker (Jacob Gelman), Ron Jeremy (Casey's Dad), Greg "G-Spot" Siebel (Ward), Mario Díaz (D.J.), Mo Fischer (Andy)

CITIZEN TOXIE: THE TOXIC AVENGER PART IV (2000)
Director: **Lloyd Kaufman**
Screenplay: Trent Haaga, Patrick Cassidy, Gabriel Friedman, **Lloyd Kaufman**, Sean Collins, Matt Levin, Corey Kalman
Executive Producers: James Coleman, Andrew Lerner, Weston Quasha, Ken Squire
Producers: Patrick Cassidy (Line Producer), Jonathan Foster (Coproducer), Trent Haaga (Line Producer), Michael Herz, Adam Jahnke, **Lloyd Kaufman,** Sean McGrath (Associate Producer), Scott W. McKinlay, Doug Sakmann (Associate Producer) Yaniv Sharon (Associate Producer), Yoni Tabac (Associate Producer), Elizabeth van Merkensteijn (Coproducer), John H. van Merkensteijn (Coproducer)
Cinematographer: Brendan Flynt
Editing: Gabriel Friedman
Costume Design: Nives Spaleta
Makeup Department: Christopher Burdett, Mara Capozzi, Tracey Faithe, Sandy Molina, James Ojala
Music: Wes Nagy (as Wesley Nagy)
Art Direction: Ali Baron (as Ali Grossman), Ana Katharina Drechsler (as Ana Katharina Dreschsler), Maus Drechsler

Special Effects: Jenny Barton, Timothy Considine (as Tim Considine), Barak Epstein, Aline Fader, Scotty Fields (as Scott Fields), Henning Hoenicke, Drew Jiritano, Matt Mastrella (as Matt Mastrelli), Lara Meda, Rachel Pagani, Mike Rappold, Rodney Sterbenz, Amy Tagliamonti, Michael Tolkle, Josh Turi, Millard Wooley, Marcus Koch
Cast: David Mattey (Toxic Avenger / Noxious Offender / Chester's Fellatio Customer), Clyde Lewis (Toxie) (voice), Heidi Sjursen (Sarah / Claire), Paul Kyrmse (Sgt. Kabukiman / Evil Kabukiman), Joe Fleishaker (Chester / Lardass), Dan Snow (Sgt. Kazinski), Michael Budinger (Tito), Lisa Terezakis (Sweetie Honey), Barry Brisco (Pompey), Debbie Rochon (Ms. Weiner), Ron Jeremy (Mayor Goldberg), Corey Feldman (as Kinky Finkelstein) (Sarah's Gynecologist), Trent Haaga (Tex Diaper), Mark Torgl (Evil Melvin), Rick Collins (Amortville Police Chief), Mitch Cohen (Lucifer)

POULTRYGEIST: NIGHT OF THE CHICKEN DEAD (2006)
Director: **Lloyd Kaufman**
Screenplay: Gabriel Friedman, Dan Bova (as Daniel Bova), **Lloyd Kaufman**
Executive Producers: Michael Herz, **Lloyd Kaufman**, Patricia Kaufman (as Patricia Swinney Kaufman)
Producers: Benjamin Cord (Coproducer), Andrew Deemer (as Andy Deemer), Jason Foulke (Coproducer), Nick Koenig (Line Producer), J. Michael Landis (Line Producer), Kiel Walker
Cinematographer: Brendan Flynt, **Lloyd Kaufman**
Editing: Gabriel Friedman
Costume Design: Brenna Traynor
Makeup Department: Dominic Alfano, Marta Estirado, Scotty Fields, Margaux Frankel, Maria Gismondi, James Ojala
Production Manager: Ryan Mead
Assistant Director: Caleb Emerson
Music: Daniel DeMauro
Art Direction: Emma Assin, Kevin Sean Michaels
Special Effects: Bitte Andersson, Kevin Barnes, Zack Beins, Benzy, Ethan Blum, Christopher C. Bowen, Jules-César Bréchet, Arvid Cristina, David Delaney, Tom Devlin, Tyler Dolph, Paul Eide, Christopher Fehring, Ken Franklin, Matthew R. Frendo, Kiel Frieden, Matthew R. Harris, Michael Huffman, Melissa McAnany, Dave Molloy, Tony Lane Norberg, Anna Gabriella Olson, Ruth Phelps, Nicholas Ruggiero, Bogdan Shepard, Gregory Paul Smith, Ian Strandberg, Richard Taylor, David Turnbull, Nikos Tzortzinakis, Nick Wolfe
Cast: Jason Yachanin (Arbie), Kate Graham (Wendy), Allyson Sereboff (Micki), Robin L. Watkins (General Lee Roy), Joshua Olatunde (Denny), Caleb Emerson

FILMOGRAPHY

(Carl Jr.), Rose Ghavami (Humus / ACB Dancer), Khalid Rivera (Jose Paco Bell), Joe Fleishaker (as Mega Herz) (Jared), **Lloyd Kaufman** (Mature Arbie), Ron Jeremy (Crazy Ron)

RETURN TO NUKE 'EM HIGH VOLUME 1 (2013)
Director: **Lloyd Kaufman**
Screenplay: Travis Campbell, Casey Clapp, Derek Dressler, Aaron Hamel, **Lloyd Kaufman**
Executive Producer: Matt Manjourides
Producers: Alex Gordon (Associate Producer), Michael Herz, Regina Katz (Associate Producer), Lily Hayes Kaufman (Consulting Producer), **Lloyd Kaufman**, René Krzok (Associate Producer), Justin A. Martell
Cinematographer: Justin Duval
Editing: Travis Campbell
Wardrobe Supervisor: Mark Finch
Makeup Department: Babette Bombshell, Jennifer Cummings, Enya Patterson
Production Manager: Regina Katz
Assistant Director: Aaron Hamel
Music: Cesar Placeres, Jason Paul Bouton, Kurt Dirt
Art Direction: Seager Dixon
Special Effects: Fernando Alle, Drew Bolduc, Kaleigh Brown, Lisa Forst, Aurelien Gendraud, Jason M. Koch, Scott Leva, Michele Lombardi, Tom Martino, Doug Sakmann, Martin Tejada
Cast: Asta Paredes (Chrissy Goldberg), Catherine Corcoran (Lauren), Vito Trigo (Leonardo), Clay von Carlowitz (Eugene "The Machine" McCormack), Zac Amico (Zack), Mike Baez (Donatello), Tara E. Miller (Rachel Ruysch), Lemmy (The President), Michael C. Schmahl, **Lloyd Kaufman** (Lee Harvey Herzkauf), Babette Bombshell (Principal Westly)

RETURN TO RETURN TO NUKE 'EM HIGH AKA VOLUME 2 (2017)
Director: **Lloyd Kaufman**
Screenplay: Travis Campbell, Derek Dressler, **Lloyd Kaufman**, Gabriel Friedman, Doug Sakmann
Executive Producer: Matt Manjourides
Producers: John Patrick Brennan (as John P. Brennan) (Coproducer), Melissa Fortunatti (Line Producer), Ashton Golembo, Alex Gordon (Associate Producer), Michael Herz, Regina Katz (Associate Producer), **Lloyd Kaufman,** René Krzok (Associate Producer), Jeff Lasky
Cinematographer: Justin Duval
Editing: Travis Campbell

Wardrobe Supervisor: Mark Finch
Makeup Department: Merritt Evelyn Christensen
Production Manager: Al Holm, Regina Katz
Assistant Director: Sam Qualiana
Music: Cesar Placeres, Jason Paul Bouton, Kurt Dirt, Ethan Hurt, Mick O'Keefe
Art Direction: Seager Dixon
Special Effects: Fernando Alle, Drew Bolduc, Evan Parra, Doug Sakmann, Martin Tejada
Cast: Asta Paredes (Chrissy Goldberg), Catherine Corcoran (Lauren), Vito Trigo (Leonardo), Clay von Carlowitz (Eugene "The Machine" McCormack), Zac Amico (Zack), Mike Baez (Donatello), Tara E. Miller (Rachel Ruysch), Lemmy (The President), Michael C. Schmahl, **Lloyd Kaufman** (Lee Harvey Herzkauf), Babette Bombshell (Principal Westly)

#SHAKESPEARESSHITSTORM (2020)
Director: **Lloyd Kaufman**
Screenplay: Brandon Bassham, **Lloyd Kaufman**, Gabriel Friedman, William Shakespeare, Frazer Brown, Doug Sakmann, Zac Amico
Executive Producer: Thomas Burr Dodd (Coexecutive Producer), Kenneth Filmer (Coexecutive Producer), Michael Herz, **Lloyd Kaufman**, Patricia Kaufman
Producers: James N. Boylan (as James Boylan) (Associate Producer), John Patrick Brennan, Flavio de Castro Barboza (Associate Producer), Thom DeMicco (Associate Producer), Justin A. Martell, Leandro Nazar Rabelo (Associate Producer), Doug Sakmann (Coproducer), George Skoufalos (Associate Producer)
Cinematographer: Lucas Pitassi
Editing: Seby X. Martinez
Wardrobe Supervisor: Jackie Koe
Makeup Department: Renata De Los Rios
Assistant Director: Allison Davidoff
Music: Louie Aronowitz, Filepe Melo
Art Direction: Patrick Klouman
Special Effects: Drew Bolduc, Kyle Corwin, Eric Fox, Nikki Freed, Stephen Lewis, Anthony R. Risen, Doug Sakmann, Gina Sandy
Cast: **Lloyd Kaufman** (Prospero / Antoinette Duke), Catherine Corcoran (Miranda's Mom), Debbie Rochon (Senator Sebastian), Julie Anne Prescott (Hippolyta), Kyle Rappaport (Social Justice Warrior), Nadia White (Gonerill), Genoveva Rossi (VIP Party Person), Alexandra Faye Sadeghian (Millennial), Monique Dupree (Caliban), Ming Chen (Busty Executive), Michael Lippert (Skeleton Pooping Man / Passed Out Partygoer), Alexander Hauck (Reporter)

Lloyd Kaufman: Interviews

Filmmakers: Cecil B. in a West Side Walk Up

N. R. Kleinfield / 1981

From the *New York Times*, April 19, 1981. © 1981 The New York Times Company. All rights reserved. Used under license.

In Hollywood these days, making movies means big money: big production costs, big advertising budgets, big stars. And, all too often, big losses to match.

On the West Side of New York, making movies means small money: Small budgets, small ads, small stars—but no losses. Troma Inc. is a tiny Manhattan movie company with large aspirations. Its total annual revenues hardly rival what Burt Reynolds or Clint Eastwood collects for a single film. Troma's two founders were once fittingly dubbed "Poverty Row Producers." Where the average movie now costs a tidy $10 million, Troma brings them in for well under $1 million. While Hollywood goes first-class all the way, Troma travels in something worse than coach. As Lloyd Kaufman, Troma's jocund president, puts it, "Our films are made on absolute breadcrumbs."

Friends and relatives pop up as extras. Stars are still aspiring. Mr. Kaufman and Michael Herz, Troma's cofounder, pitch in more than most movie moguls. They conceive scripts. They direct. They produce. Mr. Kaufman handles the camera work. Everyone fetches coffee.

Troma and its nine employees are quartered in what Mr. Kaufman freely admits is a "slum building" situated at 733 Ninth Avenue in Manhattan's less-than-fashionable Hell's Kitchen district. Troma owns the building and occupies the second floor. Several residential tenants occupy upstairs apartments. A thrift shop recently displaced a liquor store on the ground floor.

Small as it may be—Troma grossed about $1 million last year—for seven years now, the company has cranked out about a film a year and distributed a couple of others, all while turning a profit of some sort for its investors.

It has a movie scheduled to open in New York next month called *Squeeze Play!* It is a bawdy comedy (Troma specializes in bawdy comedies) dealing with suburban softball. The denouement comes when the women form a team and take on the men. The movie was shot, for the most part, in downtown Leonia, NJ.

Squeeze Play! has already played around the country, attracting mixed reviews but gross billings of about $8 million. Out of that, roughly $1 million has filtered into Troma, which is a decent sum given that a mere $300,000 covered production costs, and distribution expenses ran about the same.

How does Troma make films so cheaply? "We're sort of known for exploiting people," Mr. Kaufman says. "We don't have the dough to pay much. People look at working for us as a prestige thing. They talk about surviving Camp Troma."

Films are shot in and around New York. There is relentless rehearsing, since Troma cannot afford to film scenes repeatedly. To round up extras, Troma has several times set up recruitment stands in Central Park. In Leonia, it sent emissaries to Kiwanis Club affairs. The prestige is unlimited. The pay is nothing.

Stanley Kaufman, a prospering lawyer lucky enough to be Lloyd Kaufman's father, has now shown up in some eight Troma films. "He's getting pretty decent by now," the younger Kaufman observes. "The majors are going to be coming after him."

A foot doctor who is a good friend of Mr. Kaufman's landed a role as a "drunken lout" in *Squeeze Play!* Mr. Kaufman's mother can be spotted as an off-off-Broadway producer in Troma's upcoming *Waitress!* Mr. Kaufman was bold enough to ax her scene from *Squeeze Play!* and still live to regret it.

What does a starring role in a Troma film pay? "I'll give you an idea," Mr. Kaufman says. "The star of *Waitress!* received $400 for the job. That meant about two months of rehearsals and five weeks of filming, and those were eighteen-hour days."

What, then, does a nonstarring role pay? "Fifty bucks," Mr. Kaufman shrugs. "Ten bucks. Nothing." Still, finding talent—or at least, actors—is no great problem. Troma's offices are flooded with resumes from graduates of Harvard and Yale and Princeton. A part in a nationally distributed movie, whatever the pay, unlocks bigger doors.

Both Mr. Kaufman, thirty-four, and Mr. Herz, thirty-one incidentally, draw a salary somewhere in the mid–five figures, which is a notch above Poverty Row but many notches below Stanley Kubrick. All of Troma's profits, after the return to investors, are plowed back into development costs.

In the movie business, success is precarious, of course. "I think every day we're in danger of going under," Mr. Kaufman says. "The key is we live very modestly. You don't see too many limos parked outside. When we entertain people up here, we order some sandwiches, and we usually go Dutch. The thing is, in this business, if you just survive you're doing well. And we keep making movies . . ."

Lloyd Kaufman and Michael Herz met at Yale in the late 1960s. Mr. Kaufman majored in Chinese studies; Mr. Herz in political science. Mr. Kaufman graduated in 1969, and got into film work. Mr. Herz earned a law degree at New York University, while working with Mr. Kaufman on the side. They formed Troma in 1974. (Troma is not in fact a word, although Mr. Kaufman tells people it means "excellence on celluloid in the ancient Latin."[1])

The pair have stuck it out as independents in part because they are mightily unimpressed with the ways of the major studios. "It's all done by committee," Mr. Herz sneers, "and it's all go the least offensive, safest way. And the movies bore people. I've seen bar mitzvah pictures, pictures of my trip to Greece, that are more entertaining than many films from the majors."

Decidedly a minor studio, Troma has trouble earning prime playing times (or any playing times) at good theaters. It gets a much lower split of the box office revenues than its bigger competitors. To play first-run theaters in major markets, its films have to spend months appearing in smaller cities to build a box-office record. *Squeeze Play!*, for instance, was on the road about eighteen months and is only now hitting New York and Chicago.

Critics have not universally rushed to proclaim Troma's excellence. "We've had some dreadful reviews," Mr. Kaufman admits. "The thing is, our movies are not the sort of thing that critics can go out and discover. They're not about people discussing Vietnam."

What low-budget projects are kicking around the Troma offices? There's a comedy entitled *Split*, about relationships between men and women over a six-thousand-year period. Then there's *Carpool*, a black comedy about the impact that an automobile has on four suburbanites who share a carpool. Then there's *Welcome Home*, in which inhabitants of an old-age home rebel and take charge of the place.

At present, Troma is working on striking a deal with an established studio for some development money. It is talking with some Wall Street venture capitalists. There are cable companies in need of product to air. If things pan out, Troma hopes to start making movies that cost as much as $1 million or $2 million. It would like to corral a few "names" as stars, turn out two or three movies a year, and maybe strike it big.

"We figure that if we keep on going on in our slow, careful manner, the roulette wheel will stop on our number," Mr. Kaufman says.

Note

1. After struggling to come up with a sui generis name that had not already been registered as an LLC, Herz and Kaufman began scouring their minds for complete nonsense language that would be, as with everything else the studio would produce in years to come, their very own. Additionally, "Troma" met ubercontrarian Kaufman's alleged requirement of a company name that would be "the ugliest word we could think of."

TROMA Films: They're Not Art, but They Make Money

Jill J. Lanford / 1983

From *USA TODAY NETWORK*, October 21, 1983. © Jill J. Lanford—USA Today Network. Reprinted with permission.

If you're talking art, TROMA films definitely won't make the grade.

Critics brand them as mindless bits of fluff—a series of sophomoric comedies bound together by watered-down plots, lewd jokes, and youthful sex.

Typically cast with no-name starlets who work for little pay and with even less clothes, there are no exorbitant budgets or gala premieres for *these* movies. Special effects are kept to a minimum, as are most of the other costly tricks-of-the-trade that frequently boost today's motion picture budgets well over the $10 million mark.

But if TROMA execs are left sitting at home on Academy Awards night, it's a situation that should suit them just fine: *their* films consistently turn a profit, and that's more than the giants of the motion picture industry can say.

In a recent interview, TROMA president Lloyd Kaufman talked about his small but progressive New York company and the new moneymaker he has in the works.

"Going to a TROMA film is not an art experience," the Yale graduate readily explained, "and it's not supposed to be. We make movies that appeal to a young audience that is looking for a few laughs, a thrill or two, and some mild sex. That's it. We don't even *try* to appeal to your mind—just your raunchier senses."

At the very least, he's honest. As creator of such movies as *Squeeze Play!*, *Waitress!*, *Stuck on You!*, and now, *The First Turn-On!*, Kaufman has learned that sometimes less is better—less budget, less plot, less stars, less clothes.

This isn't bringing in big bucks according to typical Hollywood standards, but it *is* turning a profit for everyone concerned—mainly, its investors.

"We operate totally differently from most of the big motion picture companies," he continued. "To begin with, we're out to make money on a film—for ourselves and our investors—and they *aren't*."

Paramount isn't interested in turning a profit? Twentieth Century-Fox couldn't care less if its films finish in the red? To the layman this may sound strange, but according to Kaufman, most motion picture executives are looking after themselves, not the company.

"They make their money through fees," he explained. "Their budgets are tremendous to begin with, so it doesn't really hurt when $250,000 goes into a pocket here or there. It's expected, and it's a system that suits them all fine."

By the time stars are paid, production and promotions are finished, and everyone has his cut, the companies have spent a whopping sum that would be difficult to see a return on—even if the film is a hit. Only one in six sees a profit, and most of that is eaten up by tax laws.

"But, at TROMA, production money is closely guarded. We don't have the Dudley Moores and the Woody Allens, and so we don't pay our actors outrageous sums," he continued.

As an example of TROMA's thriftiness, the "star" of *Waitress!* received $400 for the job. That included two months of rehearsals, five weeks of filming, and eighteen-hour days. Nonstarring roles can pay anywhere from fifty bucks to nothing, he said, and aspiring actors and actresses are eager to snap them up just for the privilege of appearing in a nationally distributed movie.

Needless to say, the company's modest New York office is continually flooded with resumes from Harvard, Yale, and Princeton. TROMA's films may not be prestigious, but audiences *do* see them, and any leg up for an ambitious young actor is a help.

"One of the main reasons we feature so much nudity is because we don't use big-name stars in our productions," he said. "When we don't have the big names as a box office draw, we have to substitute something which will make people want to see our movies, give us a competitive edge. Nudity works just as well, and it's much cheaper."

If Kaufman is under no delusions as to why his films make money, he *does* see some merit underlying all the admittedly cheap jokes and thrills. It's all in fun, he insisted, and the movies' "basic values" are quite good.

"Let's face it: Billy Graham can make all the movies he wants, but young people probably aren't going to volunteer to see them," he theorized. "They *will* go to a TROMA production, and they could do a lot worse."

Kaufman cited as an example the recent revival of blood-and-guts horror films. "In a TROMA film, no one gets axed to death, and drugs and violence aren't glamorized. If there is a good bit of raunchy jokes and sex, at least it isn't deprecating. I believe that underneath it all, our basic values are quite good. They may be subtle, but they're there."

Kaufman also defies anyone who brands his films as sexist, despite the fact they usually revolve around young heroines who are buxom, bouncy, and *not* overly shy.

"Well, let's just say that if we exploit woman, we exploit men equally as much," he said with a laugh. "Sure, we show lots of girls nude, but they're girls who have minds, too, and are going places. I'd even venture to say that we don't stereotype women as much as a lot of the more 'acceptable' motion pictures do."

Citing the recent hit *An Officer and a Gentleman*, Kaufman continued: "The girls in those films were presented as total idiots who had no way of improving their lives unless some smart, charming soldier boy chose to sweep them up and out of their poverty. I considered that propaganda of the highest order, and have no idea how any woman could sit through a movie like that.

"The women portrayed in all of our films know what they want and can get it for themselves. True, a lot of them are silly and border on being cartoon characters, but there *is* depth there.

"But once again," he emphasized, "we have to be subtle in presenting that depth."

Does Kaufman consider today's movie-going audience that shallow?

"No, not really," he replied, "but you have to consider *who* we're making these films for. We're talking about young people—couples, mostly, who go to the movies on Friday and Saturday nights as a cheap form of entertainment. They're looking for easy comedy—not an art experience, and our films offer them that.

"Since we don't bill major stars and spend a lot in production, sex is our competitive edge," he added. "I hope it's the comedy that they end up enjoying, but it's not doubt the prospect of sex that brings them in."

Those prospects are made perfectly clear in TROMA's huge emphasis on promotion. While they may skimp to the extremes on *production* costs, the average TROMA film receives around $3 million worth of promotion. According to Kaufman, it's one of the most vital reasons TROMA films are successful.

"Most of the distributors the size of TROMA do many films each year and consequently have less money to spend in promoting each one. TROMA, however, makes only two films a year and distributes three or four more, giving us the money to get our name around. By the time one of our films is released, you'll have heard quite a bit about it. And if you've heard about it, you're more likely to turn out."

TROMA's latest apparent moneymaker is *The First Turn-On!*—a comedy which Kaufman described as "the wildest, raunchiest, most elaborate and controversial TROMA film to date."

Set to make its national debut in the Carolinas next month, the R-rated movie revolves around four campers and their counselor who become trapped in a cave on the last day of camp.

As usual, the cast consists of no-name starlets who jiggle and giggle their way through the entire project.

As usual, Kaufman expects to make money.

"We chose the Carolinas to open in because the market seemed right," he said. "For one thing, our films tend to do well there. Equally as important, however, is the fact that no other major motion pictures appear to be opening against us the week of November 4."

If the film does well here, Kaufman explained that additional prints will be made to open "territory by territory" across the nation.

The five-year-old company hasn't made a loser yet, and Kaufman said *Turn-On!* is off to the most promising start yet.

Savage Movies Don't Bloody Investors in Troma's Schlock

Patrick Reilly / 1986

From *Crain's New York Business*, March 31, 1986. Reprinted with permission.

Don't think for one minute that Lloyd Kaufman and Michael Herz are interested in winning an Oscar. The heart, soul (and schlock) they put into their New York film company, Troma Inc., results in strictly B movies.

But investors aren't complaining.

Troma has consistently made money on its low-budget films, which cost an average of $800,000 per picture compared with a routine $15 million in Hollywood. The New York film company, which grossed more than $2 million last year, is now successfully selling its film inventory to growing markets, such as cable TV, videocassette rentals, and, most recently, the TV syndication market.

Friday, Troma will be back in the theaters again with its latest effort, *The Toxic Avenger*, opening at about seventy-five theaters in the New York metropolitan area. Filmed in New York and northern New Jersey, using unknown actors, and edited in the company's ramshackle Hell's Kitchen headquarters, *Toxic* cost less than $1.5 million to make.

As with fifty other low-budget pictures Troma has either produced or acquired in its eleven-year history, *Toxic* trades heavily on raunchy language, gory details, and a bit of soft porn. If the reviews are good, or even if they aren't, Troma stands to make a profit.

"If the *New York Times* says it contains gratuitous violence and means it in a derogatory way, that's great. Our audiences love that," says forty-year-old Mr. Kaufman, who, like Mr. Herz, is a Yale graduate.

The film, about a ninety-pound weakling transformed into a sort of nuclear Rambo, already shows promise. Shown in the market portion of the Cannes Film Festival in 1985, *Variety* called it a "madcap spoof" that could be "a winner with youth audiences in all territories, but especially in the US."

In what the film industry refers to as a "prebuy," Toxic has already been sold to the home-video market before ever appearing on a theater screen. Stamford-based Vestron Inc., the country's largest independent distributor of home-video cassettes, will begin selling home videos of Toxic after six months of theatrical showings. Vestron says the undisclosed purchase price of Toxic was based on its potential sale of between ten thousand and fifty thousand units to video rental outlets.

"Toxic is great for the rental market. It won't be a top grosser at the box office, but people will be aware of it when it is ready for home video," says Jon Peisinger, Vestron president.

At the RKO Century Warner Twin in Manhattan where *Toxic* will open, Nick Constable, the theater manager, expects an "action audience—teenagers usually, male and female, and more than a little noisy. But they won't vandalize the theater or start a riot," Mr. Constable says. "It'll be a crowd that likes something like *April Fool's Day* (a horror film) or science fiction."

If that sounds like a less than desirable audience, Troma doesn't care, nor do buyers of its films.

Vestron's Mr. Peisinger says, "Troma makes no pretenses. They aren't going to make the next *Gone with the Wind*, but they have a good track record in knowing what audiences want."

In fact, Troma's *Squeeze Play!*, produced in 1979, led a new wave of teenage horror and sex exploitation films coming from Hollywood, and is a good example of how Troma makes money selling its films market by market.

Made for little more than $300,000, *Squeeze Play!*, a ribald sex comedy revolving around softball, broke even after one year, largely from box-office receipts in regional markets. After eighteen months, it returned a 50 percent profit to investors.

Success of *Squeeze* Play!

Reviewing the film in 1981, the *Times*'s film critic Janet Maslin called *Squeeze Play!* "zesty" and its actors "fresh and likeable." Shown to buyers at Cannes, the film became a box-office hit in Denmark in 1981. After five years, Troma says *Squeeze Play!* grossed about $10 million at domestic theaters alone.

After playing Europe and the United States, *Squeeze Play!* was sold to cable TV's Showtime and for home video. Box office and sale of ancillary rights included, Mr. Herz, thirty-six, says *Squeeze Play!* has made Troma investors $1 million after expenses. But it isn't done yet.

Troma is now reediting the film for sale to the TV-syndication market for about $600,000.

All that adds up to big returns for investors.

Troma offers a relatively low-cost entry to the film business. A typical Troma investor puts in $80,000 or 10 percent of the film's budget, and receives back the entire investment before the break-even point. After breaking even, the investor gets 5 percent of any profits. If the film is not what Mr. Kaufman refers to as a "dog," an investor's $80,000 could double within four years.

Financial Risks Stressed

Despite the potential profits, Mr. Kaufman stresses the financial risks to his investors, who are largely individuals, and on one occasion included Mr. Herz's mother and his podiatrist. One perquisite of investing is a bit part in Troma movies. "This is an extremely risky business. You are as likely to lose as to make money, no matter how low the budget," Mr. Kaufman warns.

But in fact, Troma has lessened the risk by never seeking financing for its films. Troma has no debt; Messrs. Kaufman and Herz work entirely with their own money or that of private investors. Mr. Kaufman admits, "Within this risky business we have eliminated a lot of the downside risk," he says. "Over time our pictures will come out ahead. Not in the short run, but as more markets open up. The Republic of China is interested in three of our films. Who would have known ten years ago China would be buying anything?"

With the growing market shares of independent TV stations nationwide, Troma has once again found a new market for its films in the sale of domestic TV syndication rights.

Troma is currently readying about twenty-five of its films for television, and expects to sell them in two groups of twelve films beginning in August. But the films must be thoroughly reedited since Troma films usually receive an "R" or "X" rating.

To make the films suitable for TV, Troma editors substitute "PG"-rated footage shot during production for the raunchy parts. The repackaging takes only the work of a film editor and keeps Troma's costs low. Mr. Kaufman says independent TV stations, the prime players in the syndication market, will pay between $150,000 and $700,000 a film.

Making Money on Film Library

"The shelf life of a good exploitation film is unending," says Mr. Kaufman. "There is always a need for the software, the film. Our major wager is in retaining and using our library of films."

Troma is working to keep its library stacks full. *Girls School Screamers*, a terror flick, *Class of Nuke 'Em High*, a comedy/action/horror film, and *Screamplay*, a black-and-white murder mystery, are all set for theatrical release in 1986. Troma will also release its most expensive and ambitious movie to date, *Monster in the Closet*, a science fiction/action picture. Costing $8 million, *Monster* features a number of "big name" actors a bit past their primes, such as Stella Stevens, Howard Duff, Claude Akins, and John Carradine.

"Monster is a new attempt for us. It's bigger and with stars," says Mr. Herz. He says that in recent years, the "sex and action" film market has been saturated with Hollywood films. Despite the overcrowding, the Troma executives don't plan to give up their low-rent ways.

"We like the films we make. We can't get Meryl Streep, so we give the public sex, comedy, action, and an acceptable level of violence," says Mr. Herz. "That's what the public wants."

Cannes 87: Mayhem, Toxic Waste—The Fun Side of Cannes

Jack Mathews / 1987

From the *Los Angeles Times*, May 12, 1987. Reprinted with permission.

Critics will argue into the night the relative merits of this or that official entry in the Cannes Film Festival. But when they really want to enjoy themselves, they duck into one of the theaters on the Rue d'Antibes, off the main drag, and become *Tromatized* with the likes of *Surf Nazis Must Die*.

Surf Nazis, one of five new films being premiered here by the New York–based Troma Inc., is a postapocalyptic gang movie set on the Southern California beaches after The Earthquake.

It is filled with bloody mayhem, sexual violence, and an unusual heroine (an obese, cigar-chomping black woman who takes on surfing Nazi youths). It is, in other words, a typical Troma feature, and at its first screening in Cannes, the audience included many of America's top critics.

"*Surf Nazis* is a terrific movie; it should have been in competition," said the straight-faced Troma president, Lloyd Kaufman, at the Troma suite at the Carlton Hotel. "We're not part of the elite here, so they never invite us (into competition). But the critics like us."

Whether or not you like their movies, you have to love Troma's titles, posters, and ad lines. A sampling:

Zombie Island Massacre: "A fun-filled vacation!"
The Toxic Avenger: "The first Super-Hero from New Jersey!"
Splatter University: "Where the school colors are blood red."
Class of Nuke 'Em High: "Readin' . . . Writin' . . . and Radiation!"
Curse of the Cannibal Confederates: "The South shall rise again . . . and again . . ."

Kaufman, a jaunty, bearded fellow, made his first trip to Cannes in 1971 to sell *Sugar Cookies* ("It was ahead of its time"). He said the eye-popping Troma titles usually are already in place when the company picks up the movies for distribution.

"People who make this kind of movies come to us," Kaufman said, as alternating images of bare-busted women, monsters, and gore appeared from a TV being used to recycle Troma promos behind him. "They know we will treat them right."

Troma, operated out of its own four-story building in New York's Hell's Kitchen, is a private company that produces a few and distributes a lot of those weird movies that appear in your local theaters almost without warning.

They are independent films that exhibitors count on to create short-term business between major studio movies.

"No question, when something falls out of bed, they call us," Kaufman said. "We usually won't last ten weeks anywhere, but for one or two weeks, our films do real well."

Occasionally, they do much better.

Troma's *Toxic Avenger*, the story of a ninety-eight-pound weakling who falls into a vat of toxic waste and comes out a disfigured giant who rips the arms and legs off of evildoers, grossed more than $12 million in the United States.

Toxic Avenger was filmed at Troma's satellite facility in Jersey City, NJ. *Toxic Avenger* and the subsequent *Class of Nuke 'Em High* were set in Tromaville, NJ, a mythical town that billed itself as "the toxic waste capital of the world." According to Kaufman, New Jersey residents loved it.

"A governor of New Jersey once took out a full-page ad in the *Hollywood Reporter* thanking Troma for making movies in New Jersey," Kaufman said. "He said he wished we had three *Toxic Avenger*s."

The governor may get his wish. A script is being written for *Toxic Avenger, Part II*. Kaufman said the gentle monster has become a big hit internationally.

"In the second picture, the Avenger will go to Japan, sort of like the James Bond movies," he said. "Women love the Toxic Avenger. He is a good person, he has a romance with a blind girl, he takes care of his mother. He just happens to be violent."

Troma is gradually moving into A movies, too, Kaufman said. *Monster in the Closet*, the first A movie being produced by Troma, will be out soon, and *Student Confidential*, a $4 million pickup starring Eric (Kirk's son) Douglas and Marlon (Michael's brother) Jackson, is premiering in Cannes.

Most of the fifteen to twenty films that Troma releases each year cost between $900,000 and $1.5 million, Kaufman said.

Kaufman, who brought along a tie adorned with erotic Oriental art for a meeting with Japanese buyers, said he doesn't associate Troma's popularity with American critics in Cannes to his films' offbeat titles.

Last year's Troma topper in Cannes was *Fat Guy Goes Nutzoid*!! "He's all action.... He's all man.... He's all over the place!"

"*Fat Guy Goes Nutzoid* is a very good film," Kaufman said, handing his guest a 1-cc vial of "Aroma du Troma," which the company is using to entice buyers to its suite.

"That's very close to being an art film. And it's a lot more fun to watch than any of those things in competition."

Among critics, *Surf Nazis Must Die* and *Fat Guy Goes Nutzoid* would fall under the category of "guilty pleasures." A more rewarding discovery is the "buried treasure."

Again, they are to be found "in the market," in rented commercial theaters where distributors begin selling foreign rights.

One of the buried treasures so far this year is Phil Alden Robinson's *The Woo Woo Kid*.

The Woo Woo Kid, which will be released in the United States by Lorimar-Telepictures this year under the title *In the Mood*, is a real discovery.

The movie is a fanciful, stylized re-creation of one of America's most entertaining World War II scandals. It's the story of Ellsworth (Sonny) Wisecarver, who at age fourteen ran off with a woman in her twenties and got dubbed by *Life Magazine* as the "Woo Woo Kid, the world's greatest lover."

The Woo Woo Kid was written and directed by Robinson, the talented author of the Steve Martin comedy *All of Me*.

It stars newcomer Patrick Dempsey as Sonny and Talia Balsam (daughter of Oscar-nominated actor Martin Balsam) and Beverly D'Angelo as his two (yup, he did it twice) wives.

Make a note. *The Woo Woo Kid*—sorry, *In the Mood*—could be one of the major sleepers of the coming summer. Then again, it could remain a buried treasure.

Green on the Screen

Andrew Smith / 1992

From the *New Statesman*, July 3, 1992. Reprinted with permission.

The company name, Troma Inc.'s loquacious president Lloyd Kaufman will mischievously explain, comes from the Latin for "excellence in celluloid." If this definition seems unlikely, it's not half as unlikely as the motion pictures it pertains to. *Surf Nazis Must Die*, *The Toxic Avenger*, and *The Class of Nuke 'Em High*—which was praised by the *New York Times* for its "exhilarating tackiness"—form part of a catalogue now extending more than one hundred titles, drawn from nearly twenty years in the business. This, allied to consistent profitability, makes Troma one of the most successful independent studios ever, and at a time when viable independents are becoming rare.

The films themselves, which run on a bizarre mix of social consciousness and unbridled misanthropy, are, by all generally accepted standards, appalling. Put together on shoestring budgets of US$3 million, the scripts are dumb, the acting unspeakable, and awareness of technical concerns such as continuity nonexistent. In one scene from *Troma's War*, for instance, the alert viewer (anyone not in a coma, come to that) will notice how, as the camera cuts between the two characters, it's raining on one while the sun shines on the other. The weather changed during filming, but film is expensive stuff and the Troma machine halts for nothing.

Nevertheless, "bad" though its product may be, Troma has a huge cult following, and, last month, a package of recent works began a four-month tour of British cinemas. At the same time, *Def by Temptation*, which did garner a surprising amount of critical acclaim, is being given its own theatrical release through the BFI, and a number of films are being made available on video.

Some of what sets the Troma movies apart from more mundane kitsch horror is illustrated by Kaufman's own story. Sounding uncannily like Mel Brooks and with an impressive line in both wisecracks and junk-filled carrier bags, Troma's president grew up in the same New York street as Oliver Stone. Firm boyhood friends, they later went to Yale University together, where their first brush with the privileged sons and daughters of America's social elite proved uncomfortable, "like a club we weren't allowed to join." They made it to the end of their freshman year, then took off; one to the African bush and the other to Vietnam.

Years later, after Kaufman and his partner Michael Herz had established Troma, he was able to offer his old chum an early break, along with Brian De Palma, Kevin Costner (whose first two screen appearances were Tromatic[1]), and Robert De Niro. The same would be true of Madonna, were it not for the fact that vice president Herz turned her down.

What is it that attracts people to these apparently atrocious movies? To begin with, offers Kaufman, it's depth. Certainly, filmmakers prepared to cite C. Wright Mills's classic political treatise *The Power Elite* as a major influence on their work are few and far between. "If you look at our movies," he continues, "most of them are about elites exerting control over ordinary, decent people, and then those people overcoming it." Often, goes the accompanying suggestion, they have been misunderstood. "All the movies Michael and I do come from the newspapers, ultimately. Usually, there's a serious theme behind the sex and violence, and that may be why the company has been able to survive for so long."

The idea for Troma's most famous creation, the Toxic Avenger, came from a combination of two headlines, one announcing the demise of the horror movie—a challenge too inviting to pass up—and another about toxic waste dumps. In a flash, the comedy-horror was born.

"Toxie," a poor chap whose accidental bath in a vat of toxic waste has transformed him into a grotesquely mutated superhuman with an adverse (chemical) reaction to evil and major dislike of polluters, has within the past two years been turned into both a Marvel comic-book character and a children's cartoon series. Already a big hit with kids across the Atlantic, this is now showing Saturday mornings on BBC1. Interestingly, Toxie's popularity seems to derive chiefly from the fact that he's a thoroughly decent bloke: environmentally conscious, loves his mother, and is faithful to his (ahem, blind) girlfriend.

"Yeah, he's a low-rent superhero," says Kaufman, "but the time was right for him. The 1980s was a period of excess and conspicuous consumption and now people are saying it's more rational to live simply." This same rationale may provide the most helpful clue to Troma's enduring appeal. At a time when one increasingly hears film-buffs commenting that, "Ah yes, the story was slight—but it looked great," it's almost a relief to come up against something this rough.

"The profligacy of filmmakers spending US$100 million on special effects seems slightly disgusting at this time. We're moving away from the form-over-substance ideas of recent years. It's for this reason we made the manufacturer put a traditional, circular face in the Toxie watches [the US is awash with "Toxibelia"], rather than the usual digital ones. We wanted to encourage kids to grow up, viewing time as a circular continuum, rather than as a linear construct. If it's linear, you want instant everything, and you grow up to be a grasping, greedy, thoughtless person, a big fat slob with bushy eyebrows and a tendency to fall off boats—that's where that leads to. With the Toxie watch, indicating time as a continuum, kids learn to take a long-term view; they work hard, they save their money, they have a full and fruitful life, and Troma eventually becomes a major studio, strictly on its own terms."

So, does Troma have pretentions to world domination and all that this might entail (primarily, a major drop in standards)? Lloyd Kaufman is having none of it. "Listen, in the whole history of the film industry, no other studio has ever survived twenty years without once having a hit. We have every intention of maintaining that record."

Somehow, you just know they will.

Note

1. Costner's screen debut was the Troma release *Sizzle Beach, U.S.A.* (1981), aka *Malibu Hot Summer*; later embarrassed by the film, Costner at one point tried to buy the rights back specifically to stop its circulation, but failed to do so. The second film mentioned here, while technically not Costner's *second* film, at least not in chronology of release, is 1984's *Shadows Run Black*, in which Costner is featured in a miniscule role.

Holy Shit! What Is All This Green Stuff?

David Carroll / 1994

From *Tabula Rasa* no. 1 (January 1994). Reprinted with permission.

It was a cold night in Sydney. We had left the Japanese restaurant early to catch *Sgt. Kabukiman N.Y.P.D.* at the Valhalla Cinema. We met Lloyd Kaufman and said, "Do you ever get up on a bad morning and want to make another *Apocalypse Now*?" He said, "No, I just want to keep exploding heads."

We never saw him again.

But we did catch up with him over the phone a week or two later, at his New York home. He said he was distracted after a day's shooting, but proved an enthusiastic and obliging subject for interview. One gets the feeling he really takes Public Relations very seriously.

And now, Mr. Kaufman talks about life, movies and philosophy. Troma style.

Tabula Rasa: Firstly, I was wondering if you could just tell us a bit about your background, and where it all started?

Lloyd Kaufman: Well, Michael Herz and I went to Yale University, and we were infected with the movie fever, and we saw such great movies as [those by] Chaplin and Keaton and John Ford Westerns, and we decided we wanted to make movies outside the studio system and try to give what we had to give to the moviegoing public.

TR: This was obviously long before video. Were there any differences in going to movies back then? Has video changed it a lot?

LK: Well, you know 1994 will be Troma's twentieth anniversary; and originally we made our movies for the movie theaters, for the cinemas, and we really are still making our movies for the cinemas. Video has come in and has democratized the movie industry quite a bit; it has made many movies accessible to the public, and it has made the public accessible to many independent film makers.

TR: Is it easier to make movies now that you can put them out on video?

LK: Well, the biggest problem—and I think we all have the same problem—is that the communication industry has become so consolidated, and has become so merged, and everything is done on such a giant scale that there are very, very few independent movie studios left. In a way, it is much more difficult for an independent movie director or an independent movie studio to get its movies to the public, because the game has become so much more expensive.

Troma, which is a movie studio, has to compete against Time-Warner, which owns TV stations, cable television networks, broadcast TV stations, magazines, *Time Magazine*, and Warner Bros. and book publishing, and its music empire. Our little movie company, which only makes movies, has to compete against that. Whereas, twenty years ago there were quite a number of small, independent movie studios all surviving nicely in and around the major Hollywood studios, before those major Hollywood studios became such giant international communication conglomerates.

TR: Is it a problem with distribution, or getting the money, or what?

LK: Well, I don't know how it is in Australia, but in America, the average movie now costs twenty-five million dollars, American, to produce, and then another ten to fifteen million dollars to market. And that is an awful lot of money. Twenty years ago, that was not the case. Twenty years ago, a movie could open in New York City, which is certainly one of the more important cities in America, and you could be the biggest movie in town for about fifty thousand dollars US. You could be, in terms of advertising, the big movie. And now, if you're going to open a movie in New York and you want to be the big movie for that week, you're talking about eight hundred thousand dollars.

So, clearly, what Troma has to do, and what Troma has always done, is to provide the adventure in movie going. The reason that Troma has survived, and just about every other American independent studio has died, is that the public who go to the Troma movies in the cinemas go not because of the huge advertising budget, or big stars, or the fact that we are part of a giant conglomerate—they go because the Troma brand name. Troma has a brand name, which means an adventure in movie watching. The person who goes to the Troma movie knows that he or she may love the Troma movie or he or she may hate the Troma movie; but the movie goer knows that he or she will never forget the Troma movie.

That's really what we give to the public: a movie like *The Toxic Avenger* or *The Class of Nuke 'Em High* or *Class of Nuke 'Em High 3: The Good, the Bad, and the Subhumanoid*; or *Sgt. Kabukiman N.Y.P.D.* These are all very high-concept Troma movies which are very unforgettable and totally different from anything that the big Hollywood conglomerates are giving to the public.

TR: In the beginning, did you have the idea of that sort of style, or did you just get into movies any way you could?

LK: Well, I love movies, period, and it just so happens, as Shakespeare said, "To thine own self be true." The kinds of scripts that I tend to write are Tromatic, and so we tended to be involved in these rather unusual projects like *The Toxic Avenger*, which basically came out of the newspapers. Most of the scripts we write, and most of the movies that we produce in-house, have their roots in the newspapers; they come out of newspaper stories.

Sgt. Kabukiman N.Y.P.D. came from the newspapers: one of the big stories is that the United States and Japan are having a great conflict now for the economic and cultural supremacy of the world, yet they love each other, and Sgt. Kabukiman is a symbol for that. Sgt. Kabukiman originally was a New York City policeman who loves hotdogs and beer, and through a quirk of fate, he transforms into a strange-looking kabuki actor with superpowers. And, you know, it's a very crazy movie, but it has a basis in fact.

Class of Nuke 'Em High, which has gone on to two sequels, revolves around the fact that nuclear power plants are built in a shoddy, corrupt manner; also a newspaper story that we read about in 1986.

TR: You've said a couple of times in interviews I've read that Roger Corman has influenced you. He was obviously very successful at making low-budget movies.

LK: Well, when I was at college, and I had to make the decision: Do I go into one of the giant movie studios and play that game, or would it be possible to go against all the odds and try to make my own movies in low-budget? Is it *possible* to make good quality low budget movies? The only example that we could find was Roger Corman; he was doing it! This is in the late sixties I'm talking about.

I saw wonderful movies written and/or directed by Roger Corman—well produced, well written, beautifully acted, and rather provocative; and that was proof that, indeed, good movies could be made on a low budget. That was enough for me, and I decided there was no reason why I could not go off on my own and create low-budget movies that would be good! And, hopefully, Troma has done that. The public has responded for twenty years and Roger Corman is one of our role models.

TR: And he's still going, as well.

LK: He sure is! He's a very good friend.

TR: You mentioned the smaller companies having troubles at the moment with the conglomerates. There have been a lot of really successful movies recently that have not come out of the Hollywood system. Is it changing, the conception of small moviemakers?

LK: I think that for every *Crying Game* or for every *Piano* or for every *Enchanted April*, the battlefield is littered with hundreds of wonderful movies that have gotten destroyed by the fact that they simply could not get decent distribution, by virtue of the fact the cartel is very, very difficult to crack.

Troma's been lucky because we have a Troma universe, we've got a brand name, and people see that Troma logo on a movie and they go, because they know what they're going to get. We have fans that we've built up over twenty years. People collect our posters and movie stills; "Tromabilia," we call it. We actually have a mail-order catalogue, and people collect it and we've got a good solid base of fans. And, every once in a while, one of our movies like *The Class of Nuke 'Em High* or *The Toxic Avenger* or, we think, *Sgt. Kabukiman*, become bigger, more mainstream hits than the typical Troma hit.

In the case of the smaller movies produced by independent filmmakers who do not have Troma's help, the only way for them to get attention, unfortunately, is to be slaves to the giant studios. Otherwise, it is impossible for them to get their films out to the public.

TR: On to actual moviemaking. You said a normal movie costs twenty-five million. What about a Troma movie?

LK: We're making movies now for between one million and three million. *Sgt. Kabukiman N.Y.P.D.* cost about three million dollars US and *The Class of Nuke 'Em High Part 3: The Good, the Bad and the Subhumanoid* cost about $1.2 million. *Chopper Chicks in Zombie Town*, which is currently playing down under, is about eight hundred thousand dollars US. But we have a brand-new movie, which was directed by a wonderful, talented first-time director, called *Vegas in Space*. And the whole budget was less than two hundred thousand dollars. We're fairly eclectic, however. I think the average now is about one to two million dollars.

TR: How long would that take to film?

LK: It depends on the movie. When Michael Herz and I direct, we spend about six to seven weeks on the actual filming, and we shoot a lot of film, we burn a lot of celluloid. We use multiple cameras. Two or three camera units, and we're filming 'round the clock, seven days a week. We don't spare film. Again, one of the nice things about Troma is that we have been empowering new, young directors, and they are shooting on smaller budgets than we are and they are more careful about how much film they use. *Def by Temptation* and *Vegas in Space*—those Troma movies by first-time directors—may move a little faster on the set.

TR: What's it *like*, making movies?

LK: Michael Herz and I love it! You know, we've been doing it for twenty years, and what's great is that if you look at all of our posters, you'll see that it's all the Troma Team. We try to gather a great ensemble, and everyone that is working with us just loves what he or she is doing. And since the actors are usually young, first-time actors—talented but new at it—everybody is absolutely committed to the project. The experience of making a Troma movie is something that everybody lives with forever. It's sort of like going to camp, or some kind of incredible bonding experience. It's very hard to describe, but it's a great "life experience." And since all of our movies are comedic, there's a great deal of improvisation. Talented young actors love working on Troma movies.

We are pretty well organized, because we have to be, and we spend a lot of time preparing our movies. Usually two or three months rehearsing. We rehearse on videotape and go to locations to videotape again, so when we get to the actual shooting the celluloid, we then throw everything away and are in a position, if we wish, to totally rewrite. But, because we are so well prepared, we can afford to improvise a lot.

Michael Herz and I codirect, which is very unusual, and we've codirected maybe twenty-some-odd movies (with an emphasis on the odd!). In the history of the movie industry, there's only been one or two codirecting teams who have even codirected one or two movies. Michael and I hold the world's record for number of movies codirected.[1] So, that gives a certain flavor, a certain energy. And on top of that, anyone else who's around, anyone on the set, is a director. Everybody is a director—it's the "Troma Team"—anyone who's got a joke, anyone who's got an idea. Until the film actually goes in front of the lens, until it's exposed, anything goes. The Troma truck driver, the pizza delivery man, we let them *all* direct if they have something to say!

TR: You were in Australia recently for Troma 2000.[2] Can you tell us about that?

LK: Columbia TriStar is establishing the Troma brand name in Australia and they have been showing four Troma movies in the cinemas: *Sgt. Kabukiman N.Y.P.D.*; *Subhumanoid Meltdown: Class of Nuke 'Em High Part 2*; *The Good, the Bad, and the Subhumanoid: Class of Nuke 'Em High Part 3*; and *Chopper Chicks in Zombie Town*. And those four movies have been showing in about ten cities in Australia. And at the same time, Columbia TriStar have been launching, each month, one or two Troma titles on video.

TR: We could only think of six titles in the shops before the current influx. So, there's not too many of them round. [*Note: actually, once we got hold of the filmography, we realized the problem wasn't quite as bad as we thought. But, was still pretty bad.*]

LK: I think it's a damn shame, because we have quite a good following in Australia. It's just been very, very difficult to get our movies to the Australian public. And now, for the first time, Columbia TriStar is capitalizing on the Troma brand name—the fact that Troma movies are fun, they're enjoyable, they're good for couples: a guy and his gal can have a great evening going out to see a Troma movie or renting a Troma movie. They're a lot of fun, and that's the key. So, Columbia

TriStar has been doing a great job getting the name out. In the United States, Troma has about a hundred and fifty movies, and many of the video shops in America have corners for Troma movies. I think Columbia TriStar is carefully establishing the Troma brand name and is looking to set up Troma sections in video stores all over Australia and New Zealand.

TR: Another aspect in getting to the public is censorship. Do you have a lot of trouble getting exactly what you want out there?

LK: Not in Australia. Australian censorship is fairly reasonable. At least for our movies. I don't think we've had too much trouble. We have trouble in the United States, because the censorship board in the United States is a privately run organization funded by the giant cartels and, in our opinion, there is a double standard. It's called the MPAA classification board—the Motion Picture Association of America—and, in our opinion, they are much more stringent on the independent movie than they are on the giant-made movie. So, as a result, the movie that has all sorts of blood and violence featuring Bruce Willis will get through; where, for our movie, they make us chop everything out. We have found that, while movies get censored, at least there is a level playing field in Australia. It seems everyone is treated pretty fair there. We have no complaints.

TR: Are there any other countries which give you a lot of trouble, besides the United States?

LK: That's the worst, because they're unfair. There's a double standard: they treat the big shots better than they treat the little shots. It's a disgrace. When I began in the movie business, there were twenty, thirty, forty, fifty small movie studios all making movies, and one of the reasons so many of them have gone out of business is that, in my opinion, the MPAA has disemboweled many good, commercial, independent movies. And they've obviously eliminated a lot of their commercial possibilities, and therefore emasculated their commercial viability.

We made what we consider our masterpiece, *Troma's War*, and the movie was entirely disemboweled by the MPAA, and we feel it was unfair. It ruined that movie. By the time *Troma's War* was shown in the theaters, it was so chopped up that nobody could understand it. That has happened to so many movies along the way. We at Troma believe the MPAA is one of the reasons why so many of the independent movie studios have died.

TR: Two movies I saw recently which weren't particularly Troma-like were *Stuff Stephanie in the Incinerator* and *Dead Dudes in the House*. Do you do a lot of this variation?

LK: Well, again, movies are art, and the spirit of the movie depends on the creators. For example, a movie like *Def by Temptation* (that might be the best Troma movie ever, and Michael Herz and I had nothing to do with creating that movie), it was a very talented young new writer/director.[3] *Stuff Stephanie in the Incinerator* was another whose movie was the first one [by that director].[4] *Dead Dudes in the House* was by a very talented director[5] who lives near New York City, and who is a Troma fan, and clearly was influenced by Troma. But, as you point out, it is quite different from the typical Lloyd Kaufman–Michael Herz directed movie.

It's part of our mission to be Troma: "the independent's independent studio." We are very proud of the fact that, in the past few years, we have empowered new directors to make movies, to get a shot at learning their craft, and also we have given some new directors an opportunity to get their movies distributed. Movies like *Dead Dudes in the House* are not big enough or commercial enough for these giant conglomerates to distribute; yet, they are worthy films, and the people who make them are worthy and talented. But they need a chance to get out there and then, hopefully, the writers and directors and actors will get an opportunity to take the next step up, to bigger and more mainstream projects. That's precisely what happened to the director of *Def by Temptation*.[6]

TR: And Kevin Costner, I do believe.

LK: There you go, that's right. He had to start somewhere, and Troma is proud to be the owner of some wonderful early Kevin Costner—his first two movies, actually.[7]

TR: You started in the horror side of movies when you saw an article called "Horror Movies are Dead" . . .

LK: That's what gave us the idea to move into that, yes. Just the fact the experts were saying that horror was dead. We knew from film history that, since the beginning, the horror film was very viable, and wasn't going to go away. We figured, well, if people weren't going to make horror movies temporarily, maybe there's an open window we could jump into and make a film in that genre, so when the vogue comes back we'll be at the forefront, and that's how *The Toxic Avenger* came about.

TR: Was that in the early eighties?

LK: As I recall, sure. We made *The Toxic Avenger* around 1982.[8]

TR: What about horror in the 1990s?

LK: I don't know. The majors seem to be doing them. I can't tell you; I'm not really an expert. Most of what we do is comedy, and even though we deal with horror, and science fiction, and sex, and war, and all the different genres, whenever we treat them, they're usually comedies. Movies like *The Toxic Avenger* are not really frightening; they are funny. They have elements of gore in them, and fear and monsters; but the end result is fun, not fear. So, I'm not really an expert on the horror format. But, I get the sense that it is a genre that has a very good following, and anyone who is able to make a truly scary movie is going to be successful.

TR: You do a lot of comic book/action sort of movies. What would you say to allegations you followed a lot of their sexist attitudes?

LK: Well, anyone who has ever seen our movies would not say that. The only people who would suggest that Troma is sexist are people that have not seen the movies. Toxie has a girlfriend who is much smarter than he is; she is the one who has the moral high ground. Toxie is always true to his gal and takes good care of his mom. He's definitely not sexist. *Squeeze Play!*, a movie we made in 1976 or '77,[9] is about a woman softball team, and it was a big hit for us, made ten years before *A League of Their Own*.[10] And, yes, the women were very bright, and they were aggressive, and they played sports, and they were upset because the men were running away every weekend to go out and play sports and be macho and the women wanted to do it. That doesn't sound sexist to me. Yes, the women happen to wear bikinis from time to time, but so what? So do the men. Besides, the bikinis in our films make a social statement. The small costumes represent the dwindling of our natural resources. We must use fewer resources.

TR: And *Surf Nazis Must Die* . . .

LK: Well there's certainly nothing sexist in that one. The hero is a fat, sixty-year-old woman. The hero of the movie. It's certainly the farthest thing from being sexist as possible. If you want a sexist movie, I was on an aeroplane with my little daughters going from New York to Los Angeles, and there was a movie called *Pretty Woman* which glamorized prostitution. I don't know what rating it was, but it was on an aeroplane for all the little children to see, and this was "Cinderella" as a prostitute. To me, that seemed a little sexist. But I didn't notice anybody going after whatever giant multinational studio made that picture. None of the woman's groups, nobody laid a finger or fingernail on it.

TR: It's a pretty dreadful movie.

LK: It's a disgrace! And it was accessible to all the small children.

First of all, Troma movies are very uplifting. The prestigious American Cinematheque in Los Angeles is doing a twentieth anniversary Troma retrospective in June, the National Film Theatre in London has done a retrospective, the San Sebastian Film Festival has done a Troma retrospective. We've had film festivals across the world. In fact, the Australian Film Institute did a Troma season not too long ago. But the point is, even if there is something objectionable, these are for the most part R-rated movies to which small children cannot possibly be exposed, and the Hollywood boys are making these movies with G and PG ratings which are more violent, and more sex-filled and more evil than anything you can imagine.

And, of course the government of the United States of America does things that are infinitely more horrendous than anything. The president, to get his ratings, bombed Iraq and killed eight civilians, for real. Any little child could see that on TV. The attorney general of the United States of America, not too long ago, barged into a religious commune and incinerated, with tanks, eighty-eight women and children in Waco, Texas. It's beyond. . . . Troma's an amateur compared to what's done in real life, and compared to what the major studios do. We're amateurs in this.

But I think the people who react to Troma in a negative way, when you ask them have you seen a Troma movie, they invariably say, "No."

TR: Do you see yourself as an escape from that sort of stuff?

LK: Oh, I don't know. I think we provide good entertainment. Good, fun, crazy movies with interesting themes. As I say, most of the themes of our movies come right out of the newspapers, so there's a rather provocative basis to them. And yes, our movies are sexy, and yes they are violent, and they have science fiction and they got monsters and they got horror, but they're fun, that's the key. They're a lot of fun.

A movie like *Die Hard*, with Bruce Willis, or *Under Siege*, these are pretty entertaining movies, but they take their violence pretty seriously. Our movies are good-natured, tongue-in-cheek, and fun, and I think that is where our success has come. We have a following, and we get a lot of women. Women love our movies, because they go with their date on Saturday evening, and they have a lot of fun, and they see something they've never seen before. And even if they know they will like it, or they'll hate it, they know they'll never forget it. That's also an attraction.

We have a movie, *A Nymphoid Barbarian in Dinosaur Hell*, that's the kind of movie that is very entertaining, and a lot of fun, and has some pretty good dinosaurs in it and a fine young "nymphoid." But some people say it's the kind of movie that's so bad that it's good. And they have fun. I think it's a great movie. I love it. *Sgt. Kabukiman N.Y.P.D.*, it's a much bigger budget, a lot more mainstream, it's got the Troma flavor to it. But it's something that's quite unique.

TR: What can we expect in the near future from you?

LK: As I mentioned, we have *Vegas in Space*, which has been playing in Los Angeles for three months, and it's opening in Japan on the Ginza.[11] *Vegas in Space* is the first space-travel musical with a transvestite cast, and it's a lot of fun. We are now developing *The Toxic Avenger Part IV: Mr. Toxie Goes to Washington*.[12] We have just written the first draft of *Tromeo & Juliet*, Troma's tribute to the bard. We have some new titles, a film from a new director called *Teenage Catgirls in Heat*; a lovely comedy, very cute.

We're good for about ten new movies each year. Michael Herz and I will direct one or two of those, and the rest of them will be by fine, new, young talent. Oliver Stone worked for us years ago on a couple of projects. And Costner, as I mentioned. There are all sorts of well-known people who have been in, and honed their craft in, Troma movies, and hopefully our new movies will bring you the giants of tomorrow.

Notes

1. Does not appear to be authoritative/official, even for 1994.
2. A distribution deal between Columbia TriStar Home Video (CTHV) and Troma that launched during 1993 in which Troma films would be released in cinemas throughout Australia and New Zealand, as well as on home video by CTHV.
3. Actor James Bond III; *Def by Temptation* (1990) featured Samuel L. Jackson just before appearing in his breakout role a year later in Spike Lee's *Jungle Fever* (1991). Bond would not direct another movie thereafter this, his debut picture.
4. Writer-director Don Nardo; although this was his one and only film, he is credited with writing an episode of the television drama *Spenser: For Hire* (1985).
5. Writer-director James Riffel; n.b.: *Dead Dudes in the House* (1989) is also known as (and listed on IMDb as) *The House on Tombstone Hill*.
6. Who, unlike the others mentioned in these grafs, did indeed go on to make a number of other (similarly low-budget, schlocky horror) films.
7. As previously mentioned, not quite true, though Kaufman here is talking about Costner's first film, *Sizzle Beach, U.S.A.* (1981) and (*not* Costner's sophomore work) *Shadows Run Black* (1984).
8. Released in 1984.
9. Released in 1979.
10. There are indeed some striking similarities between the two films, including a memorable scene in *Squeeze Play!* (1979) in which one of the female players makes a stunning and game-changing catch by vaulting herself into an impressively gymnastic split, while her caught ball is raised proudly in the air—one of the more iconic and integral scenes that would later appear in *A League of Their Own* (1992), courtesy of Geena Davis's "Dottie 'Queen of Diamonds' Hinson" protagonist.
11. Prominent shopping district in Tokyo.
12. Released six years later as *Citizen Toxie: The Toxic Avenger IV* (2000).

Lloyd Kaufman Chides AFMA on Press Freedom

Lloyd Kaufman / 1994

From *VideoAge International*, March/April 1994. Reprinted with permission.

VideoAge has obtained the following letter sent by Lloyd Kaufman to an AFMA[1] *advisory committee member.*

We are in a business where publicity is one of the most important elements. It is a part of our lifeblood. Therefore, I think we should revisit our market's policy of forcing the trade media to pay the AFMA in order to attend our (AFM[2]) market. Much favorable press coverage of AFM is needed, especially in the context of AFMA's strategy seeking new arenas for revenue and membership.

On the one hand, many AFMA members and the AFMA itself pay considerable fees to public relations firms whose job is to publicize members at the AFM and AFMA. On the other hand, we charge the trade publications (from whom our public relations firms must get publicity) for the right to cover the AFM and distribute their publications at the market. This policy seems counterproductive and cannot endear us to the media. The major studios with whom we compete do not do this. In fact, they often give the press fun-filled excursions, fancy dinners, even expensive trips to bankrupt theme parks in Paris.[3] In view of the above, if the AFMA wants coverage by the "trades" perhaps it is unwise to charge these fees (which are seen as contrary to freedom of the press).

It is in our best interests to have all the "trade papers" on good terms with the AFMA. This is not the case now. For example, *Movie/Video Age* does a very commendable job covering the worldwide independent filmmaking community. However, to protest our policy of charging $15,000 for the right to cover the AFM, *Movie/Video Age* did not officially attend the AFM In any case, even though it did a good job in reaching AFM film buyers with two well-distributed and well-read dailies, our members could have been denied important communications and publicity potential. Even worse, our association will perhaps be denied an important opportunity to get its important news message across to the world. Furthermore, *Movie/Video Age* has for some time been publishing editorials about the AFMA that are very critical of its management. We must settle this problem. It is making us all look bad and is interfering with our ability to project a good image. The AFMA needs all the good publicity it can muster if it is going to attract potential new members and new sources of revenue that are essential to its survival.

Assuming that publicity is a vital part of our lifeblood, we should do everything possible to keep that lifeblood strong. Charging the trade publications is not the proper, practical way to raise revenue. I guarantee you that I can find plenty of unnecessary expense to cut from AFMA's budget that will more than offset the revenue squeezed from the press.

Notes

1. American Film Market Association, independent filmmaker trade association, of which Kaufman served as executive vice chairman in the early 2000s; in appreciation for his vision of independent cinema's future on the internet, Kaufman was also asked at that time to help create and chair AFMA's New Technologies Opportunities Committee.
2. American Film Market, put on by the AFMA annually, is an industry-wide event in which independent filmmakers exhibit, promote, sell, finance, and work with distributors who attend for the purpose of networking and acquiring films.
3. 1994 was the year that, after two years since opening its doors, Euro Disney infamously failed, after accruing a $33 billion debt, before changing its branding/name to Disneyland Paris; according to *Forbes*, in 2022, Disneyland Paris made a $51 million operating profit on revenue that hit a record $2.6 billion.

Kaufman Brings His Mutants to Life in Tromaville

Aaron Bell / 1997

> From the *Flagstaff Lumberjack* (Northern Arizona University), October 27, 1997. Reprinted with permission.

In terms of bad movies, certain names are held sacred. Ed Wood, Steven Seagal, and Kevin Costner, just to name a few.

But lately, a new name has emerged: Troma.

Troma is not a new company. It has actually been around for a long time, putting out the some of the worst movies around. Since the midseventies, Troma has released such classics as *Rabid Grannies*, *Fat Guy Goes Nutzoid*, and *Surf Nazis Must Die*. And, as the future looms ahead, there seems to be no stop on the horizon.

With the recent release of the critically acclaimed movies *Tromeo & Juliet* and *Sgt. Kabukiman N.Y.P.D.*, Troma seems to be slowly gaining the respect it has been striving for.

"Like all of our films, we have to convince theaters to show them," Troma President Lloyd Kaufman said. "Every time we give them something different, they get scared."

This seems to be the case with most Troma movies. The release of their newest movie, *Killer Condom*, has been delayed several times; but it has finally received the green light to premiere in limited release some time in December.

The movie, based on a widely popular German comic book, follows the adventures of detective Luigi Mackeroni as he tries to defeat a sadistic cult that is trying to eliminate New York's sexual deviants.

Though it did well at the Cannes Film Festival, *Killer Condom*'s fate in the United States has been stalled.

"[*Killer Condom*] will open in San Francisco, and it if it does well there, then we hope to open it all over the country. We can always get our movies into those [stuff]-kicker theaters, but this is a great film. We want this movie in the best theaters," Kaufman says.

Although the last few Troma movies have been praised by critics and awarded at all of the major film festivals around the world, theaters still seem to shy away from them.

"They loved *Tromeo & Juliet* at the Rome Film Festival. It actually won the best film of the festival. We usually do better in the US. But, we still can't get our pictures in the good theaters," Kaufman said.

There is really no one genre that Troma movies fit into, because they could fit into just about all of them. There are some sci-fi movies, some horror, a little bit of comedy.

Just about the only things that Troma movies have in common are lots of gore, violence, and nudity, or as Kaufman puts it: "The things that make America great."

"We like to have as many different elements as possible in our movies. And I think that's what sets us apart from all of the other film companies out there," Kaufman said.

Troma has also been a platform that has launched many successful careers.

Kevin Costner got his start in the Troma Team releases *Shadows Run Black* and *Sizzle Beach, U.S.A.*, where he played a disrespectful surfer. Marissa Tomei had a bit part in *The Toxic Avenger* and Samuel L. Jackson played a preacher in the horror movie *Def by Temptation*.

There also have been some casualties of Troma. Madonna was turned down to star in the movie *The First Turn-On!* Kaufman and business partner Michael Herz did not think she was a good choice for a camping story. Oliver Stone's acting career was cut short due to the movie *The Battle of Love's Return*, which was a complete failure, even by Troma's standards.

Another not-so-common name that got his start at Troma is Trey Parker. Parker, who is now known for his Comedy Central cartoon *South Park*, wrote, directed, and starred in *Cannibal! The Musical*.

Cannibal! The Musical tells the story of Alfred Packer, the only person ever convicted of cannibalism in the US. The movie, based very loosely on the musical *Oklahoma!*, features seven original songs which were written and composed by Parker.

Aside from *Killer Condom*, Troma plans to finish off the year in style.

Two other movies, *Teenage Catgirls in Heat* and *Pterodactyl Woman from Beverly Hills*, have just been released on video. Next month will bring the release of *Femme Fontaine: Killer Babe for the C.I.A.* as well as *Tomcat Angels*, a *Top Gun*–style movie that promises a lot of guns, a lot of air combat, and a lot of naked breasts.

Also, the film rights to *The Toxic Avenger* have been "loaned" to a major motion picture company for a big-budget remake.

In 1998, Troma will release *Shlock and Shlockability: The Revenge of Jane Austen*. The movie deals with the way that great novels are being trashed by Hollywood. It features the author of *Little Women* coming down from heaven and whooping some movie director butt with her newly acquired Jackie Chan kung fu powers.

Troma Entertainment: Movies of the Future!

Doug Sakmann / 1999

From *i am an evil carrot* no. 5 (Spring/Summer 1999). Reprinted with permission.

Lloyd Kaufman and Michael Herz founded Troma Entertainment in 1974. Having met at Yale, where Lloyd was already making movies, Lloyd brought Michael onto the production of a movie called *Sugar Cookies*. The rest is history.

After working together on various productions, they came up with the idea to make a small studio that would make unique, quality films at a time when theaters needed them most. Troma was born.

After renting out an actual broom closet, they distributed some movies Lloyd made while still in college, one of them being Lloyd's first movie, *The Girl Who Returned*. Lloyd's wife Pat and Michael's wife Maris both worked for Troma, at no pay. Lloyd is usually on the creative end of Troma, while Michael deals with the business end.

It has been said that Lloyd is the independent spirit and Michael's the practical businessman. Not to say that they aren't both fully involved in all aspects of Troma.

They later acquired and distributed a movie called *Sardu: The Incredible Torture Show*. They changed the name to *Bloodsucking Freaks*. Today, it is still considered one of the sickest films in the Troma library.

After acquiring and distributing a few more films, Lloyd worked on the film *Rocky*. Then Lloyd worked on *Saturday Night Fever*. Lloyd, his wife Pat, the director John Avildsen, and John Travolta would go out dancing in many discotheques to scout out locations for the movie.

After *Saturday Night Fever*, Lloyd and Michael wanted to make their own movies. They went on to make what they called "sexy comedies." Four were made: *Squeeze Play!*, *Waitress!*, *Stuck On You!*, and *The First Turn-On!* They both produced and directed them.

After these movies, Michael showed Lloyd the headline of a copy of *Variety*. It read: "The Horror Film Is Dead." Being ones to go against the grain, they decided to make a horror movie. After working on the idea for a while, sometime in 1982, Lloyd created the Toxic Avenger, a hideously deformed creature of superhuman size and strength.

The end product was much more than a simple horror movie. It threw in elements of not only horror but comedy, sex, action, and freaky superheroes! Toxie went on to become Troma's spokesperson, their version of Mickey Mouse.

For those who don't know, the story of the Toxic Avenger goes like this:

Nerdy Melvin Junko worked at the Tromaville Health Club. A group of bullies who worked out at the club tricked Melvin into wearing a tutu, then chased him out a window and into a barrel of toxic waste. He mutated into the Toxic Avenger, the "first superhero from New Jersey!"

Using his new powers, which include Tromatons, which make him seek out and destroy any evil in the immediate area, he kills the bullies who made him into what he is now. The bullies were also the same kids who drove around Tromaville at night hitting pedestrians for points. But not anymore thanks to the Toxic Avenger!

Toxie also starred in two sequels, which interestingly enough were the same movie. Let me explain. When *Toxie 2* was made, when they went to edit the movie they realized that they shot four hours' worth of footage. They then cut it into two parts, thus *The Toxic Avenger II* and *III*!

Lloyd, Michael, and the Troma Team have made and distributed many great movies since their inception in 1974. They also created Troma Team Video, which puts out all of their fine movies on both video and DVD! Troma even have their own comic books!

Right now, after ten years, the Troma Team is working on bringing the Toxic Avenger back to the big screen for *The Toxic Avenger 4: Citizen Toxie*. I have had the pleasure of working with these fine people on this movie, first as an actor person[1] in the opening scene, now as a production assistant.

I must say that when I am there, it feels like I am part of a big family. A big dysfunctional family, but a happy family nonetheless. It is a lot of fun. But it is also a lot of work. Some conditions may be harsh, but it's worth it!

Doug Sakmann: State your name and occupation.

Lloyd Kaufman: My name is Lloyd Kaufman. I'm a filmmaker who is one of the founders of Troma entertainment and the creator of the Toxic Avenger.

DS: How did Troma come about?

LK: Michael Herz and I began Troma in 1974, and if you read my book, *All I Need to Know about Filmmaking I Learned from the Toxic Avenger*, you'll learn that we started in a broom closet with no windows. Staring across from me was a mop and a bucket, which were part of the fixings of the broom closet. About ten years later, the Toxic Avenger was born, and that mop stayed in my mind the whole time.

DS: How did you create the Toxic Avenger?

LK: Most of the Troma movies that Michael and I write and direct come from the newspapers.

DS: What is your inspiration for all this? What makes you get up in the morning?

LK: I love movies. I'm a movie nut. I was very much inspired by Charlie Chaplin, Buster Keaton, John Ford, and [Kenji] Mizoguchi, the great Japanese filmmaker. *Princess Yang Kuei-Fe* is my favorite movie. I think we take most of our inspiration from the classic cinema of Hollywood. Hollywood and Europe merged pretty much thanks to Hitler; a lot of the great European filmmakers became Hollywood film directors.

DS: What was the first movie you made?

LK: A movie called *The Girl Who Returned*, a 16mm feature length movie. It was about the world being divided up into two countries, one of men and one of women. Every four years, they would have Olympic games to determine the supremacy of the world. It was shown at Yale and other Ivy League film societies, and then it went around to a lot of colleges. So, it supported me while I was leaving college.

DS: So, you made money off of it?

LK: We would charge a dollar apiece. I also learned a very valuable lesson there: usually if people pay the money, they won't ask for it back. *The Girl Who Returned* sucked.

DS: Tell us about your new movie, *Terror Firmer*. How did your book inspire it?

LK: In writing the book, I got ideas that it would be interesting to make a movie about independent filmmaking, using it as a vehicle to deal with independent thought and art. *Terror Firmer* deals with the intersection of goofy Troma violence with genuine, realistic violence. As one critic said, "It's portrayed through the eyes of Frank Capra." So, it's probably the first serial killer movie portrayed through the eyes of Frank Capra.

DS: Have you ever killed a man in the heat of combat?

LK: No, I'm from the sixties and we believed in peace. In those days, peace was considered cool.

DS: What's the best special effect you've used in a Troma movie?

LK: I'm not really one to judge because I can see behind the scenes. But, *Terror Firmer* has some excellent special effects towards the end of the film. I don't want to give the film away, but I would say there is a lot of memorable special effects makeup and genitalia. Very disturbing. I can't speak for the audience, but I know whenever anyone sees the boy on the bicycle get his head squashed by a vehicle's tire in the original *Toxic Avenger* . . . I was just in Rome and saw fifteen hundred people react to that. The film was made in 1983, and this was a month ago and the reaction was incredible. And that was just a melon with a wig.

DS: Do you believe in extraterrestrial life?

LK: Yes. I haven't seen anything, but I believe there is. I think I saw a ghost once at the Roosevelt Hotel, in my room. It's a famous California landmark which is supposed to be haunted by, among others, Montgomery Clift, a famous dead Hollywood movie star. He was our neighbor when I grew up in New York. He actually came on to me one time. So, it might have been him. There was something in my room. It was about four in the morning and I was pretty shitfaced, so it might have been something else. But I could feel the hair on the back of my neck go up. It wasn't scary, just very eerie.

DS: What is the stupidest thing you've ever done?

LK: Well, according to my sister, I ran her over with a car. That could have been pretty stupid, or brilliant, depending on what you think of my sister. I don't remember it, but I mentioned it in the book because that was the inspiration for running that kid over in *The Toxic Avenger*. Also, we turned down Madonna for *The First Turn-On!* Six months later, she was on the cover of *Newsweek*, and our movie was becoming a nice big failure. Not really a failure, but the girl we chose was not particularly noteworthy.

DS: What is the strangest thing you've ever been hit in the head with?

LK: Well, in *Terror Firmer* there is a scene where a guy gets squibbed, and I got saturated in blood. So, we figured, "Hey it actually happened, so let's use it." So, we turned the camera around and actually used that in the movie. So, it's yin and yang, I believe in Taoism: something bad happened and it turned out good. Another thing in *Terror Firmer*: the crew was supposed to pour a cooler full of Gatorade on my head, and they let the top fall and it hit me on the head, and I got a huge cut and had blood pouring out of my head.

DS: Yeah, I noticed it hit you in the movie; it looked like it hurt.

LK: Yeah, we only did it once; that was enough, thank you.

DS: What's your favorite band? What kind of music do you like?

LK: I like almost everything except for Ricky Martin. I love opera, Rodgers and Hart, the Clash. I like Kurt Cobain, Lemmy and Motörhead, KOM; I like them a lot. I like everything! I just don't like Kenny G and Ricky Martin, stuff like that.

DS: Do you watch horror movies?

LK: Yeah, I watch good ones: *Friday the 13th, Halloween* . . .

DS: Who do you think is better: Jason Voorhees, Michael Myers, or Freddy Krueger?

LK: Well, *Halloween* was genuinely scarier. I like being scared.

DS: Yeah, *Friday the 13th* is more of a hack fest. Do you have a personal favorite horror movie?

LK: I'm partial to *Bride of Frankenstein*, but I don't have a personal favorite.

DS: What do you want on your tombstone?

LK: Check with me after this movie. If I killed myself, I would probably tie it in with that, but if not, I probably wouldn't ask for anything.

DS: Speaking of the movie, do you want to tell us about *Toxic Avenger 4: Citizen Toxie*?

LK: A lot of our fans A) Wanted Toxie to come back, B) Wanted to see Sgt. Kabukiman N.Y.P.D. and Toxie fight. And we have always listened to our fans. So, in this particular situation, we created a parallel universe called Amortville and there is an evil Kabukiman. So, the idea is Toxie goes into Amortville and the evil Toxie crosses into Tromaville. In Amortville, Toxie fights the evil Kabukiman.

DS: Does Evil Toxie fight the real Sgt. Kabukiman?

LK: No, because Kabukiman has evolved into a Kabuki-pig. He's a drunken womanizer. Sort of a frat house guy. A slob. Most of the movies we make are based in the newspapers. So, for Toxie, we saw things about pollution and toxic waste. There were toxic waste dumps in the early eighties all over the world ticking away like time bombs. Children in Brazil were playing in the dumps with what they thought was beautiful pixie dust, when in fact it was radium from hospital X-ray machines. So, we thought it would be an interesting topic around which to center a movie. In *Citizen Toxie*, we are going to deal with abortion and with Julia Roberts. Those lips she's got. What is that shit . . . ?

DS: Collagen?

LK: Yeah, exactly. All that stuff where they all look the same, like a uniform. Rene Russo has it now too. If you look at her earlier movies, she looks totally different. She's obviously had her face remade to look like Julia Roberts or whatever it is they want to look like. Maybe in her case it's just a matter of weight loss, but you can't tell. She used to look a little more . . . human. So, that theme is there: the necessity to reconfigure your face to look like everybody else. Also penile implants. Our whole fucked-up value system. So, that's how *Citizen Toxie* was born. It's pretty much fan-generated. And having written the book, and doing *Terror Firmer* in which Toxie appears, sort of got my juices flowing for the Toxic Avenger again. It seemed appropriate for our twenty-fifth anniversary to satisfy the fans. It's going to be an interesting script.

DS: Yeah, I've seen the first scene, kind of a spin on the school shootings.

LK: Yes, that's an interesting theme right there, the school shootings. They try to blame it on the media. It's constantly being blamed on Marilyn Manson, and people have already forgotten about who he is.

DS: Well the people have to find someone to blame it on.

LK: Yeah, but the truth of the matter is the values. The parents and the teachers are teaching the kids to be racist. There's a new class of white trash that has grown up, similar to the Brownshirts in Germany. They feel displaced. They think people from other countries will come and take their rights away from them. The right to be rich and stupid at the same time. The right not to be able to read or write, yet be able to go out and make a lot of money. That's supposed to be a right. But if you read the Bill of Rights, it doesn't say that. There's nothing there that says because your are a white person you are guaranteed to be rich and you don't have to know how to read or write.

There's no question that the parents and teachers are suggesting to the kids that we do have that right, and that people of other races do not. Therefore, if those other people do become successful, the implication is that they are taking away from the jerk who didn't go to school, didn't learn anything, then woke up at the age of seventeen as an intelligent but basically useless person, except at McDonald's maybe. That person suddenly thinks he has the right to shoot people. Then they blame it on the media.

DS: Well you can't blame it on anyone but the person who is doing the shooting. I know that the media will not make me kill someone. If I wanted to kill someone, I would kill him or her because I made the decision to do it. Not because the TV made me do it. If you think the TV made you do it, you should have been locked up a long time ago.

LK: Absolutely. But the kids are getting the message from the parents and the school that it is ok to do these things. Opening day of the Littleton school after the shooting, there were Nazi signs in the bathroom and outside wall. They had the preopening day where they went on *The Today Show* and *Good Morning America* saying, "We love Littleton!" Blah, blah, blah . . . "America's great!" The next day, the Nazi signs show up. Unfortunately, we have a racist, sexist society. You're right, though: the people have to be held accountable. The American public isn't gonna buy someone saying music made him kill someone.

DS: Do you have any words of wisdom?

LK: Well, Shakespeare said it all: "To thine own self be true." Do what's in your heart and don't listen to people. Do what's in your gut. No matter what you are doing. And clearly, live by the Ten Commandments, like I do.

Note

1. Tromaspeak for "extra" or "background actor."

Anything I So Desire

Roel Haanen / 2001[1]

From *The Flashback Files*, April 2001, https://www.flashbackfiles.com/lloyd-kaufman-interview. Reprinted with permission.

Here's the talk we did with Lloyd Kaufman in 2001. The creative driving force of the New York–based Troma Entertainment and director of cult classics like *The Toxic Avenger* and *Class of Nuke 'Em High* visited the Amsterdam Fantastic Film Festival where, in the early morning hours, he presented *Citizen Toxie*, to an audience of dead-tired horror fans who had been up all night during the traditional Night of Terror. Roel Haanen talked to him at that same festival (the talk was scheduled before the screening of the fourth Toxic Avenger movie). It's a sprawling and entertaining talk, with Kaufman going into every hot button topic of the time: abortion, racial violence, art versus politics, a conspiracy of elites, the hypocrisy of politicians, the hypocrisy of Hollywood, the obesity plague, and so on. In twenty years since this talk took place, not much seems to have changed. As with his art, Kaufman was ahead of the curve.

Flashback Files: Before you had success with *The Toxic Avenger*, you had been in movies for about fifteen years.

Lloyd Kaufman: My first feature was made in 1968, *The Girl Who Returned*. It was a 16-mm movie in black-and-white, made with a Bolex. And we had many successes before *The Toxic Avenger*, by the way. For instance, we had great financial success with a movie called *Squeeze Play!* It was a very raunchy sex comedy about a women's softball team, based on the women's liberation movement of the seventies. It ended up with four hundred 35mm prints.

FF: This was before *Porky's*?

LK: Oh, yes! We discovered that whole sex comedy thing in the States. It was not done before *Squeeze Play!* We made enough money with that movie to buy what is now called the Troma Building in New York. Because of that success, we made a whole string of sexy comedies: *Waitress!*, *Stuck On You!*, *The First*

Turn-On!, all of which were based on newspaper stories. Just like we do today, except that these were lighter and sexier. We didn't have a dark side yet.

FF: Is that what you learned from *The Toxic Avenger*? Combining that dark side with raunchy, anarchic comedy?

LK: I think you're right. That's what Roger Corman said about Troma. From the beginning, our brand has been famous for blending genres. In *Terror Firmer*, we not only mix genres, we turn them inside out.

FF: You seem to move along with the times. Your recent films, like *Tromeo & Juliet* and *Terror Firmer*, are more outrageous and they contain much more cruel jokes.

LK: Really?

FF: Don't you think so?

LK: Well, it's a little hard for me to be objective about what I do.

FF: I'm referring to the jokes with the fetus ripped from a woman's womb. You probably couldn't have done that in 1985.

LK: Well, in 1986 we did something similar with a pregnant woman in *Class of Nuke 'Em High*.

FF: That wasn't quite as brutal as this.

LK: Yeah, well. I thought it was important to start *Terror Firmer* with some brutal moments, because to a certain extent that is what American society is: brutal. The reality of American life is constant racial and sexual violence. My movies are a reflection of that. From *The Toxic Avenger* on, we have been involved in fighting hatred and violence and the puritanical dictatorship in America. It's always been there in our movies and these important buttons have to be pushed. In *Citizen Toxie*, the abortion button will not be pushed, it will be jammed! You'll see.

FF: What's your stance on the issue then?

LK: It's a bugaboo! It's a nonissue! It's the woman's choice. But the point is: half the world is starving and we're having discussions about abortion. It's horseshit! We did a movie called *Troma's War*. That dealt with AIDS when no one was dealing with AIDS. Certainly the first movie that took AIDS and shoved it in your face. We made it at a time when AIDS was swept under the carpet. We said: "Hey, this is here and you better do something about it!"

FF: *Tromeo & Juliet* and *Terror Firmer* deal with these hot button issues by doing provocative jokes. Not only abortion but incest and child abuse and rape. Do these jokes get you into trouble in the States?

LK: The United States is run by a cartel, as is Western Europe. It's a fixed club in which no one who is independent can enter without selling his or her soul. So, it doesn't matter which subjects I use in my movies. I'm economically blacklisted anyway. You have Pathé controlling almost everything in cinemas here in the Netherlands, right?

FF: Most of it, yes.

LK: Yeah, and everything they don't control, that fuckhead in Brussels[2] controls. And that is true of everything: television, newspapers, magazines. So what do I care what they think of Troma? What do I care what anybody thinks of our movies? Does Blockbuster have.... Do you have Blockbuster here?

FF: No, in the Netherlands the video store situation is a bit different ...

LK: Yeah, yeah! I know. We have one store—let me take you there—they have one Spanish art house movie and one Troma movie, all the way in the back! You don't have to say it. There is economic blacklisting against independent art in the States, but maybe here, I don't know, you have a free society where you can get Troma movies everywhere.

Hey, your newspaper, when they print this article on Troma ...

FF: I'm not from a newspaper. I'm from a fanzine. See? [*Shows Kaufman an issue of* Schokkend Nieuws.]

LK: Oh, well. You are the reason that Troma has been around for twenty-five years. The fans like that I do what is in my heart and you're willing to go there with me. There are millions of fans out there and they support us.

Fifteen years ago I produced *Combat Shock* and fans now are finding it. *Combat Shock* failed financially when it came out, but my partner and I knew that the public and the critics made a mistake. It's a masterpiece. We keep pushing it and pushing it. We rereleased it on video and recently on DVD. It cost us $75,000. It was one of the first DVDs of ours to come out. Now it is getting a very good following. Thanks to the fans. I'm still not making any money on it, but now people are recognizing what a great movie it is. Some will even go so far as to say it's the best post-Vietnam statement ever made in movies. *Platoon* is okay, but *Combat Shock* is the real thing.

So, over time, what we do will have its day in the sun. It just takes time for our fans to hear about it and for others to find it.

FF: So, how successful are the new Troma movies compared to the old ones?

LK: Well, to give you an example. We made twenty thousand DVDs of *Tromeo & Juliet*, but it sold out quickly. We were waiting for more orders to come in, because you have to produce them in large quantities. The stores got angry with us, because it took so long. And now, we are on our third run of the DVDs. We knew the film was successful, but we didn't expect this.

That movie took five years to make. I couldn't even get the money for it. Even our investors didn't want to invest in it.

FF: I thought the acting in *Tromeo & Juliet* was a lot better than I had come to expect of Troma.

LK: Except for the Black guy, every actor in *Tromeo & Juliet* had Shakespearean experience. They knew how to say these lines. Whereas in that Leonardo DiCaprio film[3]—which wasn't a real film anyway; it was a music video—the actors had no idea what they were saying. I don't know what DiCaprio was saying, but it wasn't Shakespeare. Claire Danes was a little better, but they didn't understand it. Our script was written in iambic pentameter. We wrote every line in Shakespeare's rhythm. You're not aware of it when you hear it, but it gives the film a mood of artistry.

FF: Would you consider doing another Shakespeare adaptation?

LK: I might. It's a real possibility. I have been thinking about it, to tell you the truth.

FF: *Tromeo & Juliet* also got some good reviews in the mainstream press.

LK: Yeah, but the major American critics have always favored our movies. *The Toxic Avenger* got good reviews. Even *Squeeze Play!* was well-received by the *New York Times*. The American Film Institute did a major Troma retrospective at our tenth anniversary. The problem is, there are fewer mainstream newspapers and fewer mainstream television critics, at least in the United States. That's because of the cartels who are eating up all the independent newspapers and TV stations. There are fewer ways to have your movie reviewed. The serious critics know what we're doing. They know that the purpose of the movies is not just to show sex and violence. The stupid ones don't. If you look at all the movies I directed in twenty-five years . . . I'm one of the few working film auteurs today. Maybe the only one who can truly do whatever he wants. In film, I can do anything I so desire.

FF: Are you deliberately trying to prove that point with each film?

LK: Good question. No, I think I'm also motivated by pissing people off. Lemmy from Motörhead is in three of our movies. He doesn't take any money. He's just a nice guy. We have a lot of well-known people that offer their services for nothing. But Lemmy asked me on the set of *Citizen Toxie*: "You do this to piss people off, right?" I hadn't really thought about it that way, but I can't deny that is part of my motivation. Last year at Cannes, a French critic compared me with Marcel Duchamp, Salvador Dalí, and Luis Buñuel. Certainly in the case of Duchamp, when he painted the mustache on the *Mona Lisa*, he did that to provoke people. Same with the urinal he put on the wall as part of an exhibition. He was a Dadaist. He was trying to stir the pot.

FF: And the pot needs to be stirred now as well.

LK: Of course! We are living in an age of excess in the US. Everyone is fat. People say I'm thin, but that's only by comparison. I can't even get into my fucking shirt. I took an airplane to Orlando, Florida, where I was a guest of honor at a convention. These people going down to Disneyland looked like elephants. It's an age of excess and pampering and smugness. People need to be reminded of certain things. They need to feel something real. The movies that you see in your theaters—I don't mean you, but most people—are *shite* like *Wild Wild West* and *Supernova*. We get this every week in the United States! We're brainwashing children and adults with hundred-million-dollar advertising campaigns to go see this shit. That's all we get. No real emotions. *Notting Hill* with Julia Roberts: absolute formulaic crap! Worse than porno. With porno, at least you have some kind of emotion. You get an erection or you find it disgusting, but there's something. What we get is no risk, no emotion, no thoughts. Nothing! Baby food!

LK: The purpose of Troma was to rail against this baby food. We are the antistudio. Antielites. Anti-Hollywood. Anti–*Forrest Gump*.[4]

FF: On the DVD of *Bloodsucking Freaks*, there is a Troma intelligence test. I took it, of course, and I got ten out of fifteen questions right.

LK: That's excellent!

FF: Well, no. Because the DVD proceeded to give me the advice to look for a job separating the brown from the green bottles. [*Laughs*] One of the questions was about you being attacked on a TV show. I was wondering if that was about your provocations.

LK: No, that was set up by a fascist, right-wing, racist, protobacco chat show guy, who used to be a Kennedy supporter, a real phony hypocrite by the name of Morton Downey. Total asshole. They called us up and said they were doing a Halloween show and they wanted Troma to be on it. But it was a set-up and I got beaten up. What they did was, he got me on the show, showed a few seconds of *Troma's War*, which we had just finished at the time, and he screams at the audience: "That was terrible! Should we get rid of this guy?" And the whole audience gets riled up. It was a real mob scene. And he wants me to get up and leave, but the only way out of there was through the audience. So, I said: I'm not going anywhere. Then the big fat security guards came in and had their way with me. This guy would do anything to get some ratings. Like I said: he supported Kennedy, and when Reagan was popular, he became a right-winger. It was live. Somewhere we have a copy of it. We'll put some of it on one our next DVDs as an extra.

FF: Isn't there a scene in *Terror Firmer* that references that?

LK: Yes! It's sort of based on that. Because my wife was in the audience. She had just given birth. This was our first night out. We got invited to a TV show and we thought we would have some dinner afterwards. "Won't this be fun?" She's in the audience with this screaming mob. It was Halloween, so everyone in the audience had masks on and they were screaming and yelling. My poor wife was in the middle of that. [*Laughs*] That's why we did the scene in *Terror Firmer*.

FF: You have a real dislike of authority, it seems. Politicians and police are mostly not portrayed in a flattering light.

LK: I have a big problem with authority. I think that we are too much controlled by so-called liberals like Hillary Clinton who think they know better. Who tell us how to live our lives. They, who have been successful by being dishonest. They, who have made millions of dollars though chicanery and tricks. They think we need to be told how to run our lives. I hate that. So, every movie we've done has reflected a subversion of authority.

We take the position that there is a conspiracy of elites. The labor elite, the bureaucratic elite, and the corporate elite. These three elites conspire to suck dry the little people of Tromaville of their economic and spiritual capital. In the States, labor leaders get salaries of a million or two million dollars a year, while the union members are working like animals for next to nothing. Government officials like the secretary of state or the environmental commissioner, they put in their three years of service and then move on to the big corporations where they make ten million dollars a year. It's all fixed. On top of that, they are preaching to us.

FF: Judging by the references you made in *Terror Firmer*, I suspect that there is a fourth elite in your view: the Hollywood elite.

LK: Yeah, because you see: I'm not going to forget. I'm not going to forget that Elia Kazan named names. They give him an award! Someone here at the festival said to me they were upset that Kazan had to fly coach to come to a festival in Europe. He should have been made to swim! He shouldn't even have been invited. He's a disgrace to humanity. He renounced his friends.

FF: But not everybody in Hollywood supported the decision to give him that award.

LK: I don't buy that whole controversy crap about him getting the honorary Oscar. I think 98 percent of the audience was all for him getting the award. Because Hollywood has sold its soul to the Devil. I used our website to picket the Oscars. I wrote an essay explaining the issue. We put out a call for people to come picket the Oscars. We have an office in Los Angeles and I had the staff make picket signs. We had about fifty people there, who had responded. The Toxic Avenger was there too. *Good Morning America* filmed it. Canal+ did some coverage. We did it again in Cannes, two months after the Oscars. You've got to keep reminding people.

Kazan, by the way, is a very mediocre director. He directed theatre pieces. He sucks. He had James Dean. Lucky him. Basically, his movies are boring. If you're going to give out awards, give one to Leni Riefenstahl. She is probably one of the five greatest filmmakers in history. She's still alive. Fly her in on business class. Give her the lifetime achievement award. Why not? If art is more important than politics.... So what if she was a Nazi? She had talent and she was a woman! How else could she have made movies back then? How else can a woman make movies today, unless they suck dicks or they're Penny Marshall?

The Oscars are absolutely disgusting anyway. I'm convinced that fifty years from now we'll look back on that as the obscenity that it is. We have an entire continent falling off the map and here's this rich Western country reveling in the wealth and prosperity of a very small minority. People wearing fifty-thousand-dollar evening gowns. Thirty thousand dollars' worth of fake breasts underneath. While babies are dying of starvation, these people, who make twenty million dollars a movie, are putting tens of thousands of dollars into their ass! To make it look smaller! Twenty percent of American children go to bed hungry. American kids are being beaten and raped by their fathers. There's child molestation all over the United States: in schools, in churches, in temples. It's out of control! Meanwhile we have this nonsense about Elian Gonzales on TV. Fuck him!

FF: Speaking of children, you have used your daughters in your movies frequently. Can they watch the movies they're in?

LK: No, because my wife is very strict. She believes children should not see these movies. She is correct, of course. So, Charlotte was ten years old when she was in *Terror Firmer*, and every time there was nudity or graphic violence, she was removed from the set. She has never seen the movie, either. But it's not like she's even asking to see it. She doesn't want to.

My oldest daughter is now at Duke University. She doesn't have any interest in my movies either. It's not like she turned sixteen and suddenly got interested in her dad's movies. She hears from her friends at college that I'm cool, but she has always thought of me as somewhat of a nerd.

FF: Are people surprised that you're such a family man?

LK: Yes, sometimes people are shocked that I'm still married to the same wife. Our domestic life is quite boring. I love drugs and alcohol, but my wife won't let me have them in the house. Well, I can have a glass of wine, but I can't get drunk and throw up. She's probably right. It wouldn't be good for the kids to see their dad waking up in the morning in a pool of his own vomit. So, I behave myself. Even at the festival here.

I might scream about the big issues, like war or Hillary Clinton or Pathé-is-the-Devil and all that. But the reality is that my family is much more important. I'm more proud of the fact that I'm still married to my wife after twenty-five years, that my kids are reasonably normal and happy, and that I'm still working with the same business partner after all these years, than getting awards from festivals.

FF: Talking about your business partner, Michael Herz doesn't seem to do any festivals or publicity, right?

LK: Michael decided about fifteen years ago that he really doesn't enjoy being in the public eye. In fact, he decided to devote himself solely to building our company. He and I both saw that the elites were getting more powerful and that independent movie companies were being destroyed or eaten by the conglomerates. So, Michael decided to focus on the business side of things. Originally, he and I codirected. We did about fifteen movies together. But he doesn't like it when people recognize him.

FF: Is that why Joe Fleishaker plays him in the extras on the DVDs?

LK: Yes. It's funny. Joe gets recognized at conventions as Michael Herz. The first time I asked Joe to play him in an interview, I thought it would get a rise out of Michael. But he loved it. He thought it was great. He said, "Can you now get Joe to come to the office as me, so I don't have to do this anymore?"

FF: I saw that you also distributed Dario Argento's *The Stendhal Syndrome* and I wondered . . .

LK: We distribute a lot of movies. We have seven hundred movies in our catalogue. Outside of the major studios, I don't think anyone owns the rights to so many movies. In India someone might have more, maybe; I don't know. But we made only about a hundred movies. The rest we bought. Now, *The Stendhal Syndrome* is a brilliant film and Troma is not good enough to distribute . . .

FF: That's not what I meant to say.

LK: No, but I agree. It's a disgrace that Troma has to distribute it. Dario Argento committed the crime of making an independent movie. Any one of the majors should have distributed that movie, but because they want to own every last bit of you, Dario had no place to go but to us.

FF: So, it's not a new strategy to branch out beyond the more apparent Troma-esque films?

LK: No. Of course I like the film. I think it's great. But I really mean it when I say that *Stendhal* should have played in major cinemas. But Dario is obviously not interested in joining their club. I asked him about that. I interviewed him twice for the DVD of *The Stendhal Syndrome*. I asked him, "Dario, it must be very disappointing for you that at this point in your career your new movie is being distributed by Troma." And he said, "Look, I am happy because I know Troma will release my movie uncut. You guys have guts and you care about the movie."

FF: You saw Pupi Avati's *The Arcane Enchanter* last night.

LK: Yes, and I loved it.

FF: So, you obviously also like more serious genre movies. Have you ever had the ambition to try your hand at that?

LK: I don't have the ambition to do anything. I get involved in a theme or concept and I go with it. It slowly develops. I'm very much interested in the subjects that interest young people. So, our next movie will be about the various political issues that concern the youth of the nineties, especially in universities. For example, you have the people who sleep in trees, who want to save the tree from getting cut down. Or lesbianism. That's big in American universities now. Troma has always been a big fan of lesbianism since the late sixties. So, we're going to focus on that.

FF: You said earlier, that given time, everything Troma does will have its day in the Sun. Does it sometimes frustrate you that Troma doesn't have the same clout as the majors?

LK: Look, when van Gogh made his paintings, nobody understood it. He had to cut his ear off. I don't know about a more influential artist than van Gogh. Troma is like van Gogh. But the difference is that Troma has been lucky enough to find an audience while we're alive. We can support ourselves by our movies. Van Gogh did not have that luck. On the other hand, he didn't have to worry about distribution. He had a rich brother to support him, so. . . . If I had a rich brother, I probably wouldn't have bothered doing anything. But I didn't have a rich brother when I started. Now I do. My brother is very rich. He's made a big business of bread.

FF: Is that the same brother who made *Mother's Day*?

LK: Yeah. He has a big bakery in San Diego. He makes high-end bread. The best. Really great baguettes and olive bread. It goes out to restaurants. It's a huge success. Horror films and bread. . . . They both have the knife thing.

The thing is, you have to be a good businessman in this business. Charlie Chaplin was a smart businessman. He owned his negatives. He was rich. Buster Keaton, on the other hand, was a contract player for MGM. Not only was he poor, bankrupt even, but MGM destroyed his career on top of it! They cut it short. He was younger than I am when he made his last movie. I'm fifty-five and still directing movies.

FF: So, what's the difference between you and, say, George Lucas, besides the obvious difference in the scale of your operations. You both are savvy businessmen and you both control everything creatively.

LK: Lucas is motivated by something else than artistic vision. Just look at *The Phantom Menace*. It's terrible. With all due respect, no one who is a true artist, no one who had a real artistic spirit, would make that movie. It's truly there for money. It has nothing to do with a world vision or anything.

And why doesn't Lucas release these movies on DVD already? Because he wants the kids to buy the VHS cassettes first and shell out twenty bucks and when everybody's got the VHS, he'll release the DVD. Don't you think that's reprehensible? These fans are just kids. They don't have any money. They're poor! Give 'em a break! How many million do you need? He gets to fuck the fans.

I actually believe that in the end, you will make more money if you treat the fans fairly. We release our DVDs region free. What the hell do I care if someone wants to buy a DVD in the States and play it in Europe? Art is for the people.

That's why we did TromaDance. Our own festival that was at the same place as Sundance, the same time. To show people that independent filmmaking is for the people. At Sundance you have to pay to send your movie in! You think they have a fair selection of movies? No way. Whichever movie has the best public relations gets in. Every movie by New Line or Miramax gets in. Miramax isn't even an independent company. They are owned by Disney!

The Sundance selection committee is 100 percent corrupt. They charge the poor filmmakers money to enter, but the selection is not done based on quality but based on politics, money, or power. We charge the filmmakers nothing to submit. We don't even charge for the tickets. It's all a public service.

You see Disney doing public service? Did you know that the US Congress, because of Disney, passed a new copyright law? Mickey Mouse was about to become public after seventy-five years and Disney lobbied for a new law. Copyright is now extended so that Disney can keep Mickey Mouse. Everyone is brainwashed. They think: "Oh, copyright law is good because it protects the artist from bootlegging." No! Copyright law has been overused to protect the elites. Because it also pertains to the world of medicine and science and education.

It means that everything is still in the hands of a smaller and smaller group of people. Because of copyright, people are dying of AIDS in Africa. They can't pay twenty thousand dollars for a pill! It should cost five cents! Universities have to pay royalties to some asshole who wrote a thesis eighty years ago! Education shouldn't be expensive. Point is: copyright should protect the artist from bootlegging while he is alive. It's fair to say that for a period of say seventy-five years no one is allowed to make Toxic Avenger movies but Troma; but after that: give it to everybody!

Notes

1. "This interview first appeared as a shorter version in the Dutch fanzine *Schokkend Nieuws*. Above is the full, unattenuated version of that conversation, edited only for clarity."—*as per the* Flashback Files *site*.
2. Kaufman in a text message to installment editor Mathew Klickstein: "I was talking bout Pres of EU, EU keeps indie movies out by supporting local and mainstream movies!! I was referring to the movie incentive laws of Europe, which come from Brussels."
3. Baz Luhrmann's *Romeo + Juliet* (1996), which, interestingly enough, was released the same year as Troma's *Tromeo & Juliet* (1996).
4. A point that fellow "pot stirrer" John Waters makes explicitly in his own cinematic tirade on Hollywood and *Forrest Gump* (1994) as the ultimate epitome of that system, the feature film *Cecil B. Demented* (2000) a year earlier.

A Tale of Two Toxies!

Neil Dowling / 2001

From *Film Ireland*, August/September 2001. Reprinted with permission.

Troma Entertainment is a name perhaps automatically and understandably linked to ultrakitsch trash and gore movies, and dime-store production values.

Neil Dowling travelled to New York to hear Troma-founder Lloyd Kaufman's profoundly serious take on the politics of US cinema.

Tromatised

Lloyd Kaufman, president of Troma Entertainment, has been involved in the production of over one hundred low-budget feature films, including almost twenty as writer-director along with his partner Michael Herz. Together, they have created the successful Troma formula that has ensured their survival. Exaggeration cannot be ruled out, but Kaufman claims Troma to be "the oldest truly independent film studio in the world." At the nerve center of the operation in New York's Hell's Kitchen, I am given the official Troma tour by Kaufman who claims to do everything "from cleaning the toilets to directing the movies."[1]

We met as Kaufman prepared for a trip to Rome to receive a lifetime achievement award at the Cinecittà Film Festival for his services to independent film. This came as recognition both for his idiosyncratic filmmaking and for his zealous thirty-year campaign aimed at preserving and creating the spaces for independent art to find its audiences. Spaces that have been, and are being, eroded at ever-increasing speed over the past two decades by what Kaufman calls the conspiracy of elites. Labor, corporate and bureaucratic institutions such as the AOL-Time Warner, the US government, and some of the film unions. "The smaller players in the industry have been at best marginalized, or in the worst scenario, rendered extinct. I'm bitter, I'm here while out there the battleground is littered with the bodies of dead artists. A lot of very talented people have been killed off."

Walking into the Troma Building is like entering a B movie about office life. The phones and computers are staffed by highly tattooed, body-pierced, black-nail-varnished young men and ladies. They sit amid parts of dismembered bodies and heads with brains spilling out that once were props. The two neat middle-aged women organizing a pile of documents look more curiously conspicuous here than they would elsewhere. Kaufman is abundantly energetic in his midfifties and excuses himself for interrupting our conversation while he chastises the staff for their complete incompetence. His affection for them, however, is only thinly veiled.

From Hippie to Punk

From across his desk—strewn with letters, photos and little plastic toys—he explains how his art and his message evolved and are inextricably linked. "I spent a year in Chad in 1966 with my 16mm camera. At one point while I was out there living in the bush, I filmed a ceremony in which all the women in the village danced around while they slaughtered a pig. When I got back, I showed it to my family and friends and they were all repulsed by it. It made me realize that I got a great thrill from pissing people off. More importantly, my experience in Chad taught me that the mainstream's value system was not necessarily the most valid."

Around this time, Kaufman came across C. Wright Mills's seminal book *The Power Elite*, which pointed out how the expansionist tactics of the big corporations would impinge on the lifestyle of the individual. Mills served as a pretext to the student movement that came to a head soon after in 1968. This would help shape Kaufman's worldview and inform his artistic output. "I'm a product of the sixties, a time when the individual was valued in society. Unfortunately that's not the case anymore."

Kaufman gained experience working on locations as production manager on various mainstream projects during the seventies, most notably *Rocky* and *Saturday Night Fever*. However, he wanted to do his own thing, and, impressed with the way Roger Corman could make low-budget films that had integrity, he and Herz decided to give it a go. He would be the first to admit that the quality of his films was not consistently of a high standard and claims to have invented a whole new genre—the goat shit genre—films that are way beyond bad.

With artistic control, Kaufman was able to subvert the ideals that Hollywood was cementing in the wider public's consciousness. There was also a spark of eccentricity that brought comparison to Woody Allen and began to earn Kaufman a following. Today, directors such as Quentin Tarantino, Trey Parker, and Baz Luhrmann are among Lloyd Kaufman's admirers.

Over time, his films became more extreme and Troma began to develop its own characteristics. "I was very taken with the punk movement; it was exhilarating, apart from the music itself. And I remember something Malcolm McLaren said: it was that you must destroy in order to create."

The new punk scene remains an important setting, notably in *Tromeo & Juliet*. The tagline of the film will give you an idea—"Body piercing. Kinky sex. Dismemberment. The things that made Shakespeare great."

Screwing George W.

The Toxic Avenger was to become Troma's greatest hit. The story of a boy who gets pushed out of a window, only to land in a vat of toxic waste and emerge with nuclear strength. Toxie, as he is known, then sets out to rectify all the injustices in his world. Toxie later became a figurehead for the Green Party,[2] and his creation was initially borne out of America's disregard for the environment. Kaufman, a supporter of the Green Party, campaigned for Ralph Nader in the recent presidential election.

"Nader has been out there working and saving lives. In his life he has saved more lives than Kennedy, Nixon, Reagan, and Bush put together have killed." Instead, he is stuck with George W. Bush, a former classmate at Yale. "There was that one night we made wonderful homosexual love, but apart from that, we didn't have much to do with each other."

Under one of George W.'s predecessors, things really began to take a turn for the worse for the independents. "During Reagan's Alzheimer's-riddled reign, the antitrust laws were altered and it suddenly became legal for studios to own movie theatres. This helped initiate the monopolistic theatrical landscape we see today."

To give a practical example of how this has affected Troma, Kaufman compares two of his films. "We had four hundred prints of *Squeeze Play!* (a 1970s "sexy comedy") in circulation. For [1999's] *Terror Firmer*, a far better movie, we only have fifty prints, because we can't get anyone to play it. Our filmmaking has progressed, every new movie pushes more buttons. We are much more widely known and more popular now than we were when we made *Squeeze Play!* But, it's becoming very difficult for the people who want to see our films to see them."

One solution has been the successful TromaDance Film Festival held at Park City, Utah, each year for the duration of the Sundance Film Festival. TromaDance costs nothing for filmmakers to enter and there is no admission charge to the screenings.

A firm believer in the cinematic experience, Kaufman saves some of his vitriol for the monolithic Blockbuster[3] in the video market. He has also campaigned to preserve the internet as the last bastion of democracy at a time when the courts called a halt to Napster's march.

The finger is pointed squarely at the baby boomer generation of which he is part. "They took control in the sixties, but somehow they are still at the helm. Every time I see Mick Jagger shaking his crusty prostate to songs written thirty years ago, I want to punch myself in the scrotum. And what's worse is that there are young people in the audience who don't even realize that they are being sucked into an egocentric festival dedicated to someone else's nostalgia."

On a hot summer day in New York, Lloyd Kaufman is a very good host. On the way out, he talks about his imminent trip to Rome while some of the interns and staff prepare to film some office hijinks for the web. The receptionist has even abandoned his runners and combats for fishnet tights, stilettos, and fake breasts.

Having organized a demonstration outside the 1999 Oscar ceremony against the Academy's Lifetime Achievement Award to Elia Kazan, I wonder how Kaufman feels about the award circus in the light of his trip to Rome. "Awards are fine when they are not bought. The Academy Awards are like an election, if you have enough money to throw into your campaign you'll probably get the result you want." And then, "I think awards are great when they give them to me, especially if they pay for the trip and throw in some free alcohol."

Notes

1. Not an exaggeration, at least at one time.
2. Yes, the Green Party and associated presidential hopefuls such as Ralph Nader did incorporate imagery of the Toxic Avenger in various campaign/promotional literature.
3. More on Kaufman's disdain for Blockbuster can be seen and heard in the documentary *The Last Blockbuster* (2020).

Lloyd Kaufman Interview

Vitorrio Carli / 2004

From *Art Interviews with Vittorio Carli*, July 1, 2004, https://www.artinterviews.org/. Reprinted with permission.

Lloyd Kaufman is the head of Troma Studios, which has released many successful cult favorites including *The Toxic Avenger, Class of Nuke 'Em High, Tromeo & Juliet, Terror Firmer, Sgt. Kabukiman N.Y.P.D.*, and the provocatively titled *Teenage Catgirls in Heat*. He also served as producer, writer, or director on many of his company's best-known works. (He did some of his work using pseudonyms such as Samuel Weil.)

The studio also distributed some notable foreign films such as Dario Argento's chilling *The Stendhal Syndrome* and Hayao Miyazaki's *My Neighbor Totoro*. Miyazaki later went on to direct *Spirited Away*, one of the finest animated films, ever.

Everyone always talks about the discovery of great stars by Corman's New World Cinema, but Troma helped launch the careers of Oliver Stone (*The Battle of Love's Return*), *South Park*'s Matt Stone and Trey Parker (*Cannibal! The Musical*), and Billy Bob Thornton (*Chopper Chicks in Zombietown*).

Kaufman is very recognizable, and he has appeared in many Troma features. His most recent notable role was as the Crap Keeper (probably a parody of the EC comics character, the Crypt Keeper from *Tales from the Crypt*).

It is expected that he will work on the script of *Poultrygeist*, which will be released in 2005 or 2006. A blurb states that the horror/comedy/musical/satire will be like a cross between *My Fair Lady* and *Dawn of the Dead*. Hopefully, the film will meat (pun intended) expectations.

Kaufman wrote several books about his filmmaking experiences including *All I Need to Know about Filmmaking I Learned from the Toxic Avenger* and *Make Your Own Damn Movie!*

I spoke to him on the phone a few days before he was scheduled to speak at the Movieside Film Festival. (That same weekend he appeared on Messy Stench's terrific internet radio show.) Lloyd had a great sense of humor, but sometimes it was hard for me to know when he was joking. He also spoke very fast, and I was not able to get down everything he said.

Question: How did you get started in filmmaking?

Lloyd Kaufman: I made the mistake of going to Yale. George [W.] Bush was in the same class. I wanted to be a social worker or teacher so I could teach people with hooks how to finger paint. My roommate was a movie bug, and I inhaled "Aroma du Troma."

Q: How did you start collaborating with Michael Herz?

LK: I met him in prison, and he was my bitch. I spent all my cigarette money on him. He wanted to be a TV moviemaker. I ended up codirecting features with Michael, and Troma grew out of that. We're the only film company that has been around for thirty years without ever having a hit.

Q: What or who were your influences?

LK: I was really influenced by the auteur theory, the whole French New Wave, and *Cahiers du Cinéma* writers. Through them (Chabrol, Melville, and Truffaut), I learned that the director is the auteur or author of the work, and he or she creates a consistency of theme and personality. This turned me to Chaplin, Ford, Hitchcock, Lubitsch, Renoir, Fritz Lang, Russ Meyer, and all the classic filmmakers. I saw the late Stan Brakhage's work *The Art of Vision*, and it was like hearing Beethoven for the first time. The little town Tromaville is like something out of Preston Sturges. Also I loved Ingmar Bergman's *The Virgin Spring*, as well as *Strapon Sally 22* [*laughing*]. Actually, I don't watch porn.

Q: The Toxic Avenger reminds me of the Incredible Hulk. Did comics influence you?

LK: Comics were a big influence on me, along with recreational drugs and masturbation. Stan Lee wrote a script with me called *Night of the Witch*. Cannon optioned it, but it was never made. Lee and I have been friends for thirty years. Lee and I also wrote a script for Alain Resnais, *The Man Who Talked to God*, but Resnais didn't like what I wrote. Fred Camper was also one of my buddies. He made the [short] film "Welcome to Come."

Q: Why did you decide to focus on horror and exploitation films?

LK: Well, I'm actually known for my mixing of genres. For instance, *Tromeo & Juliet* mixed horror, eroticism, romance, and police into a genre Cuisinart if you will. Quentin Tarantino, Peter Jackson, and Roger Corman are also known for mixing genres. I love their work because of that.

Q: How did you come up with the initial idea for *The Toxic Avenger*?

LK: One of the best places to find story ideas is newspapers. Toxic dump stories inspired *The Toxic Avenger*. Michael suggested that we move away from raunchy comedies like *Stuck On You!* and *Waitress!* The big studios started doing sex comedies with actual good scripts, so we had to try something else. I had worked on *Rocky* and wanted to make a film about the fitness craze, so I made *The Toxic Avenger*, which lampooned fitness and also dealt with the toxic dump issue.

Q: Didn't Michael Herz direct that?

LK: Well, we directed it together.

Q: Can you discuss the creation of *Sgt. Kabukiman N.Y.P.D.*?

LK: Well, we did *The Toxic Avenger Part II* which featured Kabuki Boy. The *Pac-Man* guy wanted us to create a Kabuki superhero for his games, so we made *Sgt. Kabukiman N.Y.P.D.* There was a big anti-Japanese sentiment in the country at the time because the Japanese had bought Universal Studios; but they overpaid for it. But because of this, a congressman said, "It's Pearl Harbor all over again." Of course, Sgt. Kabukiman also was featured in *Citizen Toxie*.

Q: Do you think there will be another Sgt. Kabukiman film?

LK: Probably not. He isn't strong enough to carry another feature.

Q: Which actors or actresses do you especially like to work with?

LK: Well, we have our own great stable of stars—people like Debbie Rochon, Ron Jeremy, and Joe Fleishaker appear again and again in our films. Did you know we also put out Kevin Costner's first film, *Sizzle Beach, U.S.A.*? If his career keeps going the way it's been going, he may yet work for us again.

Q: I read that you were against Elia Kazan getting a Lifetime Achievement Oscar because he named names in the Communist witch hunt. Can you talk about that?

LK: Quite simply, he was a fascist. He turned in his buddies, and then he got an Oscar. He didn't have to do it: he wouldn't have starved. He had a successful career on Broadway. That would've continued even if he got blacklisted in Hollywood. I heard he did the same thing in Turkey, too. Because of Kazan, we didn't get to see any more Erich von Stroheim films.

Q: Would you ever want to work on a big-budget film? What if someone gave you a million dollars?

LK: Oh, no. I would either make two hundred low-budget films or give someone else the money to do him or her.

Q: Can you talk about what you'll be doing at the Movieside Festival this weekend?

LK: I'll be introducing a brand new print of *The Toxic Avenger*, and I'll be answering questions from the audience. It will take place at the Biograph.

Q: What new projects will be coming out of Troma in the near future?

LK: Well, we're developing a satire of the fast-food business, and it also makes fun of phony liberals that use causes to promote themselves like Hillary Clinton and Jesse Jackson. These phony do-gooders just climb up the backside of the poor. The movie will be about a fast food chicken place built on an Indian burial ground. The spirits will rise up and possess the chickens, turning them into zombies. It's actually influenced by Takashi Miike's work, because it sometimes breaks into musical numbers. It will be called *Poultrygeist*. We're also putting out *Tales from the Crapper*, which played at some festivals and is now out on DVD. It stars Julie Strain.

Q: What was she like?

LK: She's the best. She is the film. But we had to get rid of most of the cast on the film as we were making it. They didn't work out. The film reunites Troma with Trey Parker, Joe Fleishaker, Debbie Rochon (playing herself), Ted Raimi, and even James Gunn, who worked on *Scooby-Doo* right after he did *Tromeo & Juliet* for us.

Q: Is there anything else you'd like to say to the fans or readers?

LK: Keep fighting against the devil-worshiping conglomerates like Time Warner, and keep supporting independent film.

The Art of Trash: Evaluating Troma Entertainment as Paracinema

James W. MacDonald / 2006

From Bachelor of Communications honors thesis (*appendix interview*), Edith Cowan University, 2006. Reprinted with permission.

James MacDonald: Who are your filmmaking influences and what are your favorite films?

Lloyd Kaufman: Well, the movies that have influenced me are the great movies. The movies of Jean Renoir, Charlie Chaplain, Buster Keaton, John Ford, Howard Hawks, Fritz Lang, Mizoguchi from Japan. Stan Brakhage, of course. The greatest visual artist of our century, Andy Warhol. Sam Fuller, Roger Corman.

I wouldn't put Corman in the league of those names, but the fact is he's a damn good director and his movies proved that you could make top-quality, low-budget movies with provocative scripts and good acting, and he's a very, very good director.

JM: How do you understand the label "trash film"?

LK: I don't understand it; it's a label—I don't know what it means, really. It's French, the *Cahiers du Cinéma* influenced me with the auteur theory of films where the filmmaker is the author. You know, where the filmmaker is the author of the movie and the filmmaker controls everything about the film; that's the auteur theory of filmmaking. I don't know what "trash" means. I assume it's something that's out of the mainstream, but I've never really investigated it. I know that the French do refer to Troma as trash films, and it has a good connotation.

JM: So, obviously you don't know if it applies to your work or not?

LK: That's for somebody else to say. I think if my movies weren't low budget, if these movies were the exact same movies but they had Mel Gibson in them, my guess is that people would call them something else. If *Mad Max* (1979) was "trash," then Troma's "trash," and if Troma's "trash," then *Mad Max* is "trash," that's for sure. That's certain, and I mean that in a good sense.

JM: What do you think attracts audiences to your work? Is it shock value, or . . .

LK: I think what attracts audiences to the Troma movies is that we're making movies in 35mm that they'll never forget. They may love *Tromeo & Juliet* (1996), they may hate *Sgt. Kabukiman N.Y.P.D.* (1991), but people that go to see a Troma movie in the cinema, they know they'll never forget it! They know they'll go on an adventure; they'll have a genuine emotion. And too many movies today are made with no emotion. They're made so that the AFC[1] can finance them, or they are made so that some suit in Hollywood will put the money up, or they're made as a remake of some 1980s movies with no inspiration and no heart.

I think people have come to realize that a movie made by Troma comes from the heart and that this is something that will give the viewer some kind of genuine emotion, even if it might be disturbing to the viewer, the viewer wants to be challenged. Those are the people who come to the Troma movie, those that wish to be challenged and have to do a little thinking.

JM: In your mind, what is art and do you think your films have an artistic value?

LK: Well, the Cinémathèque Française, you know they're the most serious organization or film museum in the world and they've had two [Troma] retrospectives. And the British museum, the Tokyo Film Festival . . . I mean, my movies have been feted all over the world. So, if that's any measure of what art is. . . . You know the American Film Institute has done a major retrospective. Jonas Mekas, you've probably heard of him? Jonas Mekas is one of the pioneers of experimental film; he runs the Anthology Film Archive in New York, which is the most idealistic of film museums, and they did an eighteen-film retrospective of my movies. So, I would guess that, based on what the standards of the day are, my movies are "art."

Certainly art itself is an expression of the artist's soul and an expression of what he, she or it believes in and to that extent our movies are 100 percent art. Also the fact that they endured, thirty years later, people are still watching *Squeeze Play!* (1979) and *The First Turn-On!* (1983) and *Stuck On You!* (1982) and twenty-two years later they're still enjoying *The Toxic Avenger* (1984), would indicate a certain classic status, which . . .

I think art requires an endurance, and Troma certainly stands the test of time. In fact, Troma's audience is bigger than it has ever been and it's wider than it's ever been, and my guess is that people have discovered that there is artistic value to the films like *Sgt. Kabukiman N.Y.P.D.* (1991). Just his *face* is artistic.

JM: Do you think your films contain a deeper significance for the audience to connect to?

LK: Well, I don't think Troma would still be around if our movies were only sex and violence. I happen to like sex and violence, and I happen to like nice bodies, and making a movie is a long, arduous and often times boring process where you have to stand around waiting for idiots to set lights, so it's nice to have attractive-looking people running around in small clothing. Furthermore, the small clothing is a political statement—when you see a Troma movie, the small clothing is a symbol of the shortage of natural resources. Everybody knows that.

I think people have enjoyed the political content of the Troma movies. If you look at *Squeeze Play!* (1979), it's a treatise on the women's liberation movement, when the women's liberation movement was sort of peaking. *The Toxic Avenger* (1984), of course is an environmental superhero, and it deals with the issue of both the environment and at the same time people putting their bodies into health clubs and eating organic food, the spoiling of the earth at the same time as cleaning the body: yin and yang. *Class of Nuke 'Em High* (1986) was about the conspiracy of the labor, bureaucratic, and corporate elite sucking dry the little people of Tromaville.

That's the overriding theme of all Troma movies: the overriding theme is that there is a town of Tromaville and the little people of Tromaville are perfectly capable of leading their lives. They don't need the champagne socialites, the limousine liberals, such as Hillary Clinton, to tell them how to run their lives. They're capable of doing it themselves; but there is a conspiracy of labor elite, corporate elite, and the bureaucratic elite. The labor leaders who make millions of dollars while their constituency are eating dog food, the bureaucratic elite, the upper echelons of the government who are there not to serve the people but to serve themselves and feed at the public trough. And the corporate elite, who are the big time Rupert Murdoch's of the world. They all conspire together to suck dry the little people of Tromaville of their economic and spiritual capital, and sometimes those people need the Toxic Avenger to save them, other times Sgt. Kabukiman, and then sometimes, as in *Troma's War* (1988), they must do it themselves.

Troma's War (1988) being a very good example of a movie that has endured with time. It was the first movie to deal directly with AIDS, it deals with terrorism, it treated the Ronald Reagan era of glorification of war.... These are issues which are universal issues and which are not going to go away. *Troma's War* (1988) has a much bigger audience now, people are rediscovering it. There's a TV show called *Lost* (2004), which has some very similar attributes and blah, blah, blah. So, I would suggest that there is a lot more to Troma movies than sex and violence, otherwise they wouldn't be here.

The battlefield is littered with the bodies of dead movie careers who thought that the way to make a successful movie was by formula, and that doesn't work. If you're going to make film interesting, you need to do something you believe in and that's what we've done. My guess is that is that has a lot to do with why audiences are still with us and why people like Peter Jackson and Quentin Tarantino, and Gaspar Noé in France, and Álex de la Iglesia in Spain, and Takashi Miike in Japan, and the guys who did *Shaun of the Dead* (2004), and, you know, people all over the world have been very respectful of Troma. James Gunn, Eli Roth, all these guys are very, very fond of Troma. Major, major mainstream directors who have grown up with Troma. You know, we've opened the doors for them.

JM: Do you think your films succeed more on theatrical display or narrative and themes, then?

LK: Well, Marcel Duchamp: What did he succeed on? If anything, dadaism. And the French newspapers have compared me to Marcel Duchamp. For example, with *Tromeo & Juliet* (1996), they suggested that I was to Shakespeare as Duchamp was to the *Mona Lisa*. When Duchamp painted the moustache on the *Mona Lisa*. So, I would guess that the overriding factor is probably the Dadaesque quality to our movies; but certainly the primary consideration when I write and direct is to be entertaining, so that people have something to see.

Poultrygeist (2006), the movie I'm working on, is far more entertaining and will have a much bigger impact on its audience than the rather pretentious *Fast Food Nation* (2006), which is on the same subject. Furthermore, *Fast Food Nation* (2006) is aimed at people who are older and already believe it, already have been converted to the evils of fast food, whereas *Poultrygeist* (2006) is aimed at young people who are the people that change the world. The old people don't have any influence on the world. It's the younger generation that go out there and stop eating fast food. So, I think that *Poultrygeist* (2006) is a good example of the politics, the entertainment factor, and the demographic. Young people are the people that make a difference.

JM: Do you think your films are anticinema, and what elements of conventional mainstream cinema do you reject?

LK: What do you mean anticinema?

JM: Well . . . anti-Hollywood.

LK: Well, we make independent movies. We make movies "to thine own self" to the extent that we have marched to our own beat. To the extent that I am one of the few genuine, American auteur artists. We are procinema, 100 percent. It's Hollywood that's anticinema, its Hollywood that are making movies by committee and making movies by focus groups. Making movies for a hundred million dollars where you have to appeal to all people at all times, hence they're making baby food. And you can live on baby food, but it's very, very boring. I think we are producing films according to Shakespeare's maxim "to thine own self be true." Shakespeare was that guy who wrote that bestselling book *101 Moneymaking Screenplay Ideas*, otherwise known as *Hamlet*.

JM: What do you think of the concept of "bad taste," and do you think that your portrayal of sex and violence distances yourself from a cultural elite?

LK: No, the intellectuals love our movies! The ones who are educated are the ones who go to see our movies; they are the ones who get it. The ones who don't get it are old people, and people who are uneducated. Certainly our movies are cult movies. Although, I guess they have a wider reach than cult movies. I guess that you could suggest that in the history of cinema, Troma is probably the most powerful cult movie studio ever, because there has never been an independent movie studio that's lasted for thirty-some-odd years. Clearly, the reason for that is that we have this amazing, very dedicated cult audience, this core audience, and then our movies do spread out to the mainstream population to some extent. I don't know if that answered the question or not . . .

JM: That answered the second part of the question; the start was "What do you think of the concept of 'bad taste'?"

LK: Well, what is bad taste? Why would Troma movies be in bad taste? There might be elements that some people find shocking, or disgusting or in bad taste, but certainly the themes of our movies, [*Class of Nuke 'Em High Part 3*:] *The Good, The Bad and The Subhumanoid* (1994) is a movie that . . . certainly the theme of which is rather democratic. The third Toxic Avenger movie, *Last Temptation of Toxie* (1989), is a Faustian thing where Toxie has to fight the Devil, has to fight the giant corporate conspiracy, the big conglomerate which is, in fact, Satan. I don't see how any of the Troma movies could be in bad taste, other than certain elements within it. Certain blue nosers might find the close-up of the hermaphroditic genitalia in *Terror Firmer* (1999) is in bad taste, so I can certainly admit that there are pieces of it in bad taste.

But, we are amateurs in obscenity; we are amateurs in bad taste. General Electric, who own NBCUniversal, they made a movie called *United 93* (2006). That's bad taste! Making a film that exploits the death of all those people in the. . . . Two planes crashed into the World Trade Center: *Did you hear about that?*

Yeah, so they're taking advantage of that and making money with it, and to make it even more obscene, Universal is giving a percentage of the opening week's gross to the survivors of the dead people, who now number like eighty-two thousand. You know, everybody's related to someone in the World Trade Center. So, Universal is going to give 10 percent of the opening week's, and *only* the opening week's revenue to the dead people. So, that means the dead people should go out and flag for the movie too, they should go out there and promote a movie that is exploiting the dead people on the airplane. That is obscene. That is in bad taste, in my opinion.

If you want bad taste, it's spending one hundred million dollars on one fucking movie, and then having the major media, who are also owned by the movie companies, suggest to young kids that this is a good thing, this is what glamor is, glamor is wearing a fifty-thousand-dollar gown to the Oscars, and borrowing eighty-thousand-dollar diamonds for your ears, whilst a brief jet plane ride away you've got two hundred thousand people in Darfur getting corn holed and beaten to death, and starving to death. *That* is obscene, that's the obscenity. Mary Antoinette was nothing compared to the value system that is in place and in the fullness of time. My guess is that this era will be looked upon as one of the most disgusting and profligate eras, and dwarf Marie Antoinette.

JM: When you make films, do you make a conscious decision to make the film "raw"?

LK: Make it what?

JM: . . . Unrefined?

LK: Well, when you're making a movie for no money, you're going to have to make it raw. You can't have all the refinements. You know, we have to make concessions on the quality of the acting, on special effects, on the look of the film, on the lighting of the film, and we're still shooting in 35mm which is very expensive and we're making movies for. . . . Even your Aboriginal, AFC, politically correct Australian movies, even they seem to be costing a million to two million dollars. I'm making movies for three or four hundred thousand dollars, five hundred thousand dollars. So, of course they're raw, there's going to be rough edges and it's going to be not the best lighting but our audiences sort of like it. We are very Brechtian.

Jonas Mekas—you have to look him up, too—he was a survivor from the concentration camps who came out to America and started Cinema 16 and made a movie called *The Brig* (1964) and lots of experimental movies and hung out with Stan Brakhage. . . . Anyway, he's ninety now, and he says that my films are very Brechtian and they take down the fourth wall a lot and talk to the audience, and indeed characters in my films do. I got that from hanging out around the Warhol Factory. And I'm a big fan of Warhol's movies, and Warhol's actors talk to the camera quite a bit. Anyway, breaking the fourth wall. . . . Part of the fun of that is letting the audience share with you the rough edges. For example, we have been using the same car flip in several movies—the car flip from *Sgt. Kabukiman N.Y.P.D.* (1990), where a car goes up in the air and flips around and crashes and explodes—we have reused that special effect, that stunt, I guess you could call it, numerous times.

The audience at this point in the game, they really enjoy knowing that it's from another movie. They have a good time with it, and in a sense they're making the Troma movie, they're participating in it, and when they see the latex, or when they see the blood that's coming out of somebody is coming out the wrong way, like in *Terror Firmer* (1999) where the blood is spurting out with the force of a geyser or an oil rig, the blood is not coming out the way it normally would, they have fun with that, they enjoy it, the audience becomes part of the filmmaking experience.

So, I think we have turned a liability into an asset. But we don't deliberately make a raw movie; we don't deliberately make a movie that's technically incompetent.

Note

1. Founded in 1975, the Australian Film Commission was an Australian government–based organization whose goal was to promote, distribute, and produce films about and imbuing the heritage of Australian heritage. In 2008, it became a similar agency called Screen Australia.

The Den of Geek Interview: Lloyd Kaufman

Sarah Dobbs / 2008

From *Den of Geek*, January 17, 2008, https://www.denofgeek.com/movies/the-den-of-geek-interview-lloyd-kaufman/. Reprinted with permission.

Lloyd Kaufman is the president of Troma Entertainment, and the chairman of the IFTA.[1] And we managed to steal half an hour of his time . . .

Troma Entertainment prides itself on being a truly independent movie studio. Even if you've never seen one of their movies, you'll definitely have seen movies by one of their alumni—people who've begun their careers at Troma include James Gunn, Trey Parker and Matt Stone, Eli Roth, and lots and lots of others. Lloyd Kaufman has over thirty movies credited to him as a director, but dozens more that he's produced, and more than a hundred that he's appeared in. He's a busy man. Not that that stopped us from asking him about everything under the Sun . . .

Den of Geek: Your recent MySpace blog mentioned that Troma is about to move into a new building in New York . . .

Lloyd Kaufman: Yes, indeed, we have bought a new Troma building; we have renovated it, and it's going to be a whole new era! It's in an even crappier neighborhood and a crappier building. We managed to find an even worse building.

DG: And the neighbors are worse? [The old building was next door to a McDonald's, to which Lloyd attributes the building's rat infestation.]

LK: That's why we moved! We wanted to get away from McDonald's!

DG: So you've checked out the rat situation at the new one?

LK: The area is so unusual, there's nothing there. Nothing lives. But there is the Museum of the Moving Image, which has rats of a different sort. And there's two big movie studios very near us, one of which has the name Kaufman, too. So it'd be kind of fun to call our building Kaufman, too. It'd be funny if Robert De Niro was directed to the Kaufman building and it was the Troma building. That'd be great! His first movie was a Troma movie called *The Wedding Party* directed by Brian De Palma.

DG: Let's get to why we're here: you're one of this year's Zone Horror CUT![2] competition judges . . .

LK: Yes, I had the honor of judging last year's competition and the movies which were submitted were terrific. I'm hoping that this year there will be more sex and violence . . . errr, that the movies will be even better!

DG: What will you be looking for in a winner?

LK: I think, basically, originality. But, you know, horror has traditionally been a way in to a very, very closed and elitist industry. Horror has been the most democratic genre—other than porno, of course, but I have never seen a porno so I wouldn't know. In terms of the elite and in terms of prestige, horror and comedy ride the back of the bus. But what a great way for young people to break into an industry which is still fairly sexist and racist and elitist! It is an industry controlled by a small number of devil-worshipping international conglomerates. So, horror is a way in for young people and if there's any way I can be a part of democratizing our industry, I would like to do it.

For CUT!, the movies must be two minutes long, or thereabouts, and they must have references to what a warm and sensitive person Lloyd Kaufman is—be sure to put that in the rules, that's very important!

DG: So what's going on with *Poultrygeist* now?

LK: *Poultrygeist* had a test screening in Peckham, and since they didn't burn the theater down, and because the audience liked it so much, there's going to be a tour. It'll start in Northhampton, and then go to, I guess, mostly university towns, and then presumably end up back here, at the Prince Charles. The test was very successful, so the film will be hatching around May, maybe. Something like that.

DG: Do you still feel it's the best movie Troma's made?

LK: I would say so, yeah. It's the most daring, that's for sure, it's the most intelligent, too, I think. And it's got singing and dancing, which is great. The film clearly is not going to be for everybody, but our fans will love it, and I think if intelligent people come and see it, they will find that they learn a lot and have a very entertaining ninety-five minutes.

DG: Which is what matters, at the end of the day.

LK: Indeed, yeah, it's about entertainment. But also, it has very provocative themes. I'm not a big fan of fast food, but the satire is not only about fast food, it's also about the millionaire phony left-wing people, too. It satirizes the corporate side as well as the phony Al Gore types who are using the populist movement to further their own millions of dollars. Even though it's full of chicken Indian zombies and explosive diarrhea and people getting their faces grinded off in the meat slicer, the movie has a lot of very, very interesting points to make. And that's why Troma's been around for thirty-five years.

DG: Warner Bros. choosing to go Blu-ray exclusive was just big news, but more importantly—which way is Troma going to go?

LK: Well, we are more homosexual ourselves, but we could be persuaded to go another way . . . I don't know, really. You know, I'm just trying to make the movies.

DG: So you don't have much interest in the high-definition formats?

LK: Well, certainly it looks great, but the bigger issue for us is that we are economically blacklisted. The television markets are blacklisting independent movies unless those movies come in through the vassals of the major conglomerates—Disney Miramax or Fox Searchlight, and these feel-good independent movies like *Juno*, which is of questionable moral theme; but that's the kind of stuff that will get on TV. The real shit-disturbing independent movie won't get on TV because it's not coming in through the strainer of one of the divisions of one of those conglomerates. So that's really our concern.

I was just elected the Chairman of the Independent Film & Television Alliance, which is the trade association for all the independent movie companies. The reason I got elected is that I ran on a platform of fighting industry consolidation and trying to protect net neutrality[3] on the internet, because the internet is the last level playing field. Nobody thought I'd win because it's a very controversial platform; many of our members live off the crumbs that fall from the table from the cartel that runs the industry. But I won and we're going to try to see if we can insert ourselves into the process in Washington and, to some extent, here; to see if we can make the media and the public aware of the fact that we are really getting our art through the strainer of five or six giant conglomerates. We are not really getting the information to find the truly independent art; we are being denied access to it—not just Troma, but many, many other important artistic creations. That's a big deal, really, and I'm very serious about that.

Blockbuster has never had a Troma movie, not even the *South Park* guys' *Cannibal! The Musical*, which has sold a couple of hundred thousand DVDs with no advertising. And yet it's never been in a Blockbuster. We're blacklisted, and it has nothing to do with the content. It's because we've committed the sin of being truly independent. We want to own our movies, we want to own our intellectual properties, we don't want some studio to come along and take the library and start censoring and chopping up the movies for some kind of silly TV thing. It's a tough world. The internet is the last way and we have to fight for net neutrality because the phone companies and the big media companies are trying to create Big Media, and they're already colonizing MySpace and Facebook and YouTube.

DG: MySpace has been useful for Troma, though, hasn't it? There are so many Troma promotional sites out there; the official ones and the fan ones . . .

LK: There are many, many fan websites. Even my Lloyd Kaufman website is fan-based; it's fan-driven, it's fan-created. The fans do it; I don't do it. The TromaDance website is by fans—the TromaDance festival, which is starting next week. Oh, by the way, very important announcement: the winner of this year's CUT! competition will have automatic acceptance into the tenth anniversary TromaDance festival in Park City, Utah, which takes place at the same time and same place as Sundance. So, that'll be a nice thing in terms of getting exposure for the winner.

DG: Is there any possibility of having a TromaDance festival in the UK?

LK: Well, again, it's all fan-driven. In Utah, it's very expensive, so Troma and our fans have contributed the money to do it. Here, you could do it easily: you just get a venue somewhere. It's very simple and it doesn't cost a lot of money. But unfortunately in this small town where Sundance is, because there are so many perfume companies, and jewelry companies, and Mercedes-Benz, they've rented all the space, so it's like $20,000 for one day to rent a venue to show your movies. It would be wonderful to do something in the UK; actually, there was a TromaDance in Edinburgh for a couple of years called the Troma Fling, and it took place during the Edinburgh Festival. It took place for two years, but I don't know if they're doing it again. In the States, there's TromaDance New Mexico, there's a TromaDance Canada, Denver... and then there are the TromaPalooza concerts, which raise money for the festivals. We had the third year this year of TromaPalooza concerts in Las Vegas, and in Dallas, Texas. Basically, bands donate their time and then they get publicity. And if any money is made, then TromaDance gets it. Because TromaDance is all free—there's no entry fee, the tickets are free and there's no VIP policy, so it's not a very good business model. We need sponsors and we need the fans to also donate money to make the budget.

DG: *Den of Geek*'s Duncan says his lifetime ambition is to remake *The Toxic Avenger*. How would you feel about potential remakes of Troma movies?

LK: If Eli Roth or James Gunn wanted to remake *The Toxic Avenger*, I'd probably give it to them for free. But Brett Ratner wants to remake it, and remake *Mother's Day*, and a guy like that has to pay big money.

DG: So it would all depend on who it was that wanted to remake the movies?

LK: Absolutely. You know, I'm an auteur director and it would all depend. It wouldn't be about money, it would be about making sure it would be interesting. By the way, *Poultrygeist* is actually a shot-for-shot remake of another gore slapstick comedy called *Schindler's List*.

DG: While we're on the subject of Toxie, what's happening with the Toxic Avenger comics?

LK: Devil's Due Publishing out of Chicago has created a graphic novel and it's *The Toxic Avenger and Other Tromatic Tales*, and it's very good. That just came out about a month ago. I'm sure you'll be able to get it off the Troma website. It shouldn't be hard to find.

DG: There was a previous Toxic Avenger comic done by Marvel, right?

LK: Yes, Marvel did *Toxic Avenger* and *Toxic Crusaders*. They were very successful.

DG: But there was never, like, Toxic Avenger vs. Spider-Man?

LK: Well, they wanted to do something like that but then they went bankrupt. Ron Perelman bought them—not the actor Ron Perlman, but the billionaire, the bald guy with the many rich wives. He bought them and drove Marvel into the ground. So, that was the end of that. And they wanted to own Toxie, they want to own everything, so that's a big problem. I was buddies with Samuel Arkoff, who founded AIP and started Roger Corman and so many others, and he told me his biggest mistake was to sell his company to a bigger company because they totally chopped everything up. The whole identity, the whole interesting patina of his library was destroyed. He says that's his biggest regret, even though he got a lot of money. Except for meeting me, having to have lunch with me was worse. He was a good guy.

DG: Has the WGA strike affected Troma at all? What's your position on the strike?

LK: Well, it certainly hasn't affected Troma: we've never had any writers. I don't know how to write. I'm actually on strike against myself because I don't pay enough, and I don't even give myself a decent health plan. I did write a blog where I pointed out that the writers do have a gripe, most of the writers are eating dog food and they do need more money, and they're not getting a fair shake and they should not be excluded from internet sales. But the problem is that they are marching side by side with actors that no one wants to see who are making a million dollars a movie or more.

I can understand that Bruce Willis would be profitable, or Tom Cruise, or Tom Hanks, but there's two hundred other actors there, and no one wants to see them in a movie and they're marching side by side in the picket line so they can get their faces on TV. The writers ought to be picketing these useless actors who are well overpaid, and if they weren't so overpaid, then the writers could get more money. So, that would be my advice. But the Writers Guild has no affect on us. We're so blacklisted that nothing can affect us.

DG: Do you think that'll ever change?

LK: The blacklisting? No. Never. If I get hit by a bus, then they'll swoop in and try to buy all our movies. They're hoping we'll go out of business so they can get their hands on *Toxic Avenger* and have Michael Bay direct the remake. They'd love to have Brett Ratner steal *Mother's Day* and make it into *X-Men*.

DG: Doesn't bear thinking about really, does it?

LK: Well, hey, if he wants to pay us a lot of money, or not even a lot of money, just some money, fine, we're desperate, we need money. But for us to give the rights away? These guys never pay you; it's almost an insult to suggest it. But if Eli Roth or James Gunn or Neil Marshall, or someone like that wanted to do a remake—any of those guys, I'd give it to them. It's just about the only movie of that type that hasn't been remade. They want to remake *Class of Nuke 'Em High*, *Toxic Avenger*, *Mother's Day*. . . . There's about four of our movies that they want to remake, and it would just be awful. We've got a fairly high price just to prevent that. And we need money, so it would be wonderful if someone paid us that.

DG: Do you think the original movies would become more available if they were remade, though? Would it help with getting them on TV and into Blockbuster and all that?

LK: That would be the good thing, yes. All the little nerdy fanboys who've never heard of *Class of Nuke 'Em High*, when they do *Jason vs. Class of Nuke 'Em High*, then they might say, "Hey, what was the original . . . ?" That's the one good thing about all these crappy remakes: a lot of young people who didn't know the original *Halloween* will go and look at it. Although, actually the *Halloween* remake was pretty good. Did you like it?

DG: I didn't see it.

LK: It was pretty good! Rob Zombie: good for him. Because *Devil's Rejects* was not terribly great and the other one, the first one, was unwatchable.

DG: That was what put me off.

LK: *Halloween* was good, it was well written, it was very good. So, then these *Jason vs. Robots* and *Jason vs. Freddy*, whatever, those things are horrible, awful. But if they get young kids to go and look at the old movies, hey, nothing wrong with that.

DG: Had you considered doing that kind of thing with Troma characters? Toxic Avenger vs . . .

LK: When I was on my book tour for *Make Your Own Damn Movie!*, every time I did a Q&A, someone would ask what would happen if Sgt. Kabukiman fought Toxic Avenger? So, it's in *Citizen Toxie*. Except they're both good guys, so they would never fight each other, and we had to create the alternate universe with Evil Kabukiman. That allowed us to satirize that whole genre. That was very cool: our fans basically came up with the plot for *Citizen Toxie*. We do have the Troma universe, so our characters do meet each other, but not like that kind of stuff, not *Freddy v. Jason*.

[At this point, Emily Booth[4] and the Zone Horror crew come in and start setting up cameras on the other side of the room. I'm concerned about time, but they tell me to just carry on . . .]

I'm about to go to meet with the Minister of Culture right after this. That's why I have to leave early. I've been told not to bring the Toxic Avenger mask, which I do have with me.

DG: What's the meeting about?

LK: Because I'm chairman of the IFTA, we want to discuss the issues of industry consolidation and net neutrality. The MPAA, which is the trade association of the big studios, state that they are the representatives of the entire movie business. Well, they're not. Everything they do hurts the independents; they do nothing to help us or the public. Our association is twenty-five years old, and I felt it was time that we present ourselves to the public and the media as representing the independent film industry, and we embed ourselves into the process.

We have a lobbyist in the States, the same one that Google has actually, and the lobbyist has set us up with various congressmen. We met with the chairman of the Federal Communications Commission to explain to them that Miramax is not an independent movie studio; HBO is not independent, it's owned by Time Warner; that NBC, Universal, and General Electric are all the same company and they don't know that.

They don't know that all the regulations against monopoly have been done away with in my country. Because, most of them were elected since Clinton and his phony populist wife and administration did away with all that stuff, because they accept massive donations from the Hollywood film studios. As do the senators from California.

If we can create a little bit of noise, maybe we can frighten them—the one thing that the conglomerates fear is the US government. So, if we can create hearings or maybe get the attention of the media, and get the story out that independent art and commerce is basically blacklisted in our country and in most of the world, it might embarrass the big boys so that they won't blacklist independents anymore.

Troma owns almost a thousand movies. We probably have one of the biggest library of films outside of the majors. And, yet, Comcast, which is our big cable company, won't talk to us. We have to go through a middleman, which is owned by the majors. And then if there is any revenue, they will take most of it. That's the problem.

DG: Are you hoping the situation will be easier to sort out in the UK than in the US?

LK: Well, you guys have better treatment of your independents, because you have the Lottery[5] and your government, and I think that you encourage more independent—you have movies like *This Is England*. Did you see that, by the way?

DG: Yeah.

LK: That's a great film, huh? That kid is great. It's wonderful, it's so original. It's terrific. So, in fact, I think the United States is the only country that does not subsidize in any way the true independent. They do subsidize the major conglomerates with the tax system, and most of the incentive system is for the big, big, big, big guys. And they throw out a few crumbs if you make a movie, you know, about left-handed lesbian mattress workers. You know: something that's politically correct but has no commercial opportunity, then you might get some money.

DG: Speaking of politics, you're working on a documentary, *Splendor and Wisdom*, about George W. Bush?

LK: Yes! How did you know about that?

DG: Well, because I looked it up on the IMDb this morning.

LK: Oh, thank you!

DG: There's virtually no information about it, though. Which is why I wanted to ask you about it today . . .

LK: It's about the Reverend William Sloane Coffin. He was a blue blood—a rich guy—who was in the CIA, and then he switched around to become . . .

And that's where we ran out of time, and Lloyd had to go and film his stuff with Emily Booth. So—thank you, Lloyd Kaufman, and also huge thanks to George Mills for arranging this interview for us!

Notes

1. Independent Film & Television Alliance. The trade association for all the independent movie companies.
2. Zone Horror being a popular UK horror TV channel (part of the Chello Zone TV network) of the time, and CUT! being its two-minute short film festival/competition that was going into its sophomore year by this point.
3. Via the FCC: "Net Neutrality policies are a national standard by which we ensure that broadband internet service is treated as an essential service. It prohibits internet service providers from blocking, throttling, or engaging in paid prioritization of lawful content."
4. Zone Horror host/presenter.
5. The British Film Institute uses National Lottery funds to help finance British films. Such pictures in the past have included: *The King's Speech* (2010), *Gosford Park* (2001), *Billy Elliot* (2000), and *The Last King of Scotland* (2006).

Lloyd Kaufman

Sean O'Neal / 2008

From the *A.V. Club*, May 8, 2008. Reprinted with permission.

For more than thirty years, Troma Entertainment has operated outside of the studio system, churning out cult movies (among them, the *Toxic Avenger* series, *Class of Nuke 'Em High*, and *Sgt. Kabukiman N.Y.P.D.*) that trade in visceral shocks, slapstick, heavy puns, and grotesquely satirical takes on deeper social issues. While the critical response hasn't always been kind, Troma's impact can be seen in nearly every independent filmmaker who cut his teeth in the video era, from Peter Jackson and Quentin Tarantino, to *South Park*'s Trey Parker (whose debut, *Cannibal! The Musical*, was a Troma production). And the Troma universe has a devoted worldwide fan base to rival that of any comic book. As head of one of the longest-running independent film companies in history, president Lloyd Kaufman has added more than eight hundred films to the Troma library, many of which he either personally wrote, directed, or starred in.

Kaufman's latest, *Poultrygeist: Night of the Chicken Dead*, may be his most ambitious yet, boldly incorporating trenchant anticonsumerist statements, singing lesbians, zombie fowls, and—of course—buckets and buckets of diarrhea. *The A.V. Club* recently spoke with Kaufman about his latest opus, working with a young Oliver Stone, attending school with George W. Bush, dallying with the Warhol scene, and the things young filmmakers can learn from his long, bloody, shit-stained career.

A.V. Club: A lot of your movies are ripped from the headlines. Was that the case with *Poultrygeist*?

Lloyd Kaufman: Well, we're living in an age of remakes, so we decided we'd do a shot-by-shot remake of that hilarious, slapstick-gore movie *Schindler's List*. But instead of the Jews, we put in several hundred chicken Indian zombies, and instead of the concentration camps, we've got concentration coops. Liam Neeson wasn't quite up to the task, so we hired the very famous Shakespearean actor Ron Jeremy. I predict *Poultrygeist* is going to be very favorably looked upon by the *Schindler's List* crowd.

AVC: Well, it definitely has better songs.

LK: We certainly have better dancing. Like so many of my movies, *Poultrygeist* has one foot in serious political and sociological themes, but it could have also been the Hantavirus I got when I was cleaning up all this rat shit that occurred shortly after McDonald's moved in next door to the Troma building. In fact, I begin my book *Make Your Own Damn Movie!* with me in the basement cleaning up rat shit—and I wasn't even meeting with Blockbuster executives! But that's a metaphor for what you have to do if you're an independent filmmaker: You have to do things nobody else will do.

AVC: So, was *Poultrygeist* spawned directly from your enmity with your new neighbor?

LK: We had a new employee who had worked in fast food—obviously Troma is a step down for him—and he suggested it. McDonald's had behaved in such an ugly manner, putting their garbage in front of our door—which our employees liked at first, because they could have lunch, but then it became too much. Then I read *Fast Food Nation*, and indeed, what a horrible industry. Of course, in [Eric] Schlosser's book, he *wanted* to put in chicken Indian zombies, but was apparently persuaded against it. So we put them back in, sort of like when we made *Tromeo & Juliet*. Shakespeare wanted to have car crashes and dismemberment and hot-bodied lesbians, so we put them back in.

AVC: Is this the movie that *Fast Food Nation* should have been?

LK: *Fast Food Nation* was boring and aimed at yuppies, and yuppies don't eat fast food. *Poultrygeist* is aimed at the younger market, and at fat Al Gore riding around in his private jet with his big fat wife who wants us all to feel guilty about using up a little gas or smoking cigarettes when his family made its money off of tobacco. The hypocritical limousine-liberal crowd. The phony-baloney global warming bullshit artists. We're skewering them. It's satire, like what I've been doing for thirty-five years.

AVC: Do you consider all your movies to be satire?

LK: Peter Jackson and James Gunn, who did *Tromeo & Juliet* with me, suggested that I created the "slapstick-gore" movie with *Toxic Avenger*. *South Park* comes out of that too; Trey Parker and Matt Stone used to have Troma parties in college. I've brilliantly managed to combine the two least prestigious genres. Whereas horror rides the back of the bus, I have added the comedy element, so that I ride on the back bumper—or, actually, I'm being dragged by the bus, as if I was that poor bastard from Texas who was dragged from the truck.

AVC: What made you decide to make *Poultrygeist* a musical?

LK: I've always been a big fan of Rodgers and Hart and Rodgers and Hammerstein. Being a gay married man, I love Broadway musicals. Of course, this isn't a musical. *Poultrygeist* is a chicken-zombie satire with some singing and dancing, and probably—I would venture to say—the first slapstick-gore satire with chicken Indian zombies that has singing and dancing. I may have to do some more research, because I think Eric Rohmer may have made a couple of chicken-zombie movies with dancing. But I don't think he had any singing.

AVC: Would you ever want to do a Broadway version of one of your films, like Mel Brooks?

LK: Here's the thing: I'm not against piracy. There were a couple of playwrights and composers who wanted to put on *Toxic Avenger: The Musical*, and one group did it in Oregon and another in Nebraska, and I never asked for a cent. What harm is it going to do? It may actually help sell some DVDs. And lo and behold, the producers of the Broadway hit *Dirty Rotten Scoundrels* optioned *Toxic Avenger* to try and develop a musical. I don't think this has ever been announced before. Bon Jovi's keyboardist, David Bryan, he's written the music—wonderful songs, very catchy, hilarious lyrics. Who knows? Maybe it'll actually be presented someday. And they paid us some money, so how cool is that?

AVC: You're open to people pirating your films?

LK: I think it's actually helped. I've written essays about copyright law and the Digital Millennium Copyright Act that Clinton pushed through, which basically gives perpetual copyright to giant devil-worshipping media conglomerates. Mickey Mouse should be in the public domain by now. What a better world it would be if other people were doing things with Mickey Mouse!

If Shakespeare had lived in our age, he would have been sued for writing *Romeo and Juliet*, because as everybody knows, he plagiarized that from an Italian play. With the Clinton act, Shakespeare would have had his rosy red ass sued right off. That DMC Act is a disgrace. And the problem with independent art in this country is that independent artists have been economically blacklisted.

HBO hasn't bought any independent movies for God knows how many years, and if they do, they get them from Fox Searchlight or Warner Independent. Believe it or not, Warner Independent—I did a lot of research on this—is actually part of Time Warner. And IFC,[1] which has never played a Troma movie, is actually owned by Cablevision and the Dolans, who are horrible people as far away from the independent spirit as you can get. The nice thing about piracy is, it allows the public to get independent art, to get a variety of music and movies.

I was recently elected to be chairman of the Independent Film & Television Alliance, and I ran on the platform of lobbying in Washington to educate the lawmakers and FCC that independent art is under assault in this country—and under a pepper, too, but that's beside the point. Comcast won't talk to Troma. We've been in business for thirty years and have eight hundred movies, and they won't talk to us. If we give one of our movies to some middleman at Time Warner or whatever, then they'll talk to *them*, so there's another layer of revenue that we lose.

The limited access to the marketplace is economic blacklisting. If you're an independent, you don't get on TV. And in the rare instances that you do get on, you get a fraction of what that very same movie would get if it came in through Fox or Viacom. With *Poultrygeist*, Troma didn't even have the money to put up, so my wife and I had to put it up. I of course told her she was investing in *Transformers*. Don't tell her.

AVC: No problem. So, did she get to have any say in the film?

LK: She made me censor the toilet-cam shot of the big fat guy—which is an amazing technical achievement—where he has the infested crap coming out his behind. She made me censor the actual departure of the turds. Since she put up the money, I had to go with that. On the turd where it says "Censored," I wanted to put "Censored by director's wife," but it would have cost too much.

AVC: Does having a wife who's the New York State Film Commissioner come in handy?

LK: By law, my wife has to recuse herself from anything to do with Troma—and I think she would probably like to recuse herself from anything that has to do with me, period. [*Laughs*] But her office did find us this abandoned, bankrupt McDonald's in Buffalo, and we got it for very little money. What was fascinating about our production was that we recruited our crew as volunteers off the internet. We put up a post saying we were doing our next movie, and you'd have to pay for your own travel expenses. We got volunteers from all over the map.

Maybe three months before we started shooting, we put a call out for someone to make vein-covered, pulsating eggs, and a gal in Stockholm responded. We never got them, so I just assumed that—like most people in the film business—she was a slacker, but we found out that she had sent them, but the United States Customs confiscated them. After 9/11, there were apparently new laws about importing mysterious, vein-covered, pulsating eggs.

We got about eighty people from Australia, Canada, France, England, Germany. Anyway, people from all over the map converged, and we lived in this Buffalo church. Most of them slept on the floor, ate cheese sandwiches three times a day, and had to learn to defecate in a paper bag, because we only had one bathroom. It was quite an interesting United Nations of idealistic young people. The auditorium of the church—we didn't ever go into the sanctuary, of course—was used as a rehearsal hall, and we had two kitchens that we put special effects ovens in so we could create masks and beaks and things.

AVC: Speaking of special effects, how much fake blood and shit do you think you went through?

LK: I don't know the exact amount, but the Australian guy—the blood boy—said that he was certain it was more blood than Peter Jackson's *Dead Alive*. We certainly had more explosive diarrhea. Every special effect had to be organized and filmed way ahead of time and shown to me to prove that it worked. With the big fat guy who's having explosive diarrhea, I specifically told the special-effects department to use Baby Ruth candy bars and get the normal size, but they came back with the miniature ones, so I had my little diva moment and stopped shooting. It was like [Masaki] Kobayashi on *Harakiri*, where there was a big samurai battle and he wouldn't shoot because the clouds weren't right. I don't take myself seriously, but I take my movies very, very seriously.

AVC: Do you think that serious approach sometimes gets lost under all that explosive diarrhea?

LK: Our fans are pretty intelligent. The dean of the American Film Institute has written that I'm one of the very few auteurs in America. I've had freedom for forty years to create art that is totally personal and is what I believe in. The Cinémathèque Française, the British Film Institute, the AFI at the Kennedy Center have all had Troma retrospectives. Vincent Canby—one of the all-time great *New York Times* critics—he chose to review *Toxic Avenger* when it came out instead of the big Hollywood movies that came out that day, because he loved *Squeeze Play!* and *Waitress!*, those raunchy early comedies we made. When we went to his memorial service, Janet Maslin told me that he always talked about Troma and how we were underappreciated.

AVC: Speaking of your early days, you started out working with Oliver Stone, yet when he recently spoke at the Austin Film Festival, he basically denied those early films, as though they were beneath him.

LK: Oliver Stone would not be making movies if I didn't make movies. My roommate and I at Yale made two feature-length movies with a Bolex—which is a wind-up camera, not a social disease—while Oliver would hang out. He was writing this horrible, crappy novel—he was trying to be James Joyce or something, but it was awful. But as a result of hanging around us, he went to film school. I've known Oliver forever. We grew up together, from second grade on. We lived a couple of blocks away from each other in New York. In fact, we used to have sleepovers as kids, and he used to beat the shit out of me. He was a bully! [*Laughs*] He's better now. He's still a psycho, but much nicer. But at Yale, he would hang out while I was making movies.

He's in my first color movie, *The Battle of Love's Return*. And with *Sugar Cookies*, he was associate producer. Oliver had very good instincts on that movie. There were scenes I'd written that the director wanted cut, with a big fat kid—my first big fat kid!—dressed in a woman's nightgown and lipstick, running into the street. Oliver said, "No way," and we kept it in and it became the conversation piece for the movie. He also saw the need to try to have some kind of name actor in the movie, so he got us Monique van Vooren. I had been hanging out with the Warhol gang, so I got some of the Warhol people.

AVC: Were you part of the Factory scene?

LK: I hung around the fringes of that Factory crowd, just observing. I'd see Warhol at Max's a lot. I think he knew my face, but I don't believe he ever saw any of our movies. He's a big influence on my work, no question about it. Anyway, Oliver's early films . . . *Seizure!* is a very interesting film. *The Hand* with Michael Caine is great. He shouldn't be ashamed.

AVC: He basically just said that he doesn't appreciate horror, like that's just not his type of film. Is there any cinema *you'd* consider unworthy?

LK: I would only make a movie that I believe in. If I didn't believe in it, it would be unworthy. *Squeeze Play!* is very entertaining, but it's also about the women's liberation movement. *Stuck On You!* is about palimony. *Toxic Avenger* is about the environment. You know, I don't think I would make a biopic comparing Hillary Clinton to Abraham Lincoln, even though she might have a thicker beard. That kind of stuff would be beneath me. But luckily, I've never been offered a directing job that was lucrative, so I've never had to make that decision. I've never heard, "Here's $800,000 to remake *Sisters*." [*Laughs*]

AVC: Your distaste for the Clintons and Gore—that wouldn't have anything to do with being classmates with George W. Bush at Yale, would it?

LK: Well, Bush *was* a classmate in 1968, and I distinctly remember in freshman year, he was running around campus looking for weapons of mass destruction. We couldn't figure out what that was all about, but now we know.

AVC: You weren't in Skull and Bones,[2] were you?

LK: I was invited! But I didn't know that there was money involved. I didn't know you get taken care of for life, and whatever career you choose, you get. I just saw these jerks. I wish I had joined Skull and Bones. I probably would have had six Oscars by now. Maybe it would be me in the White House. Maybe Bush would have been directing *Poultrygeist*. [*Laughs*] But I was kind of an oddity at Yale.

AVC: How so?

LK: I was making feature-length movies. In the sixties, everybody was doing short, psychedelic stuff, but I was interested in the long form. I showed my movie, *The Girl Who Returned*, at the Yale Film Society, where I learned two very valuable lessons. One was that once people have paid, no matter how bad the movie is, they don't ask for their money back. And there were two movies shown that night. One was *Moonrise* by [Frank] Borzage—which is a masterpiece—and the poster on campus just had the title on it. Not a lot of people there. But *The Girl Who*

Returned had a photograph of a gal lying on her back, with her love pillows stretching her T-shirt. We had about three hundred and fifty people show up. So, I learned a little about marketing. The movie wasn't erotic, per se, but I was heavy into Warhol, so the film had these long periods of this girl with nice jugs jogging around.

AVC: You didn't go to Yale for film.

LK: No, I majored in Chinese studies. I'm probably the only director of chicken Indian zombie movies who can speak pretty good Mandarin. But if I hadn't gone there, I would not have made movies. It was the sixties, and I was going to be a teacher and improve the world. Teach people with hooks for hands to finger paint, and teach bums to draw happy faces on beads. But through fate, I got put in a tiny bedroom with a movie nut who ran the Yale Film Society. Our beds were head to toe, and at night, I would inhale his Godard-stinkin' feet, and the "Aroma du Troma" was born. I didn't even know what a film director was.

To me, Charlie Chaplin was a goofy clown, and John Ford—what? Never heard of him. Howard Hawks, Stan Brakhage. Warhol, I'd seen his soup cans. Anyway, I started going to the Society screenings. One night, I saw Ernst Lubitsch's *To Be or Not to Be*, and I remember being so knocked out by that film. I decided right then and there that I would make movies. It was as easy as getting up out of the La-Z-Boy and opening up a fresh vial of crystal meth.

AVC: How did you start looking for film work?

LK: The first time I took acid, I made the decision that I would stay in New York and find an independent film company to get a job with. I had two possibilities: to work on *The Owl and the Pussycat*—with the whiniest actress in history, Barbra Streisand—or I could work with Cannon in New York. On acid, it came to me that I would stay and work for the tiny company. I got lucky there, because John G. Avildsen—who went on to do *Rocky*—was about to do *Joe* with Peter Boyle. It was Boyle's and Susan Sarandon's first movie. I got on it and learned a lot from Avildsen. Originally, Lawrence Tierney was cast in the part of Joe, and he had a bit of a drinking problem. I was assigned to take him to get some costumes in a department store, and we were going up the escalator, and the guy started taking a piss. [*Laughs*] It was my first job, and here's Lawrence Tierney taking a piss on my leg. This was my film school.

AVC: You actually teach a master class at various film schools now. What's the first thing that you tell your students?

LK: The first decision is, "Do I want the big mansion in Hollywood? Do I want the hookers? Do I want to be on the cover of *People* stepping out of a limousine with no underwear?" If that's what I want, then I gotta go out to Hollywood and fight my way up the food chain. But if that's not necessary, then no need. One can stay in New York or Chicago or Memphis or wherever and make your own damn movie the Troma way. The other very important thing is, "To thine own self be true"—which is a phrase coined by William Shakespeare, who wrote the bestselling book *101 Moneymaking Screenplay Ideas*, otherwise known as *Hamlet*.

AVC: Do you think most of your students want to create films or just "make it"?

LK: I think the people that show up for my classes are already predisposed to be independent. I think they come as much to be inspired, to hear that it is indeed possible to work outside the system and survive. Even though there is economic blacklisting—even though whenever I, Lloyd, have penetrated the hymen of the mainstream, I've been the one to get fucked—they can see that one can have a satisfying creative existence without selling out. I think they want confirmation of that.

It's a lonely world, being independent, and they can come away with the idea that if Lloyd Kaufman can make movies with people getting their heads squashed, with hard-bodied lesbians, women masturbating with pickles, graphic diarrhea, and singing and dancing chicken zombies—if he can do that for forty years and put his kids through Yale, Columbia, and Duke—if that idiot can do it, anybody can do it.

Notes

1. Independent Film Channel.
2. Infamous secret student society at Yale University whose members have become extremely high-profile/powerful personalities over the course of multiple generations.

Lloyd Kaufman's San Diego Comic-Con 2009 Roast Retort

Lloyd Kaufman / 2009

From roast of Lloyd Kaufman, San Diego Comic-Con,[1] July 25, 2009. Transcribed from video/audio with permission.

Lloyd Kaufman: By the way, it's a little-known fact that Joe [Lynch] saved all that vomit from the Toxic Avenger mask, and that became the script for [Lynch's film] *Wrong Turn 2*. It's a little-known fact. Don't tell anyone!

[*Laughter, applause*]

Well, it's been a wonderful. . . . Is [SDCC staffer] Mimi Cruz here? Thank you, Mimi, for insisting on this miserable bore fest. Fuck you! Fuck you very much! By the way, Mimi, the Troma team has an award. They're replacing the Eisner[2] now. And we have the 2009 Baster[3] Award. The Baster Award for the best roast ever. And, of course, you are the master baster, so—Mimi Cruz, ladies and gentlemen!

[*Applause*]

Well, anyway, people think that my being dragged through the mud is going to bother me. I've had forty years of being shitted on and pissed on and vomited on. This is nothing. This is Troma 24/7.

Our company is kind of famous for having influenced many of today's luminaries, and famous directors, and actors, and many famous alumni have come out of Troma. And it's just a pity that none of them are here right now. But, maybe at the eightieth anniversary, who knows?

Now is Adam Green. . . . Where is Adam Green? Who is Adam Green? Oh, Adam Green, right. His middle name, you know, is "Straight to Video."

[*Laughter*]

He made a very good movie, by the way. It's called *Hack*. No, I'm just kidding. It was actually called *Hatchet Job*.[4] It's about a young gay film director who blows as many people, as many online film reporters and critics as he can. "He finally got some good reviews!"

[*Applause*]

Adam Green! Oh, by the way, Adam, that was my shit you licked off of [filmmaker] SpookyDan [Walker]'s dick.

[*Applause, laughter*]

Hey, look, it's Mick Garris. Who would have guessed? Mick Garris. Thank you so much for being here, Mick. Stephen King wrote all of Mick's jokes tonight, but Mick didn't do a very good adaptation.

[*Laughter*]

What's that smell? It smells of bullshit here. Holy cow, Joe Lynch must have burped. I don't believe it. Unbelievable. Incredible.

Well, who else have we got on this fine dais? Oh, my heavens. Made a few notes here. Is Batton Lash here? Who's Batton Lash, by the way?

This was just passed, this important note. [*Kaufman holds up folded up piece of paper upon which is messily scribbled: LLOYD HAS AIDS*]

I don't know what it says, but I don't read the newspapers or watch TV very much. One thing I know is when I wake up tomorrow morning, I'll be able to see a live concert with Michael Jackson.[5] That's all I know.

[*Applause*]

Batton Lash, though? All I have to say is, "Who?!" Who? Mimi, how far down the barrel did you have to scrape to come up . . . to get to that point of obscurity? That's unbelievable. What was that thing with the chicken? That was a fowl movement.

[*Groans, laughter*]

By the way, if some of you people feel something weird in your ass, the famous people out there, it's probably Joe Lynch's nose. So, don't worry about it. It'll go away.

[*Groans, laughter*]

Anyway, Jim Salicrup is here. Jim Salicrup, the first man to use Vagisil in his hair. That's pretty cool. Can't beat that.

Hey, Ron Jeremy! Ron Jeremy's here. You know, they have a buffet in the green room. And Ron Jeremy went over to the baloney wrap and fucked it.

Where's John Rogers? John Rogers is the only dummy here stupid enough to show Troma movies on the TV. The good news is that John Rogers has a full. . . . He's filming tonight. He's filming this event tonight. It's so nice of you, John. There's a big camera crew here, and. . . . Hey! What the fuck? Where's the camera? What? Fuck!

You know why John chose movies on G4 television? The Troma movies? You know why he's showing Troma movies? Four words: Tijuana, donkey, blow job . . . [*Waits a long beat, nods head knowingly*]

John Rogers, everyone! Any rate, thank you, John, for such beautiful, beautiful words.

Who else is here? Who else is here? Is Tim Seeley still around? Yeah, Tim Seeley is here. Oh, my God. [*Shuffling through papers*] I got something I wrote down about him, but I can't find it. Have I used up my two minutes?

Adam Green: [*Standing, shouting*] Two minutes!

[*Laughter*]

LK: Tim Seeley, you should be at your job over on Front Street giving out blow jobs, shouldn't you? Anyway, Tim Seeley has a comic book called *Hack/Slash*, and it's going to be a movie. It's about a crappy director and the guitarist from Guns N' Roses . . .

[*Laughter*]

I also hope they change the title. *The Adam Green Gets Fucked in the Ass Life Story*.

[*Laughter*] Well. . . . Hey, Richard Saperstein! I can't believe you're here. It's amazing. Richard has made quite a name for himself out of making crappy remakes out of classic movies like *Mother's Day*, and he's up for a big job now at Xerox.

[*Laughter*]

You know, Richard, they insist on *good* carbon copies at Xerox.

[*Laughter*]

Hey, Ron Jeremy: You know, we told him it was a roast, and he brought his own bib.

[*Laughter*]

Ron, we got you an apple. Come on, man, this is a roast. Where's the apple, you pig?

[*Laughter*]

Well, all I can tell you is that Joe Lynch is here. Joe Lynch. Hold on a second. He did the most talking, so [*mumbling while shuffling through papers*].

Hey Adam, Adam! Just because you made friends with a bunch of zeroes who run shitty little websites, that doesn't make you a respected filmmaker. If that were the case, I'd be the driver of the Bang Bus.[6]

Well. . . . Did I leave anybody out? Uh, oh. Oh, time. Okay. Well, any rate, thank you. . . . Oh, four minutes!

[*Laughter*]

We just have enough time for . . . [*shuffling through papers*] *The Joe Lynch Story*.

[*Laughter*]

Crowd Member: Have any new books, Lloyd?

[*Laughter*]

AG: [*Standing*] He wrote *all* of this while this was going on. This is what I was talking about!

LG: Hold on one second here. I thought I had another Joe Lynch tribute.

CM: Three and a half minutes!

LK: Uh, oh. Three and a half minutes. Well, any rate. I think that's about it. [*Shuffles hopelessly through notes*] Uh.... Any questions from the audience?

[*Laughter*]

Speaking of all the wonderful male directors, great to have Penelope Spheeris, with that incredibly visual tribute. Oh! And Alan Carroll! You know you've made it when Alan Carroll from Night Flight Comics *sends* a video. You've hit the big time. I've got some film of Alan Carroll that I could show later in my room at the Motel 6.

Well, thank you very much. I think that just about wraps it up, Adam Green. And thank you to this wonderful audience. Thank you, Mimi Cruz. Thank you, Comic-Con 2009! Troma!

[*Cheering*]

Notes

1. Seventy-minute long roast held at the San Diego Convention Center during San Diego Comic-Con, hosted by filmmaker/actor Adam Green; with roasters including: filmmaker Joe Lynch, filmmaker Mick Garris, adult film star Ron Jeremy, Marvel head honcho Stan Lee, legendary cartoonist Batton Lash, comics artist/writer Tim Seeley, comic editor Jim Salicrup, film producer Richard Saperstein, longtime SDCC president John Rogers, and Kaufman's wife Patricia (as well as prerecorded messages from various special guests broadcast to audience of more than two thousand live audience members).
2. Long considered "the Oscar of the comics" world, with a presentation held annually at SDCC.
3. As in "turkey baster"; and, yes, Kaufman had created and held up an actual plaque with the picture of a turkey being "basted" on it for all of the crowd to see.
4. A play on the actual title, *Hatchet* (2006), a slasher film that spawned three sequels and a comic book series.
5. Jackson had passed away a month earlier.
6. Popular adult film website/gimmick in which filmmakers portray themselves as drivers traveling around looking for young participants in pornographic films they produce from inside said bus.

Produce Your Own Damn Movie!

Beth Accomando / 2009

From KPBS-FM, December 1, 2009. Reprinted with permission from publisher's own transcription of radio broadcast.

You gotta admire Lloyd Kaufman. Okay, maybe *Class of Nuke 'Em High* and *Dialing for Dingbats* aren't Oscar-caliber fare. But you have to respect the fact that for more than three decades, Kaufman's Troma Studios has been successfully turning out independent films, and has been providing a film school for people like Trey Parker and Oliver Stone. Troma has been producing a consistent product that not only keeps its fan base happy but keeps them begging for more.

Kaufman himself is also quite a character. When you speak with him, you are never quite sure where the showman/salesman ends and the real person begins. He quotes Shakespeare and Pascal and then, with seamless kill, plugs his latest film *Poultrygeist: Night of the Chicken Dead*. His series of books—now known as "Your Own Damn Film School"—serves up a mix of hilarious anecdotes and observations along with genuinely helpful information about making films outside the Hollywood system. So, as much as Kaufman jokes around, he's serious about passing on useful tips to a new generation of filmmakers.

Kaufman's latest book, *Produce Your Own Damn Movie!*, was recently released and is currently available—the perfect gift for any wannabe filmmaker this Christmas. I spoke with Kaufman last month while he was attending the American Film Market (AFM). You can read my review or listen to the man himself.

Beth Accomando: This is Beth Accomando, KPBS film critic, and I am speaking with independent filmmaker and author Lloyd Kaufman. Hello Lloyd, how are you doing?

Lloyd Kaufman: Welcome and greetings from Tromaville.

BA: You are actually at AFM right now, correct?

LK: Yes, the American Film Market. I'm actually the chairman of the Independent Film & Television Alliance, which is the trade association for the independent entertainment community. This is the only major film convention that is owned and operated by the two hundred members of the trade association.

BA: And you are there celebrating your thirty-fifth anniversary?

LK: Yeah, this year is the thirty-fifth year and that's why *Produce Your Own Damn Movie!* came out a couple of weeks ago and everybody's talking about it, because it's all about producing independent art.

BA: This book is part of a series of books—What is it, "Your Own Damn Film School"?

LK: Yes, Beth, indeed . . . indeed it is. It follows *Make Your Own Damn Movie!*, which then was followed by *Direct Your Own Damn Movie!*, and because many people would like to produce, the publishers, Focal Press . . . so, *Produce Your Own Damn Movie!* is aimed at young people who'd like to try and be independent and have control over what art they are creating.

BA: How did this book series get started?

LK: There was a retrospective in New York by the Avignon Film Festival. And the curator of the Avignon Film Festival did a panel with me. I think this was for our twentieth year. And I'm kind of the Jerry Lewis of the French underground. And Avignon is a well-known French Film Festival that takes place oddly enough in Avignon, where the Châteauneuf-du-Pape[1] runs like water. And after doing the Q&A with me, he thought, "Gee whiz, Lloyd's life is kind of interesting." So, he suggested that I write the first book, which was actually kind of a memoir. And I told him go ahead and find a publisher. And he did. So, he became my literary agent[2] and the books have done well.

And *Produce Your Own Damn Movie!* is the fifth book I've written. Three of them are in the "Make Your Own Damn" series, and one was a novel called *The Toxic Avenger Novel*, and the one before that was called, *All I Need to Know about Filmmaking I Learned from the Toxic Avenger.*[3]

BA: Tell me a little about the style you write these books in, because on the one hand, they are often hilarious and loads of fun to read, but they are also packed with a lot of very practical information.

LK: Well, so many of these books that tell you how to make your movies or how to direct or how to write screenplays: they're written by people who don't actually do that, and I've actually been writing and directing and producing movies with no interference; I've had total freedom for forty years.

And the only parimutuels, as Pascal used to say, the only sort of wager, is I have a very low budget. . . . Half a million bucks is kind of the budget I've been working on. I've got kind of a cachet to be able to tell young people how to do it, since I've been doing it for forty years. And it's part of my crusade to continue and keep alive the independent arts, because we are living in an age of giant media conglomerates, and they are strangling everybody, they're eating everybody's lunch. . . . That's part of our crusade is to try to . . .

It's very discouraging to young people, breaking in today, because so much of the media is vertically integrated and controlled by a small number of giant devil-worshipping international media conglomerates headed by people like Rupert Murdoch, where they own the newspapers and the TV stations in the same market, and they control everything, and the rules that used to protect the public against monopolies have been done away with and that is a big, big problem.

So, my motivation in writing the books is to try and inspire young people to go out and try to make their own art and not worry too much about conforming or try to make something that will appeal to Burger King; or that van Gogh didn't necessarily sell any paintings but he did eventually in the fullness of time become the most popular artist in the history of the world.

So, I think that's kind of my mission. Just to try and give people the inspiration to make their own damn movies.

BA: But you have a nice balance between keeping the book entertaining and helpful.

LK: Well, thank you very much and indeed I was aiming at young people. In fact, I've gotten many emails where they say, "Dear Lloyd Kaufman, I'm a junior in high school and I never read books and I read *Produce Your Own Damn Movie!*, and now I'm interested in reading books. And I really had a good time reading it."

You know, a lot of kids think books are scary. They are afraid of books, because they watch too much television and they see Jay Leno and idiots like those on *The Today Show*. Not enough of them listen to NPR.[4] Or they don't read proper journalism, they don't read the papers, they watch baby food television, and then they see *Transformers Part 6*. And they are scared of books.

And why shouldn't they be? Our whole society has been against teachers, against nurses, and in favor of Paris Hilton. That's been the whole value system. So, we at Troma, all of our movies, all the movies I write and direct are usually an attempt to raise the spirits and the psyche and the motivations of the underdogs. Inspire people to fight against the conspiracy of elites.

BA: Keep a spirit of rebellion alive?

LK: Well, not rebellion for the sake of rebellion. But, we really do live in this age of "limousine liberals" and people telling us about inconvenient truths and winning Nobel Peace Prizes that they don't deserve. And then leaving things out of *An Inconvenient Truth* that might be inconvenient like: don't eat meat, like more global warming is created by bovine flatulence than by any human made thing. But, God forbid we put that in *An Inconvenient Truth*, because that would be an inconvenient fact that might make us unpopular.

Or that maybe we shouldn't be watching oil-based DVDs and CDs. Maybe we should be getting our movies from Amazon.com so we don't use up all those oil-based discs and then throw them away, because they never break down. Those things take thousands of years to break down. But the folks who are scare mongering us with the so-called "green message," they don't talk about the bovine flatulence or the DVDs that are polluting the groundwater. They don't talk about that. And that's the thing that's so depressing about the world we live in. That's why it is wonderful that Beth Accomando is interested in independent art. Thank you so much.

BA: I have to say that I have always enjoyed when Troma has had panels at Comic-Con. My favorite was showing how to crush a skull using a watermelon.

LK: No, no I must correct you.[5] It's very important, not a watermelon. In fact, we fired people when we had to crush . . . Trey Parker, he started. . . . Troma discovered many famous people and Trey Parker of *South Park* is one of them. He made *Cannibal! The Musical* at Troma. But, he had to have his head crushed in *Tales From the Crapper*. And I told the young people over and over again, it must be a cantaloupe, because the skin of the cantaloupe in a quick one-second shot is more human-like than the watermelon.

The watermelon cracks. The skin of the cantaloupe gives the way a human epidermis would give. So, those people were fired on the spot because they used a watermelon. So, please: it's a Crenshaw melon, a cantaloupe perhaps, and of course many of the Troma special effects are world-famous because they are quite inexpensive. And very, very effective and rather amusing at the same time.

BA: And then Styrofoam cups to use for crunching bones?

LK: Well, for sound effects. Yes, we use them for sound effects. But, we can talk about the evils of Styrofoam cups not necessarily from the environmental point of view, but people tend to leave them in the middle of a scene. Some crew guy will be drinking out of a Styrofoam cup on *Poultrygeist: Night of the Chicken Dead*, and leave it on the set. And then if nobody sees it, then when the movie is projected, there is nothing that says this is a movie more than a Styrofoam cup in the middle of a scene where there's nothing to do with a Styrofoam cup.[6]

By the way, the other thing about Styrofoam cups, and I talk about this in one of my books, is: don't have big Styrofoam cups, because people tend to take soda or juice or coffee and they'll fill up the cup and then they'll only take two sips and then they put it down and they waste so have very small cups.

And I discuss this in a movie called *Terror Firmer*.[7] Because it's a movie about the making of a Troma movie. So, it's my most personal movie. So, it deals with a sexually confused serial killing hermaphrodite.

BA: You mentioned Trey Parker worked on a Troma film. Are there any others?

LK: Trey Parker and Matt Stone made *Cannibal! The Musical*. *Cannibal! The Musical* was a wonderful film. And Troma is still distributing it very successfully. Although, it's never been on American TV. Because of the media consolidation that I referred to earlier. But, those guys went on to do *South Park*. They have been very supportive of Troma and appeared in *Terror Firmer*. Trey got his head squashed in *Tales from the Crapper*. They have been very nice to us. They are the essence of independence and they are totally brilliant, obviously. They single-handedly revived the art of American satire.

BA: I was wondering if there are any other Troma graduates that you might want to mention?

LK: There's a movie *Def by Temptation*, which Michael Herz, my partner and I, financed. Other than that, we had nothing to do with it. We put up money for it, and Samuel L. Jackson's first movie was *Def by Temptation*.[8] And the fact that we had nothing to do with the artistic side means *Def by Temptation* is an amazingly good movie.

Vincent D'Onofrio's first movie was *The First Turn-On!*[9] *The First Turn-On!* is about summer camp. He played a character called "Lobotomy" in *The First Turn-On!*, and if you see him on TV, he acts as if he's had a lobotomy. So, he owes a lot to us. To Troma.

And Fergie, Fergie from Black Eyed Peas, was in *Monster in the Closet*. And Oliver Stone, who's a big-time director, he came into movies through *Battle of Love's Return*, my first movie in sync sound, the first time I had direct sound on my movie, and Oliver Stone had a part in that. There are a lot of people; Kevin Costner's first movie was *Sizzle Beach, U.S.A.*, a Troma movie.

And when you go to the American Film Market, you can see so many different offices, so many different companies that have executives that started with Troma, and it's quite interesting. Troma is sort of like half film school, half camp, half hippie commune, half artist center, and that's a lot of halves. I was never good in arithmetic.

BA: Now, for your book *Produce Your Own Damn Movie!*, you spoke to and interviewed some other filmmakers. How did you decide who you wanted to include in your book?

LK: Well, I've been lucky enough to produce movies for forty years. Troma's always had the wherewithal and the cash to do it. I have not gone out and done things like preselling movies or putting together packages of stars and then based on the package getting the financing. I've never had to do that kind of stuff. So, I wanted to interview people who . . . for example, Mark Harris who won an Oscar for *Crash*,[10] I wanted to interview him because he's very independent. And he has also come out of the earlier movies when he was young—I don't want to say Troma, because that would insult him, but lower-budget. And he did *Million Dollar Baby*, he did *Crash*. But he's financed them independently, so he had total control over it.

I interviewed Kathy Morgan who is an executive producer/producer's representative who has packages of movies where there are big stars like Scarlett Johansson and Tom Cruise's wife[11] and a big-time director and a bestselling book and a wonderful script, and she can presell those rights to enough companies so they raise $40 million. But they do it independently. It's not through a studio.

And then I interviewed Paul Hertzberg who has a company called Cinetel. And he makes movies for SyFy Channel. And he finances them through Canadian banking and government subsidies and is preselling independent foreign distribution rights. And Steven Paul who's been independent for a long time. As a filmmaker, he did *Ghost Rider*, which was financed independently. He's now working with Steven Spielberg on *Ghost in the Shell*.

I didn't really know much about producing, so I interviewed all of these producers, including Roger Corman. I talked to him about why he stopped directing and only produces. I talked to some of the no-budget producers too who are making movies like. . . . Sometimes I act in people's films, like the guys who did *Crank 2*. I acted in a little part. They are Troma fans, so I interviewed them. They also did *Gamer*. Then there is a guy who did *Bloodbath in the House of Knives*, which is kind of an homage to the *giallo* Italian movies of Argento and Fulci and those guys. And he was making a no-budget movie and I interviewed him.

So, I think if you read *Produce Your Own Damn Movie!*, you can get a sense of producing movies from no-budget all the way to Oscar-winning $80 million movies. All of the producers I talked to raised their money independently. Some of them distribute independently. Some of them do their own distribution like Troma, and some of them are distributed through the movie studios, through the big conglomerates.

So, a young student or an old student or anyone can read *Produce Your Own Damn Movie!* and not just get the Troma way. But half the book is how Lloyd Kaufman produces his or her, its own movies. But also you can learn from up and down the food chain of people producing movies independently from the no-budget movie produced at home to the $80, $90 million that has big, big stars. All of them are independent, however.

BA: You mentioned that you had gotten some feedback about how young people had gotten inspired to read more books, but have you gotten any feedback from young people who are filmmakers who have been inspired and felt they learned something?

LK: Yeah, and in fact a lot of young filmmakers have read my book and write that they carry my book in their ditty bags, in their kits. And when they are on the set. . . . And if you talk to people like James Gunn who—he actually worked for Troma—he says he channels me. He wrote the *Dawn of the Dead* remake, he wrote *Scooby-Doo*, he directed *Slither*. He's in Louisiana now writing and directing a big movie.[12]

Eli Roth is a major director. He did *Cabin Fever* and *Hostel*. And Tarantino has read my books. So, there are some people who are kind of well-known who read my books and then there are a lot of students. And I get a lot of . . . a huge amount of emails from young people who are shooting their first film or just shot their first film who say, "I just finished my movie and your book was in our ditty bag the whole time and the whole crew was constantly referring to it." I also have *Direct Your Own Damn Movie!* and *Make Your Own Damn Movie!*

And a gyno-American—and, again, I don't say "girl," because at Tromaville, we are very politically correct, so "girl" is a bad word and "woman" has the word "man" in it, so "gyno-American"—a gyno director wrote to me recently that has all my books on the set all the time, and has her crew read them, gives them out to her crew to read at night or when they are not filming for inspiration. She said if someone as idiotic as Lloyd Kaufman can make movies for forty years with head squashings and arm rippings and hard-bodied lesbians, then anyone can do it. So, she gives out her books on her set to the young people to read.

I think it's very important for young people to know that they don't have to work for Viacom, Paramount, VH1, or NBC, General Electric, you know, Universal. . . . They don't have to work for a big conglomerate and operate a Xerox machine. They can go out now and, through the magic of the digital revolution, they can go and make their own damn movies, and it's not beyond the reach. And they just have to have the attitude of what Woody Allen says: "Success is about 88 percent[13] just showing up."

We keep going. Troma is here at the American Film Market, we've got *Poultrygeist: Night of the Chicken Dead*, we've got a new Bigfoot movie[14] that's really, really good. We are just starting to write the fifth *Toxic Avenger*[15] movie that involves Toxie's Toxic Twins. And the Toxic Avenger, he gets older in each movie. So, my books, depending on the subject, they have a lot of my own experience, and my own how-to. But in the case of *Produce Your Own Damn Movie!* more than half of it is the interviews and sidebars with successful producers as compared to me.

BA: What do you think is the key to the success of Troma?

LK: I think in all honesty, the secret is that Michael Herz and I are.... Even though we are two different people, we totally kind of channel each other. We are lucky partners. That we really respect each other and basically trust each other. We've never had a contract, we've never had anything in writing, and we abide by the "to thine own self be true" maxim coined by one William Shakespeare. Who wrote that great bestselling book *101 Money-Making Screenplay Ideas*, otherwise known as *Hamlet*.

So, I think that's the lesson. Do what you believe in, "to thine own self be true." Don't listen to people. Do what you believe in. And, again, Troma would not be here without the fans. The fans are very, very, very loyal to us and aggressive. And hardworking. And there's no question that the reason that Troma is the oldest independent movie studio is because our fans have kept us going. They help us, they spread the word.

Notes

1. A French wine.
2. With a name so perfect for representing Lloyd Kaufman and Troma's literary output, he must be pointed out here: Jerry Rudes (n.b.: a New Yorker who lives in France, and hence: the name is pronounced phonetically).
3. The aforementioned memoir, Kaufman's debut book, put out in 1994 by Penguin; cowritten by James Gun.
4. KPBS is an NPR affiliate.
5. This is not the only time Kaufman will "correct" an interviewer about the "watermelon" mistake... Though, in all fairness to them, there *is* an entire chapter in *All I Need to Know about Filmmaking I Learned from the Toxic Avenger* (1994) called "Is That a Crushed Watermelon You Have for a Head, or Are You Just Unhappy to See Me?"... Granted, within said chapter, Kaufman *does* explain that the best way to fabricate a cheap and easy head crushing in a film is with a *cantaloupe*.
6. Interested viewers can see Kaufman fulminate profusely at a crew member for leaving behind a Styrofoam cup in *Poultry in Motion: Truth Is Stranger Than Chicken* (2008), the *Poultrygeist: Night of the Chicken Dead* (2006) feature-length BTS documentary.
7. Kaufman's metafictional doppelganger, the blind indie filmmaker (making *Toxic Avenger 4* for Troma, no less) "Larry Benjamin" (which he plays himself) does indeed harangue a crew member about this very issue in *Terror Firmer* (1999).
8. Not quite; Jackson had in fact been making movies for nearly twenty years before *Def by Temptation* (1990) came out, including Spike Lee's *School Daze* (1988) and memorable roles as both the radio DJ in Lee's *Do the Right Thing* (1989) and the crazed robber in the original *Coming to America* (1988).
9. True.
10. The 2004 Paul Haggis film, not to be confused with the more Troma-adjacent David Cronenberg erotic thriller from 1996.

11. At this time, actress Katie Holmes.
12. The 2010 comedic pseudosuperhero film *Super*, starring Rainn Wilson, Elliot Page, Kevin Bacon, Liv Tyler, and Michael Rooker.
13. Eighty percent, but close enough.
14. Bob Gray's aptly titled *Bigfoot* (2009).
15. Though the script, which would have the latest installment of the Toxic Avenger story taking place in Chernobyl, is finished around 2015, the funding of the project falls apart due to its financing largely running through the auspices of a Troma fan and her Ukrainian billionaire father who, shortly after the 2014 Russo–Ukrainian War broke out, disappeared.

Lloyd Kaufman Interview

Robert Ziegler[1] / 2011

From *Horror DNA*, May 10, 2011. Reprinted with permission.

Since 1999, the TromaDance Film Festival has annually showcased truly independent cinema. Founded by Troma Entertainment, the festival was originally held in Park City and Salt Lake City, Utah, showing counterprogramming at the same time as the Sundance Film Festival. In 2010, TromaDance relocated to Asbury Park, New Jersey. *Horror DNA*'s Robert Gold got a chance to sit down with Lloyd Kaufman, President of Troma Entertainment, who is entering the twelfth year of the TromaDance Film Festival.

Horror DNA: Lloyd, I want to thank you for sitting down with me for a minute.

Lloyd Kaufman: It's a pleasure. Thank you for taking me to the transvestite glamor show at the fabulous Empress Hotel. It was almost as good as the TromaDance after-party last night. Almost.

But it was a good transvestite party and thank you for letting me accompany you.

HDNA: Sure. Wouldn't miss it. How has TromaDance changed over the years?

LK: Well, I think the most important part of the metamorphosis is that we started TromaDance when Trey (Parker) and Matt (Stone) brought me to Sundance and we were so disgusted by the haughtiness and smugness and elitism and nastiness, and we created TromaDance to sort of be a poke in the eye to Sundance. It was more developed to be a festival, but in large part to screw around with Sundance.

But, over the years, Sundance kind of cleaned up their act, I believe, and they seem to actually be showing some independent movies these days, and I think they heard our message. Now that we've moved to Asbury Park, we're really a nice little idealistic festival.

What hasn't changed about TromaDance, of course, is that you don't need to pay money to submit your film to the festival, you can see your movies for free, and there's no VIP policy. . . . Although, if you're an attractive young transvestite and if [Robert Gold] wants you to get into the TromaDance Film Festival and *Horror DNA* is a part of it, then we let them in. We give them precedence.

HDNA: Now that you are on the East coast, do you have any beef with Tribeca or do they run a tight ship?

LK: I think Tribeca is a bit schizophrenic and I don't quite understand it. I think they're too mainstream. They ought to be more . . . real. I don't think they're a real festival. I think they're more American Express . . . I think it was more star fucking for the first few years. But I think recently they're showing some genuinely interesting independent movies.

They had the Olsen Twins and Alec Baldwin and, while those are great people, I just don't think a festival needs to promote celebrities. A festival should be promoting John Goras (*Chirpy*) or maybe Bill Plympton (*The Tune*) . . . or Troma. With all due respect, we've been in New York for almost forty years. If I were Tribeca, I might look into perhaps showing some of the forty years of Troma movies. Trey and Matt are in town with *The Book of Mormon*—Tribeca could show *Cannibal! The Musical.* Maybe you show a movie by Eric Rohmer (*My Night at Maud's*) or a film by Takashi Miike (*13 Assassins*), because most of the public I don't think know those guys. But I just don't think we need to be showing movies that are opening at three thousand cinemas the next day.

HDNA: You are always making appearances at conventions, festivals, etc. Where do you find the energy?

LK: Troma has no money and we are economically blacklisted, so we have no money to advertise. *Poultrygeist* is a very good movie, but the major media totally ignored it. Troma had its thirty-fifth year in New York City and not one word of ink was spilled, even though we own a building. We have had a payroll all these years of New Yorkers who clearly would have been on welfare if it wasn't for us.

The only advertising we can do is getting out there, and if there's a retrospective, I have to go. . . . Or if I'm invited to give a *Make Your Own Damn Movie!* master class, I go . . . and I enjoy it. I get a chance to meet the fans and hear what they like and what they don't like.

HDNA: Where is your biggest international audience?

LK: The only revenue we get is from the United States. We have a huge fan base in other countries, but we have no distribution. I'm sort of the Jerry Lewis of the Underground in France, but we have no distribution. In England and Japan, we have no distribution other than piracy. File sharing keeps us alive in the archival world, the museum world, and the festival world. So, Troma's got a big footprint around the world; I don't think we have much going in Africa. But, on all the other continents, there's a big Troma following, and we have a big influence on the more mainstream young directors who are coming along.

HDNA: How is Troma doing?

LK: Troma has never been more famous, but we've never had less revenue. We are economically blacklisted. The media has become vertically integrated so that Rupert Murdoch and three or four other media conglomerates control everything. *Cannibal! The Musical* has never played on American television, not even on Comedy Central or Skinemax. *Citizen Toxie* sold about three hundred thousand to four hundred thousand DVDs and cassettes. It's never been on American TV. The only reason we're still around is because our fans keep us alive, and that's it. We have a small number of very aggressive, hardworking, and loyal fans who keep Troma alive by spreading the word on Twitter or Facebook.

HDNA: You've always been an early adopter of new technology. You guys were some of the first ones to offer titles on DVD, Blu-ray, video on demand, and now your library is available on Xbox.

LK: We got into DVD actually before the machines were even in people's homes, which was pretty stupid. But we got a head start and we made a few bucks. Because we are a small company, we can move fast. In 1993, we started our website long before anybody else. There was something called CompuServe [an early form of AOL], and Roger Ebert said that Troma is the only studio that had a website [that early on]. Thanks to that site, Troma has a huge following online.

Usually when new technology develops, the major conglomerates take it over and preempt it, and they're trying to take over the internet now. They're spending hundreds of millions of dollars 24/7 in Washington; the MPAA and Rupert Murdoch and Disney and Sony and all those guys, they're all down in Washington, trying to get rid of net neutrality on the internet, so that we and you and *Horror DNA* cannot have equal access to the internet.

Right now, the internet is the only level playing field—it's the last level playing field in the world of media, and the big guys want to stop that, because they don't like having to get up in the morning and compete. They want to be able to put out crappy Adam Sandler movies, and brainwash the public, and open them in four thousand theaters, and make their money and go home. They don't want to have to actually come up with something original or interesting, and the internet makes them have to do that.

The more originality on the internet, the more the giant media have to compete. So, they're trying to screw up the internet, and they want to get permission to have a superhighway for themselves and slow down everybody else's service on the internet so that the internet becomes kind of like the television of today, where you have everybody playing *Law & Order* 24/7. Just click your dial—*Saved by the Bell, Full House*.... That's the way the internet's going unless we fight it.

As chairman of the Independent Film & Television Alliance (IFTA), I am down in Washington lobbying. We don't have the kind of money the MPAA has, but we are doing a pretty good little guerrilla campaign, and we threw a monkey wrench into the Comcast/NBC/Universal/GE merger, and we got that held up, and we got an agreement between that giant conglomerate and the independent filmmaking/television world where Comcast has got to answer the phone when we call.... So, that's nice.

HDNA: When you were on the *Make Your Own Damn Movie*! book tour in 2003, you were concerned about the conglomerates destroying the little guy. Now, almost ten years later, how do you encourage new filmmakers?

LK: The good news is now anybody can make a movie, the making of cinema is democratized. You can make a movie for no money and TromaDance proves it with movies like *The Taint*, which I had not seen [before last night], and it's quite a revolutionary film. *The Taint* was great. It's in my head. It may be an influence on me.

There are millions of people who are able to make films thanks to the digital revolution. They can make very wonderful movies for very little money, or no money. You don't have to make your living from making the movie; you can be a schoolteacher or work in the Holocaust Museum, or be a big shot at *Horror DNA*. You don't have to have a hundred thousand dollars or two hundred million dollars or pounds or euros to make a movie, and that's a good thing. Unfortunately at Troma, we have a payroll and we have to pay people, so it would be nice to have a little bit of revenue.

The bad news is that, because the industry is so consolidated, if you want to live off your art, you probably have got to work with the giant evil people. Technology has not gotten to the point where we (Troma) can pay you enough money so that you can have a roof over your head or send your children to school and all that kind of crap. You'll have to make *The Toxic Avenger* and then you can send your kids to school.

HDNA: And four sequels ...

LK: Exactly. I'm making *Toxic Avenger Part V* now and I still have kids going to graduate school. So the point is, yes, you can be an artist and the good news is you don't have to go to Hollywood and drive the Disney parking lot van or do Xeroxing for William Morris or suck dick for Miramax. You can do your own thing and be a teacher; you can have a useful life. You can be a nurse, save people's lives, and contribute to society, and then you can still make movies.

I don't think it's as hopeless as it was. But, on the same point, it's ugly that the public is kept in ignorance of so many amazing movies, that the gatekeepers are so elitist and domineering. The *New York Times* and the big festivals are not doing their jobs. They are not unearthing the brilliant new talent that is all over the world. It's everywhere ... in every nook and crevice. TromaDance is proof.

These movies that are playing TromaDance, most of them are better than what's being shown at the New York Film Festival, they're definitely better than what's being shown at Tribeca—without a doubt. Without a doubt they're better. They're more original, their themes are more interesting, and for the most part, they are all unknowns.

When I tell people "I just saw this great movie called *All About Evil*," they ask, "Who's in it?" It doesn't matter who's in it. If anything matters, it's who directed it (Joshua Grannell), and even that doesn't matter.... The point is that it's a good movie. *All About Evil* is a movie that should be seen, it's interesting, it's got a great point of view, and not enough people are seeing it.

HDNA: Does an overflow of shoddy material hurt the independent spirit?

LK: I think everybody should make a movie. I think it's a good idea, but the biggest problem is so many people making movies don't read books, and they don't read the newspapers, and they've got nothing to say. They're not educated and they haven't traveled, they haven't done anything, or they haven't killed anybody, or they haven't read *Moby-Dick*. You need to read. You need to travel, and have inner resources and have something to say, something to express . . . It isn't all about zombies. Although, maybe 80 percent is about zombies.

HDNA: Going out on a light note, who would win in a fight? You or Mel Brooks?

LK: Mel Brooks would beat the crap out of me for sure.

HDNA: But, you have a more ravenous fan base that would come and kick his ass after.

LK: I'm not so sure. My fan base is very peaceful, they're lovers. But, it would never happen. I'm a pussy. I run fast, and I would run away. I've got a big mouth, and I've said some provocative things to various people . . . I saw Kirk Douglas once cock his elbow, and I thought he was going to punch me . . . but he did not. That was about as close as I ever came to getting punched.

Once, I was at a gas station and I called a guy a cocksucker, and he came after me, and I ran away. I ran around the car and it was like the Three Stooges. I kept running around the car and he couldn't catch me, so he eventually gave up.

HDNA: Very cool. Thank you, Lloyd.

LK: Thank you to *Horror DNA* for continuing the good fight for independent cinema and world peace through celluloid.

Note

1. Credited as pseudonymous Robert Gold (permission granted to mention real name here).

Lloyd Kaufman Interview with James Rolfe

James "The Angry Video Game Nerd" Rolfe / 2013

From *Cinemassacre*, January 24, 2013, https://www.youtube.com/watch?v=dLsl5GRE8No. Transcribed from video/audio with permission.

James Rolfe: Hello! I am here at Troma headquarters with Lloyd Kaufman. For almost forty years now, Troma's been paving the way for independent filmmakers and making films that we'll say are usually more extreme than most filmmakers would dare to do. In a Troma film, you're likely to see lots of blood and shit. I've done a lot of shit in my videos, too. Would you like to share shit recipes?

Lloyd Kaufman: Well, I know *Sizzle Beach* has got Kevin Costner in it. Are you talking about that? Oh, *Tales from the Crapper*: Maybe that's what you'd like to.... You'd like to know *Tales*.... Check out *Tales from the Crapper*; that says it all. And ... and James, by the way, we're big fans of yours here at ... we're big fans of The Angry Video Nerd here in Tromaville. Very big fans. We masturbate to you constantly.

But, let me say this about that. If you need recipes for shit, just check out the Troma bathroom here. And after Friday, we have free lunch for the employees with some amazing shit. And my books *Make Your Own Damn Movie!* and *Direct Your Own Damn Movie!* have secret recipes with for shit, for blood, for vomit, for urine, for jism.[1] So, I think you young people have a lot to learn. Michael Herz and I went to Yale University where we learned all those things.

JR: Speaking of the books, some of the most entertaining and inspirational books about filmmaking I actually read were *All I Need to Know about Filmmaking I Learned from the Toxic Avenger* and *Make Your Own Damn Movie!*, but now there's also *Produce Your Own Damn Movie!* and *Sell Your Own Damn Movie!* You want to tell us about those, the newer ones?

LK: Well, *Sell Your Own Damn Movie!* I think is the most visionary of my books. It's better than *Direct Your Own Damn Movie!*.

JR: What are you working on right now? What's the newest from Troma?

LK: Well, right now we're touching up the sound on *Return to Nuke 'Em High*, which is, as you know, the shot-by-shot remake of Ingmar Bergman's *Virgin Spring*. *Return to Nuke 'Em High* is being made in association with Stars Media, and we're about to mix Volume 1.

Return to Nuke 'Em High is an event film, James. An event film similar to *Kill Bill*, with a Volume 1 and a Volume 2, and we're about to sound mix Volume 1. We saw the trailer to *The Angry Video Nerd: The Movie*, and most of what's in that trailer you will see in *Return to Nuke 'Em High*. And thank you for letting us, how shall we say it, file share your movie.

JR: Do you have a favorite movie monster?

LK: I would say Frankenstein, the original Frankenstein, by far. And if you check out *All I Need to Know about Filmmaking I Learned from the Toxic Avenger*, which is a book that James Gunn wrote, that I wrote,[2] you will see that there's a lot to do with Frankenstein, especially in the creation of the Toxic Avenger. Because, like you, James, we always wanted Frankenstein to live. We feel sorry for the guy, for the monster. So, Toxie is very much inspired by letting the Monster live among . . . and just the whole mood of James Whale, and the combining of horror and humor and all that kind of stuff.

JR: Very cool. I made a video one time about all the filming locations in the *Rocky* films, and you were involved with that, the first *Rocky*. And you were the, the drunk guy who Rocky picks up and carries into the bar. And that happened to be one location that we couldn't find. Do you remember any of that? Or just tell us about your experience on *Rocky*.

LK: Well, the director, John Avildsen, had made *Cry Uncle*, which Troma distributes. Which is. . . . If you haven't seen it, *Cry Uncle* is a great, great movie. It's a takeoff on the film noir, but it's full of sex and violence and . . . and it's hilarious. And, in its day, it's still the . . . The screenplay is brilliant by David Odell who wrote *Dark Crystal* among other movies. At any rate, Avildsen didn't have enough money to film on location, so the, the producers were—

JR: In LA, you mean?

LK: No. No, he wanted. . . . No, they didn't have money to film in Philadelphia, and they were going to try to fake LA as Philadelphia. But, Avildsen and Stallone both wanted Philadelphia. So, they hired our crew, which had just done *Squeeze Play!*, I think,[3] or. . . . Anyway, they hired our crew. Yeah, I think. . . . Well, I know we had just done a movie, and they hired our nonunion crew with us to line produce it.

And Michael Herz and [Herz's wife] Maris were syncing up the dailies from the eight days of filming in Philadelphia, and they were wondering . . . we had an upright Moviola, and we . . . they kept wondering, "What the heck is this?" But my mother-in-law, my mother-in-law read the script to *Rocky* before I started working on it. She said this would be the next *Marty*. *Marty* with Ernest, with the late Ernest Borgnine. Which I didn't pronounce right, but directed by, I think, Delmer Daves[4]—an Oscar-winning movie. My mother-in-law saw it; she was right.

And, when Avildsen got his Oscar, what a good guy. Because, most people, when they get the Oscar, they either thank their lesbian partners or—which I would, of course—but, they mostly butter up, you know, kiss ass and thank Harvey Weinstein and all that. Avildsen thanked me, which is pretty cool, because all I did was set up Philadelphia. You know, organized it. And it was all nonunion, so we shot for eight days and then the, the Teamsters found us and then they brought, they brought everything back to LA. But, by that time we had the, the running up the steps of the museum. We. . . . All the great stuff in *Rocky* that—

JR: —and the bar were you were at: Was that Philly?

LK: The exterior was in Philadelphia. The interior was in LA. And, but the Pat's Steaks was Philly. . . . All the stuff—the pet shop, the fighting, the punching the meat carcasses—was in Philadelphia. We got away with about eight days of nonunion filming before we got caught, and then they went back to Philadelphia, and the Teamsters then came and broke my legs.

JR: The first time I ever heard of a Troma franchise was actually the cartoon show, *The Toxic Crusaders*. I was only a little kid at the time, and it wasn't till later on when I learned of *The Toxic Avenger* and what it was based on. And when you go from the, you know, the film to the cartoon: very, very different. You have one that's more, you know: with lots of sex and violence. And then you have one that's, you know, more for children. It's like, how did something like that get made into a show?

LK: Well, when you're in this business, every once in a while you get lucky. It's like if you stay at the tables long enough, you'll get lucky. And for some reason, the people making the toys, the Teenage Mutant Ninja toys, wanted to get an environmental cartoon. And Kevin Eastman[5] is a big Troma fan. So, somehow they decided to make Toxie toys and—

JR: Is that where they got the idea of the mutagen, from the toxic waste?

LK: Probably they thought of it on their own. I don't know. You know, I can't imagine that they didn't do it on their own. But I'll tell you, a lot of mainstream. . . . You watch *RoboCop*, you watch everything from *RoboCop* on—including *South Park*—and you see a huge influence of Toxie, *Class of Nuke 'Em High*, and the Troma. . . . You'll see plenty of Troma in all of, much of today's pop culture.

But, the cartoons were very well done, mainly because they kept me out of it, and I thought they were very original. As is the *Toxic Avenger* musical, which came out last year here in New York, ran a year, and I think they're bringing it to Philadelphia, actually. It's very good, and they . . . It has the spirit, and the, the cartoons both. . . . And the musical . . . have retained the spirit of Troma humor. But they've been able to mainstream it—the Bon Jovi guy, and, and the people who did the cartoons for *Toxic Crusaders* did a great job in presenting the Troma universe in a really very kind of mainstream-ish way. But very entertaining.

JR: You ever played the *Toxic Crusaders* NES game?

LK: I tried to play it, but it was much too difficult for me. It just wasn't as good as the *E.T.* Atari game. You know, after *E.T.* Atari, I—You know, that was so good that I couldn't play Toxie anymore.[6]

JR: I once saw *Toxic Avenger* on TV and they didn't censor any of the nudity. But, they censored the gore. Like the, you know, the watermelon with the kid getting run over everything? That was all cut out. It was on demand, but. . . . What could we do to get Troma movies on TV in their full glory?

LK: Well, the good news is that. . . . First of all, may I correct you, James? That [child's head being smashed by the car tire] was not a watermelon. People have been fired because they've used watermelons for squashed heads on *Tales from the Crapper*. Trey Parker's head gets squashed, and they. . . . The kid brought a watermelon out—It's a cantaloupe, because the cantaloupe skin has more flexibility. The watermelon skin cracks and breaks open. So, it's clearly a melon. Cantaloupe, if you let it ripen a bit, even though it's smaller than a head, it's, it's much more effective. But—

JR: The honeydew before.

LK: Well, honeydew also. Honeydew, if it's really ripe. But, again, it cracks open and, and it's, it's, it's. . . . But, it could work if you load enough stuff in it and let it get a little bit rotten. Honeydew is . . . it's bigger, it's closer to the head shape. But, I stay with a cantaloupe. Or maybe the Crenshaw melon. The Crenshaw melon can be pretty good, too. We could talk about how to make blood. There's—

JR: And a crushed head.

LK: There's so many different ways to do the head crushing—

JR: And the shit.

LK: Well, shit . . . shit . . . it depends—well, yeah, shit, too. But, blood, especially. Blood. I could talk an hour on the blood for squibs, the blood for wounds, the blood for dead people, interior blood, exterior blood, blood in the hair, they're all different formulas for blood. It's pretty interesting.

JR: You know, blood always photographs differently sometimes. Sometimes it's just a weird-colored red. What movies do you think had the right blood color? Right hue?

LK: Boy, you know, I. . . . Blood is tough. But what, what's really awful is that the MPAA rating board—no matter what we did, they would chop our movies up. And if we had any kind of blood in our movies, they would cut it out, even though *Die Hard* and, and violent mainstream movies were permitted to keep the blood. So, we. . . . That's why you'll see in *Class of Nuke 'Em High*, the monster has yellow blood. And that's where we started using green fluids rather than red fluids. Because, no matter what, the MPAA would chop it up, and we then, we couldn't get our R-rating, which meant we couldn't get movie theaters. And in *Class of Nuke 'Em High*, the MPAA made us cut out the one spurting yellow fluid coming out of a goofy-looking monster. They made us cut that out in order to get an R-rating.

JR: So they don't like the color yellow also, then.

LK: Well, I think they don't like Troma. They don't, the MP. . . . The purpose of the MPAA rating board is not to protect the public from movies; it's to protect the big studios from competition from people like the Angry Movie . . . I mean The Angry Video Game Nerd. I took a lot of acid in the sixties.

Well, at any rate, the point is the, the system is there to protect the cartel that runs the entertainment and the media. So, they'll have a different standard for the major films, and they'll, they'll cut out and disembowel the Troma movies. And they've pretty much won. They've pretty much. . . . There are virtually no independent movie studios that have lasted for forty years. There are none like us. And most of them come and go. It's not that they make bad movies. It's that they, they can't compete with the, with the, with the vertically integrated cartel that runs our media and entertainment industry.

JR: Okay, Troma films are like party films. They're great to watch with a large group of people. Are they anywhere near as fun to make as they are to watch?

LK: Troma films are not fun to make in any way. They're a nightmare to make, and the reason is because we've got thousands of people in them, they tend to have transformations, they have special effects, they've got special effects makeup, and now we've gone into CGI with *Return to Nuke 'Em High*. But the main thing is, they're very complicated and it's hell.

And if you want to see it, check out *Poultry in Motion*. *Poultry in Motion* is the documentary of *Poultrygeist: Night of the Chicken Dead*. It's hilarious, but you can see the pain and suffering of everybody in the film. It's totally unvarnished. It's actually. . . . *Poultry in Motion* would be a good thing for students to watch, because it really gives you the real world of Troma filmmaking. There's no fun whatsoever, but very creative and, and it's totally devoted. . . . The team is totally devoted to the cause, which is rather inspiring. But, it ain't fun.

JR: I second that.

LK: Yeah, welcome to my world.

JR: With independent films, they seem like they just go on forever, because you always got that one shot that you still need and it just goes on and on and on. With Troma, how do you keep such a steady machine going and move on the next film and keep, you know, keep it going?

LK: Well, the great thing about the digital age—and I've discovered this with *Return to Nuke 'Em High*—is you can. . . . I'm a terrible director; like, I make huge mistakes, and we get to the editing room, and we cut the entire film and then we realize, "Holy Christ! The highlight of the movie, nobody understands it! It's incomprehensible!" I somehow missed the most important point of a film. But, with digital, you can go back and take a [Canon] 5D [camera] and go here and film the people, or bring them . . . I mean, it's amazing what you can do that you can't do with 35mm if you're on a low budget.

With 35mm, we always. . . . In fact, I met Woody Allen once, and he said the same thing. He saved some money in the budget to film in postproduction. But for 35mm, it becomes thousands of dollars. With the digital, how nice is that that you can keep, keep fine-tuning and filming.

You know, we take a long time to edit. Always. I mean, *Poultrygeist* took at least two years to write the script and another full year to produce. At least. It was—and *Tromeo & Juliet* was five years to write the script. So, we're pretty slow.

We do produce other films with other directors who are more straightforward and know what they're going to do, and, and by the time they come to us, we've agreed on the script and all that kind of stuff. But, it does take me a long time, and the digital revolution is really a democratization of filmmaking and allows you to have a lot more freedom and to not be rushed if you don't have it.

It's sort of liberating: Nobody wants our movies, and that's very liberating because we don't have to deliver *Return to Nuke 'Em High* for Christmas. You know, we finished shooting Volume 1, basically, back in August and September. It's now January. We have finished shooting, and we've got kind of a rough cut, and we'll be mixing probably toward the end of February; we'll have the movie finished. But, we didn't, you know. . . . We don't have to have a deadline, because nobody wants our movies. Peter Jackson, that's his job. He's got to get the movie ready for Christmas. That's got to be pretty stressful. The big problem is, is that, since I've been in the business, since we started Troma in 1974, the industry has gotten so vertically integrated. All the rules that used to protect the public against monopolies.

JR: Yeah, and also not only making films, but you're also very active. You know, doing a lot of interviews like this one and taking a lot of time. How are you able to keep so active without stretching yourself too thin?

LK: When Michael Herz and I got Troma to the point where we didn't think we'd disappear, we wanted to do what we could to encourage independent cinema. And, so, the books are mainly for that purpose, and I act in a lot of movies, and I've been trying to get a part in The Angry Video Game Nerd film. I did offer my lips like a woman to James, but he. . . . So far, I haven't gotten anywhere. But, I'm still hoping to get a part. And anything we can do to help the cause of independent cinema.

And right now, we're hoping to make another documentary to go along with *All the Love You Cannes!*, which we did ten years ago. We're hoping to do another documentary teaching students about the importance of international film festivals as sales tools. Not just art, but selling your film. And also to try to expose the, the hypocrisy of the Cannes Film Festival and the fact that it has become the private plaything of the giant worldwide conglomerates.

JR: Another thing about independent films is that they get compromised a lot. Is that, you know, you have the idea in your head, and you know exactly how it's supposed to be, but every day as soon as you start shooting, you're facing all kinds of problems and it starts getting, like, watered-down until it becomes a very different film than what you originally imagined, even if it comes out real good and everybody likes it.

Still, it's never going to live up to your imagination on how good you, you know, you expected it to be. And do you feel the same way when you're working on films? Like, do you deal with a lot of compromises?

LK: Well, certainly on a modest budget. . . . You know, *Return to Nuke 'Em High* has got thousands of people. It's a very ambitious project. It's in two volumes. And, in fact, Volume 2, we're still filming. So, maybe we can get The Angry Video Game Nerd to play a cameo in Volume 2. That would be terrific.

It's more, I think, that you have the kind of yin and yang—I majored in Chinese studies at Yale—and you have the yin of total artistic freedom. We've had forty years where nobody's been telling us what to do. But the bet is that, the kind of bet that you make is that you will make a movie for a small amount of money. So, therefore you can't have honey wagons, you can't really feed the crew what you'd want to feed them, you have to sleep on the floor, eat cheese sandwiches three times a day and learn how to defecate in a paper bag in order to work on a Troma movie.

And we, you know. . . . On the one hand we don't shoot SAG—Screen Actors Guild—so we don't have to deal with if you shoot with somebody on a Monday and you and you don't use them until Friday and they're sitting around just picking their nose. With SAG, you got to pay them for that time. We don't have to do that.

When we filmed *Return to Nuke 'Em High*, people were living in Niagara Falls, New York. We had about eighty people living there for two months and literally sleeping on mattresses on the floor in a funeral home. But, we could—Anything that went wrong, we could say, "Okay, we can't shoot. The costume is not ready, so we can shoot with those two people." Or, oh, gee, the. . . . We had an outbreak of spider bites, oddly enough, on this movie.

There was like. . . . Niagara Falls seems to be the epicenter of spiders—all different types—and we had two or three people who had go to the hospital; so, we couldn't use them on certain days. But, we had everybody there, so we could say, "Okay, we'll shoot over here and cover sets." And I don't think we had to compromise too much, other than we obviously can't compete with *Inception* in terms of the special effects.

But, our fans kind of enjoy the Brechtian aspect of Troma movies, because they sort of enjoy being part of the creative. . . . They understand that they can see backstage with our movies. They can see some of the makeup, they can see the, the bald caps don't quite work, or the, the blood coming, the fluids coming out of people's ears. Maybe they'll see a piece of tape. They like that. They kind of like it. You know, it's part of the Troma magic, the Troma technique. That, it's. . . . Brecht did the same. Bertolt Brecht did the same thing, and Andy Warhol. I'm a big fan of Andy Warhol, and he would be doing a scene, and all this, and suddenly the actor would say, "Andy, I want to have lunch. I'm hungry," and Warhol would leave it in the movie. You know, he was great, he was terrific for that. You know, that kind of. . . . And, I think the audience. . . . I mean, I always liked that, to be kind of backseat, backstage a little bit. And behind the scenes. But, you do have to compromise. But, better that than Michael Bay.

JR: It seems, you know, movies, our favorite art form, has been turned into such a big business, really, and, you know, we have movies nowadays that cost, you know, more than two hundred million dollars, and all kinds of, you know, obscene amounts. Do you feel that Hollywood makes it kind of difficult for independent filmmakers to, to be able to compete, you know?

LK: Well, it's not just Hollywood. The media is international, the conglomerates, the small number of giant devil-worshiping international conglomerates, are international. Sony's Japanese, [News Corp's] Rupert Murdoch is from some other planet, [Viacom's] Sumner Redstone is the creation of [four-time Academy Award-winning special effects master] Stan Winston.

I mean, these people . . . these are a small number of old, old, old people and conglomerates, and, and they control everything. And the rules that used to protect the public and used to let independents like us enter the market in the seventies and eighties, it's almost impossible to do that now, because the rules have all been changed to, to help Viacom, and help Sony and help to control the marketplace. And we all better be real careful.

I've written about this in my books and essays. We better protect net neutrality on the internet, because the big guys are down in Washington. The MPAA is spending a hundred million a year to get rid of net neutrality. They don't want net neutrality. They do not want the free, open, and democratic internet. They want to control the internet as long—as do the phone companies and the ISPs.[7] So, we need to fight and make sure that no more, no more of these laws try to get sneaked in. They usually try around Christmastime when people are asleep, you know? We were big on—

JR: Two Christmases ago, yeah.

LK: We closed down the Lloyd Kaufman fan site and other stuff, as did Google, I think.

JR: As the blackout thing,[8] when that was going on?

LK: Yeah. So, I think we have to be very vigilant. But it is indeed very difficult to compete in this world with the conglomerates. But, may I also suggest that the line . . . it's interesting, because the line between filmmaking and home movies, on the other hand. . . . There's so many people making films that the line between filmmaking and home movies has been blurred. So, you have, in other words . . . to get noticed . . .

You have, for example, the tender and the searing, interracial, controversial film by Kim Kardashian, *Superstar*.[9] Of course, Ryan Seacrest made Kim Kardashian into America's Sweetheart. A sex film, basically. But, now she's America's Sweetheart. And how about the, the beautiful love story created by Paris Hilton, *1 Night in Paris*,[10] or whatever it is? In other words, it's a different world. How . . . they got noticed. They sure as hell got noticed. But I don't think it's, you know, helping the art of film. But, at least you can get noticed.

How did Justin Bieber get to be Justin Bieber? I believe it was just a YouTube video. And probably The Angry Video Game Nerd who has immortalized. . . . I know I've done my bit, I discovered that he's wearing a training bra and that he stuffs it. Not The Angry Video Game Nerd, but Justin Bieber apparently stuffs his training bra. I've done my little bit to help him.

JR: When you're making an independent film, how do you compete with all the options of what there is to watch, because people have such a large choice. What do you, you know, do to get, to get noticed, really?

LK: Well, I think the most important thing is to make a film you believe in. It's an art form, and that's. . . . There are easier ways to make money, right? You can be a congressman.

JR: Going to, yeah, either going to law school or become a doctor or something. Yeah, people going into independent filmmaking, no. You're gonna go into debt if you do that.

LK: Well, also don't expect to be rich. You can be rich. I mean Harvey Weinstein is very rich, and Tom Cruise is very rich, and . . . but, most, you know . . . I mean, what are the odds of that? You have to. . . . If you want to make a lot of money, you should not go into moviemaking. And if you want to make a lot of money in moviemaking, you probably ought to go—and you want the Oscar, and you want the cocaine and the hookers—go to Hollywood and be part of the mainstream. But, I believe in the auteur theory of cinema, as do you, and we want to control our movies. As Shakespeare said, "To thine own self be true." And he also wrote that amazing book *101 Moneymaking Screenplay Ideas*, otherwise known as *Hamlet*.

JR: Yeah, you know, talk about how it's changed when, you know, with YouTube and everything, it's so easy to upload something to the internet and get it out into the public. But before it was just, you submit to film festivals, and that was really the only way. And it was usually kind of a blind guess if you were going to get in or not. You'd pay the entry fee and then you wouldn't even get any feedback, you wouldn't really know.

LK: Well, when Michael Herz and I began Troma, there was only theaters. There were only cinemas. And 35mm. *Squeeze Play!*, *Waitress!*, *Stuck on You!*, *Sugar Cookies*, all these movies that we made in the seventies, we could compete in the theaters, because they were building the multiplexes, so we could get out there.

There was no DVD, there was no VHS, no TV, none of that stuff for independent cinema. And now there still is none of that stuff, thanks to the fact that the FCC and Clinton—actually Clinton and Reagan, between the two of them, got rid of all the rules that opened up the field to independent, to truly independent filmmakers.

So, the internet is a great, great place that. . . . The public . . . if you make a thing that is good, the public will find it. I mean we've been doing it for forty years. We don't have a huge fan base, but our fans are extremely loyal. They support anything we do. That's why if I'm in a new filmmaker's film and if there's no budget, I act for free, and the Troma fans will support anything that's Troma-related, and so that's really valuable.

And word-of-mouth, there is no way that the major studios can buy word-of-mouth. They've tried. It doesn't work. And even when something works on the internet—*Snakes on a Plane* is perfect, because it had this huge internet presence before the movie came out, but the, the mainstream people, the cartel behind it, didn't know how to use it and the movie sucked. And I don't know that it was commercially successful. I imagine that, because it got on HBO, and it, that maybe it did all right, but . . .

In other words, the internet, the public will find it. If it's interesting, and different, and true-to-your heart and all that stuff, the public is pretty good about finding. It may take time. *Combat Shock*: one of Troma's best movies. We were deficit on that for a long time, and we finally broke even about fifteen years after the movie was made, and thanks to the word-of-mouth, *Combat Shock* actually is pretty . . . it's an evergreen for Troma: we keep making, not a lot, but a bit.

And, certainly, when *Cannibal! The Musical* came out, nobody got it. We were the only. . . . Trey Parker and Matt Stone had no interest. Troma was the last stop on. . . . They were fans of Troma. But, they knew we were underground. But we were the only ones who got *Cannibal! The Musical*. And once *South Park* came out, of course *Cannibal! The Musical* was a huge home video success, as well as in the theaters. And thanks to the fact that Troma is blacklisted by most of the TV stations, including Comedy Central, *Cannibal! The Musical* has never been on TV. So, American TV at least. So, our home video keeps going pretty strong because people hate us. And they'll hate you, too; don't worry, you'll see. No, no! They're gonna like you. They will love you.

JR: If you were to do anything over again, would you ever go into a different genre or something? Or do you feel, you know, this is what it's meant to be, or . . . ?

LK: That's a good question, James. I think the only regrets I have are when I've compromised, and I compromised on *Toxie II*, *Toxie III*, *Sgt. Kabukiman N.Y.P.D.* And I don't think we made any more money with them, and I don't think that we made better films because of the compromising, and I don't think we got a bigger audience.

They're good movies. I mean, they. . . . Some people think *Toxie Part II*—the one we did in Japan—is the best of the *Toxic Avenger*s. But, to me, I see where I tried to make. . . . And we had partners on those movies, and we had to get the R-rating, we had to get an R-rating. So, we clearly had to compromise, and I regret it. *Sgt. Kabukiman*: I talk about it in my books. *Sgt. Kabukiman N.Y.P.D.*, we had Namco, the video game, the *Pac-Man*, yeah, and. . . . They were our partners, and they wanted kind of a family-oriented movie that they could . . .

They had these little amusement parks in Japan. They wanted Kabukiman in those places so families could come and enjoy him, and I didn't get it. I didn't get it, so I kept pushing: "No, he's got to eat the worms! And we got to kill children!" You know: "The little babies have to be killed!" And we sort of, you know . . . that we sort of compromised during the. . . . They were very understanding and they let me do a lot that they didn't want, and I kind of shaved the, the corners a bit, and I don't think it helped the movie. I think we didn't get a full-fledged Troma movie, and they sure didn't get the, the mainstream *Kabukiman* that they wanted.

And, and I think the lesson is: either you have total freedom—you just let yourself go and make some art—or you become a hired hand and just do what they tell you to do and take a big paycheck. And I think John Sayles does this. I think John Sayles—and there are a few others who . . . they'll make a movie for the mainstream, and they'll do whatever it is that is wanted, and then they'll go out and make a brilliant John Sayles movie.

JR: Last question. Probably the one that has no answer. Going back to one of the first things I asked you, you know, you talked about how hard it is to make films. You know, you have that burning desire to make a movie. But when you go to make a movie, you put yourself into debt, you lose all your spare time, you lose touch with, you know, personal, loved ones. And, really, making a film, it just takes over your life. So, if people make films and, you know, you get sick of it and everything, but still you want to make it, you want the end result, why do we make films?

LK: Well, it's an art form, and in the same way that Picasso painted or van Gogh painted, you want to give something in your soul to express it. You know,

Kubrick spent ten years on [the unproduced] *Napoleon*. He had a project called *Napoleon*, and he had a file card.... There's a Kubrick show somewhere, and it's in LA, I think, and he had file cards for every day of *Napoleon*'s life. He spent.... Obviously obsessed about it.

I mean, again, I think you have to be a bit eccentric. I know that in my own personal life, I put filmmaking way ahead of my wife and family, and I regret doing it. But there was no other way to make the movie. And I've been married for almost forty years, and my partner Michael Herz and I have been together for forty years. So, some . . . and my close childhood friends, I'm still with them or they're with me; however you want to put it. And I see that you guys are schoolmates, and your group has been together for a long time and are good buddies.

And I think that's kind of . . . if you can have sort of a base, and then build up. And you've got that fan base, so you really.... It's very discouraging to be where Troma is. Forty years, nobody really, nobody.... There's no.... The *New York Times*, for example.... We've been making movies in New York for forty years and employing.... You know, we've had a payroll, we own this building, we own the building on 9th Avenue, we've got a library of eight hundred movies, we've probably produced a hundred of them mainly in New York City, in New York area, New York City.

Well, Manhattan, you know.... We were in Manhattan for thirty years and in Hell's Kitchen. And, yet, the *New York Times*.... We had our thirtieth anniversary. Not one, not even a line, you know? And when they review our movies, they review our movies in the Shit Department, you know? With that section where they put somebody's first movie or some documentary about left-handed mattress workers or, or, you know, they put us—

JR: The left-handed mattress workers?

LK: The *New York Times* gave that one a lot more attention than they gave *Poultrygeist: Night of the Chicken Dead*. Even though the review was very good. But they.... Because we don't advertise.... We can't: We have no money. How are we going to advertise? And we have one theater on *Poultrygeist*. *Waitress!* opened in New York in 1980 with ninety-two theaters. Okay, we could advertise and amortize. With one theater in New York, how much could we advertise?

And, even so, we had the highest-grossing single screen in the country the day that *Poultrygeist* opened. And yet, now we beat *Speed Racer*, which was the big movie that weekend. And yet, they yanked us out I think three weeks later. Or two, after two weeks, because *Indiana Jones: Skull Fucker* needed every screen in the world. So they kicked us out.

And, by the way, the good people at the Tribeca Film Festival—the very wonderful, independent cinema festival—they wouldn't let us put the poster, they wouldn't let us put the *Poultrygeist* poster up the week before *Poultrygeist* was opening at the Clearview Cinemas downtown, because I-don't-know-why. I have no idea. I'd love to know why they wouldn't let us put the poster up. Because, you know that Tribeca is supposed to be this independent New York based.... But, this is what you go through if you don't, if you don't have a lot of money to grease the skids.

JR: Well, anyway, Lloyd Kaufman: Thank you so much for, for the interview, and for inviting me to Troma and everything. This has been great. *Cinemassacre* fans love Troma.

LK: And, again, thank you, James and *Cinemassacre* fans for supporting independent cinema. And, we at Troma can't wait to see your film, and please give me a part, and I have lips like a woman. I know how to use it.

JR: Okay.

Notes

1. For those interested, he's not kidding.
2. Cowritten by both; (at least credited as such!).
3. Although there tends to be a large gap between many Kaufman films' production and their distribution, this is unlikely, as *Rocky* (1976) came out three years before *Squeeze Play!* (1979); more likely, the film he means is *Sugar Cookies* (1973).
4. Delbert Mann.
5. Cocreator of *Teenage Mutant Ninja Turtles*.
6. 1982's *E.T.* Atari video game was infamously such a monumental boondoggle that it in effect ended the product line of the company and nearly collapsed the entire video game industry right before it really took off three years later with the rise of Nintendo (which had to at first market itself as an "entertainment system" as opposed to "video game").
7. Internet service providers.
8. It was shortly after Christmas 2011 that major websites, platforms, search engines, and outlets (including Google, Reddit, Mozilla and Flickr) temporarily shut down their operations in protest against two proposed laws in the United States Congress: the Stop Online Piracy Act (SOPA) and the PROTECT IP Act (PIPA). Concerns arose that the bills would not so much as aid in protecting copyright as infringe on Freedom of Speech along with further concerns that they were biased against smaller, more independent, and user-generated web content hubs.
9. Kim Kardashian's 2007 illicit "sex tape" that made the media rounds during an unfortunate period in which such tapes became a popular way for certain celebrities or those aspiring could become celebrities could actually accomplish their goal of gaining enough public attention to, indeed, become celebrities or revitalize their careers. The gambit seemed to have worked in the case of Kardashian.
10. Kardashian's friend, hotel scion and celebutante Paris Hilton's own sex tape from 2004.

Lloyd Kaufman on *Squeeze Play!*

Lloyd Kaufman / 2013

From *Trailers from Hell*, July 1, 2013, https://trailersfromhell.com/squeeze-play/. Transcribed from video/audio with permission.

Lloyd Kaufman: Greetings from Tromaville. I'm Lloyd Kaufman, legendary film director you have never heard about, and I'm here at *Trailers from Hell* to talk to you a bit about a little movie called *Squeeze Play!*

[*Audio clips from* Squeeze Play! *trailer / VO: "Everyone's asking: 'What is a squeeze play?'"*]

LK: Like many of my films, *Squeeze Play!* is based on a political theme ripped from today's headlines. In this case, the women's liberation movement.

What made *Squeeze Play!* kind of unusual was that it took sex, which back in the seventies. . . . When I was coming along, the early seventies, sex was considered a serious subject. The sex movies were there to spur on the raincoat manufacturing industry, and the rule was you shouldn't mix sex with comedy.

But, Michael Herz—my partner—and I knew that there was such a thing as vaudeville, and comedy and sex were mixed together. In fact, the title *Squeeze Play!* . . . The "squeeze play" refers to squeezing a part of woman's anatomy: boobies. Well, how delighted was I when I found out that "squeeze play" is actually a term that's used in softball? And so the title actually makes some sense.

Also, it fit on the marquee. In the early seventies, the marquees . . . your title had to fit on the marquee. So, the shorter and catchier you your title was, the more room on the theater marquee you could have.

Squeeze Play! is about a women's softball team and how they are trying to gain parity with the men. The men run off and play softball and leave the women in the house, and the women want to go out and form their own softball team. This was fifteen years prior to the much-inferior *A League of Their Own*, which featured somebody named Madonna, or I guess it was a religious movie.

Squeeze Play!, of course, had some amazing humorous moments, such as a man who catches a softball between the cheeks of his behind. Gets the biggest laugh of the film, of course.

The main actor who was supposed to do that shot did not want to have a softball taped to his behind, have a string pull this off and fall away, have the camera upside down so that the material in 35mm would be recorded backwards, and when placed in the editing room, it would then come forward, and you'd have a hilarious moment. So an extra did it. A guy who was a kind of a walk-on took the part and had the ball tape taped to his behind, and went down in history with the biggest laugh in *Squeeze Play!*

Another lesson that I learned was that you've got to get rid of actors who were uncooperative. Woody Allen, I believe, has had more Oscar-winning performances than any other director. I've had probably the least. But Woody Allen would get rid of actors. He got rid of Emily Lloyd in *Husbands and Wives* after he shot the movie. In this case, I didn't have the guts to do that. In *Squeeze Play!*, one of the actresses, Melissa Michaels, told me two days before we were gonna film that she would not do nudity. And we had gone through the drill, she rehearsed it, we had filmed rehearsals in Super 8. I should have fired her. I should have given her a part that required no nudity. I did not. I didn't have the guts to fire her. This led to a cancer on the presidency, because later on when there was supposed to be a shower scene, she and some of the other actresses ganged up on me, and we filmed the only shower scene in history with women in bathing suits.

Squeeze Play!, like many Troma movies, has one foot in a serious political issue. *Toxic Avenger* was about the environment. *Squeeze Play!* was about women's liberation. So, the metaphor of softball and the women wanting to have parity with the men and have their own softball league was kind of an interesting theme, and maybe that's the reason the film was quite successful.

When we tried to get it into movie theaters, because it had ample doses of crass sex, the MPAA was giving us a hard time and the movie theaters wouldn't accept it. But, it did get a sneak preview in Virginia. We had a sneak preview with *The In-Laws*—Peter Falk and Charles Grodin—and people loved *Squeeze Play!* And the next Monday, AMC decided to play the movie in a lot of its theaters, and the film went from one print, I think, to three or four hundred prints.

Troma's Lloyd Kaufman: "I Hope the MPAA Burns in Hell"

Simon Abrams / 2014

From the *Village Voice*, January 15, 2014. Reprinted with permission.

Lloyd Kaufman is a staunch defender of American independent cinema. He's also the guy who, with business partner Michael Herz, codirected *The Toxic Avenger* and *Class of Nuke 'Em High*. As the cofounder of the now-forty-year-old Troma Entertainment, Kaufman produces, distributes, and directs no-brow comedies about, for, and by a new generation of juvenile delinquents like *South Park*'s Matt Stone and Trey Parker, and *Guardians of the Galaxy* director James Gunn. This month, Kaufman's latest film, *Return to Nuke 'Em High Volume 1*, had its New York premiere at the Museum of Modern Art. The *Village Voice* talked to Kaufman about too much urination, stoner-friendly kids' shows, and the Toxic Avenger's Christlike qualities.

Question: How did you sneak into MOMA?

Llyod Kaufman: They liked [*Return to Nuke 'Em High Volume 1*], I guess! I keep wondering if they've got me mixed up with Charlie Kaufman.[1] But I do believe that both *Return to Nuke 'Em High* films will be, when completed, my Sistine Chapel. This recognition may be because of Troma's fortieth anniversary. But I've been making movies in New York since 1968. It's nice to get this recognition. When I was five years old, my mother put me in the art class at MOMA, so I spent a lot of family time there.

Q: You usually rank *Troma's War* as your favorite Troma film, right after *Tromeo & Juliet* and *Toxic Avenger*. How do contemporary Troma fans respond to [*Troma's War*]?

LK: I believe *Troma's War* is one of Troma's best movies, but *Poultrygeist: Night of the Chicken Dead* is a much better film, and I certainly like both *Return to Nuke 'Em High* films better—*Toxic Avenger IV: Citizen Toxie* ... *Terror Firmer*! Troma's

115

War is a very underrated movie, and it got totally fucked by the MPAA. Richard Heffner, who just made a noise like a frog and was president of the MPAA, told Michael Herz over the phone that our movie stunk. The MPAA is not supposed to do that, and they disemboweled our movie. They took out punches and jokes and things that were perfectly acceptable in movies like *Die Hard*. I think Heffner's words were, "No fuckin' good," or something. It was very unpleasant.

Our violence is, as you know, cartoon violence. That movie followed *The Toxic Avenger* and *Class of Nuke 'Em High*, so we had built up some steam. But the only way we could get into movie theaters in 1986 was with an R rating. And the film[2] was cut down to something like a G-rated movie. I'm very bitter about it; I hope Dr. Heffner burns in hell, quite frankly. And I don't like to speak ill of the dead, but the nerve, the arrogance, the hubris of his comments! There are very few movies studios that have lasted and remained independent for a long time. And the MPAA is one of the reasons.

Q: Moviegoers generally can't distinguish independent or exploitation films from mainstream films. On Netflix Instant, if you search "Troma," the first two options are Troma films, and the third is *Tora, Tora, Tora*. And Michael Haneke used footage from *The Toxic Avenger* in his film *Benny's Video* as an example of typical Hollywood filmmaking. Is that a basic literacy failure on his part, or a victory for Troma?

LK: [*Laughs*] I have no idea. That's insane. Troma now has brand-name appeal. Troma and Disney have name-brand recognition. People don't go to see a Paramount movie, I don't think; people don't go see a Warner Bros. movie; they go see a Leonardo DiCaprio movie. But people go to see a Troma movie because it's a Troma movie. So when the MPAA unfairly censored *Troma's War*, they totally ruined us. Our fans were pissed off at us! They don't know the MPAA fucked it up. They think we tried to sell out.

Q: Troma has had a lot of alumni infiltrating big corporations, like James Gunn. Pretend you're a proud mother showing off embarrassing baby pictures of your favorite son. What can you tell us about some of his rookie mistakes?

LK: I spent five years writing *Tromeo & Juliet*, but he solved it! We cowrote it together, but most of the dark brilliance of that screenplay is James Gunn. James came to us through a friend, and he wanted to be a novelist, not a screenwriter. I liked what he had written, and gave him $100.

Q: $150.

LK: Oh wow, how generous. Well, it was back in 1996; $150 was worth $100, back in those days. The only thing I remember is . . . he put a lot of urination scenes in it. Too much of that. Other than that, I think he did a great job. It was his idea to put in the line, "What light through yonder Plexiglass breaks?" That set up a stunt with Plexiglass that almost blew me up. They used too much dynamite, or whatever they use for stunts like that.

Q: Speaking of too much blowing up, almost all of the movies that you either directed or codirected since *Sgt. Kabukiman N.Y.P.D.* recycle that one car crash. When did that stop being a good way to save money, and start being an inside joke?

LK: When the fans asked for it. The first time may have been with *Tromeo & Juliet*. And then with *Citizen Toxie*, we weren't planning to use it, but we had a big sequence with a car chase, and we decided it would save us a lot of anguish if we reused that shot. Only problem was that *Kabukiman* has a clown running around that movie on a unicycle. So, with *Citizen Toxie*, we had to write in a clown on a unicycle. [*Laughs*] Somehow, when we started editing the movie, we managed to edit, to cut the clown out. Now the fans are waiting for it. And wait till [*Return to Nuke 'Em High Volume 2*] comes out; there's a major riff on that whole thing.

You know, Bertolt Brecht is a big inspiration, and Andy Warhol. I don't think they ever met, but they both broke the fourth wall a lot, and I like that stuff. So I think the running gag with the car flip works on various levels. When I was at Yale, I hung a bit with the Warhol gang. I used some of his superstar types in early movies. I can't say I had any conversations with him, but I did pass him at Max's Kansas City. But I was a big fan of his movies.

Q: In the past, you've said that the "stew" of influences on *The Toxic Avenger* includes *Silent Spring, Mondo Cane, Hail the Conquering Hero,* and *The Power Elite*. What were some of *Poultrygeist*'s influences? That seems like your most incensed film since *Troma's War*.

LK: The same influences have persisted throughout my career: Stan Brakhage, Warhol, John Ford, Chaplin. Toxie's blind girlfriend is straight out of *City Lights*. And Preston Sturges's *Sullivan's Travels*; the school for the blind in [*Toxic Avenger Part II*], that's from *Sullivan's Travels*. Most of what influenced me were classic American movies. I like Renoir a lot; I like Fritz Lang's American movies. In fact, I tried to reenact the first shot of *The Big Heat* in *Terror Firmer*, where the guy blows his brains [out]. I failed. But it still happens in *Terror Firmer*! I made it goofy, of course.

Q: That suggests that there are certain things people expect from a Troma movie. I want to talk about a movie you made before there was such a thing as a Troma movie. It's a movie that you joked was "the worst thing to happen to the Jews since *Mein Kampf*": *Big Gus, What's the Fuss*? It's never been officially released on DVD or home video except as an Easter egg, but it is on TromaMovies' official YouTube Channel under a "Directed by Lloyd Kaufman" playlist. Have you watched this thing recently?

LK: [*Laughs*] I can't look at it. It's so horrible. The Israelis that helped make this film were crooks. They never gave us the negative back, they never gave us statements—not that the film was worth anything. We had a beaten-up 16mm print, and we had a list of synagogues and Jewish organizations, and we got one reply back, one rental. The guy sent back a really nasty letter—he hated it! I think it was somewhere in the Midwest. The lesson for *Big Gus* for young people is: Don't listen to anybody. We got lots of advice on that film from older, more experienced people. But the film stunk; it's a disgrace. What you saw was made from a half-inch video that somebody from Israel brought to us. I went to Israel in 1974 on my honeymoon to try to get the film back, but I just got a lot of double-talk. The movie opened in Tel Aviv, but it opened the week of the Seven-Day War.[3] So bombs were raining down outside, but we had a bomb inside the movie theater.

Q: Some of Troma's acquisitions have developed a life of their own in spite of—or maybe because of—their negative reputation. For example, *Fatty Drives the Bus* has become something of a secret handshake among the Troma faithful.

LK: That's a great movie! It's just very hard to get attention. Look at the money they spent on this little movie—a wonderful film—Joseph Gordon-Levitt, *Don Jon*. It was terrific. I'm sure they spent a couple million making the movie, and a couple million trying to sell it. But it went nowhere, and that's a great movie. I guess whoever was selling it chickened out, and it still has ads all over the place. The movie cartel basically brainwashes the public. We're supposed to think that this three-hour Martin Scorsese film is supposed to be good. And *Anchorman 2*. That guy was everywhere: every newspaper, every Twitter—it was on my Twitter! I didn't ask for it to be on my Twitter. So how is *Fatty Drives the Bus*, a wonderful film.... We lost money on it. We have no money, that's the problem.

We can't get any traction. You're the only major publication interested in the fortieth anniversary of Troma. The *New York Times* is busy sucking the teat of the major studios. They twist themselves into a pretzel when *Kumar and Schmumar Go to White Castle Part III*. They say, "Oh, the farts are such a statement about American culture! It's such great satire!" It's bullshit. Troma paved the road for farts! But we don't exist. In Russia, they used to kill people. Then they got a little nicer, and all they'd do is take away people's passports. That's where we are.

Q: Another project that never took off: What the hell were you guys thinking when you made *Doggie Tales*?

LK: One of the people who worked for us, his significant other worked at this dog daycare center. He convinced Michael and me to make this. It didn't turn out to be very successful. But did you notice who did the voices? James Gunn.

Q: Wasn't that Trey Parker?

LK: I forget.[4] But there's also Jenna Fischer. And, by the way, when we go to horror conventions or fantasy conventions, the stoners love *Doggie Tails*. We can't keep it in stock. And the little kiddies, the five-year-old crowd, they love that show. I have so much positive reinforcement from parents about kids that watched *Doggie Tails*. But perhaps because it came from the loins of Troma, people assumed it was not appropriate for young people.

Q: There's a lot of singing in your films, and also a surprising number of people crying out to God in anguish. But since this is a Troma film, those prayers seem rhetorical. If you're the authorial God of these films, what kind of God are you: Old or New Testament?

LK: [*Laughs*] I'm Jesus. I forgive; I think he was the best. I love Jesus, though I'm a Jewish person. But that's why Toxie's a unique superhero. He's upset, but he doesn't want to kill people. His Tromatons are programmed to destroy evil, so he can't help it. I believe in the Golden Rule, so I think I'm more New Testament.

Notes

1. The Academy Award–winning idiosyncratic writer and writer-director of such films as *Being John Malkovich* (1999) and *Synechdoche, New York* (2008); not to be confused with Lloyd's filmmaking-cum-baker brother Charles Kaufman.
2. *Troma's War* (1988).
3. Lloyd is either completely making up this nonexistent war to crack an off-color punny joke about bombs, or is misremembering his dates. The Yom Kippur War took place a year earlier in 1973. And there was also a *Six*-Day War in Israel . . . back in 1967.
4. Kaufman beats out the *Village Voice* here: It *was* James Gunn, *not* Trey Parker.

Getting Tromatized with Lloyd Kaufman, an Interview

Ed Sum / 2015[1]

From *Otaku No Culture*, October 25, 2015, https://otakunoculture.com/2015/10/25/lloyd-kaufman-interview/. Reprinted with permission.

Getting to talk to Lloyd Kaufman, the cheerleader for Troma Entertainment, is a treat for this journalist. He's very knowledgeable about the industry and he has more than forty years of experience in entertaining the masses. One of his long-standing philosophies in life is to share what he knows and not play with the evil conglomerates. His work in the independent B-movie scene is well respected, and perhaps the best way to summarize his thoughts is in when he said, "We're all friends of the underground and it's very important to help develop each other's wellbeing."

That's not only in reference to lifestyle changes needed to emotionally succeed but also in how he conducts business at Tromaville, or rather, "Troma Central." When considering all that he's experienced in his road to recognition and the fact the *Toxic Avenger* franchise put Troma Entertainment on the map, people are asking, "What's next?" The big question is in what's happening about the big screen treatment that's been limping along in development. Sadly, Kaufman is not in the loop with every detail. He notes that Steve Pink is a fervent supporter of Troma products and that a script exists. Kaufman knows that the product is in very capable hands and when it does go into production, he will have a cameo in it, much like how he appeared in *Guardians of the Galaxy*, directed by James Gunn (also a supporter, since Troma was where Gunn got his start).

Kaufman is very happy that a handful of films his company produced does have moguls in Hollywood interested. Just when the big-budget *Toxie* will arrive will depend on the ultimate thing that plagues this business: *Where's the money?* Until that comes, TromaMovies has a YouTube channel offering two hundred and fifty of their films for free and lessons in how to get into the film industry.

"We're doing this to thank our fans who've supported us over the forty-three years we've been operating," said Kaufman.

Both he and Michael Herz founded this studio, and together they will conquer the world. They are the dynamic duo of the B-movie world. Kaufman's wife, Patricia Swinney, has also helped. As Kaufman likes to note, she's a retired New York Film Commissioner. Together, they make for an interesting dynamic of how both sides of a film industry can work together.

I had a chance to really chat with the Kaufmanator to get his take of what's going on in the industry today.

Ed Sum: When you were last present in the Pacific Northwest, it was in Vancouver, BC, for TROMAFEST last summer. What can you tell me about that event, since not everyone was able to attend?

Lloyd Kaufman: This group really understands what we do. They celebrate Troma and they get the sophisticated themes that are buried within what some people might say [is simply about] sex and violence. They get the political statements being made, and that's really satisfying for me to know.

The fans who attended also gave great ideas generally on what's going on in the world of underground film, so there was a really intelligent fan base here. It was really great, it was terrific.

ES: And now that you'll be appearing at Island Fantasy Convention this Halloween in Victoria, BC, what can fans expect from your presence there?

LK: We're going to have the Canadian premiere of *Citizen Toxie: The Toxic Avenger IV* and quite possibly the debut of *Extreme Jukebox*. I'll be bringing the original mask too. Of course, I'll have my special selection of stuff to sell. I'm going to have at least twenty different video titles along with T-shirts, mugs, beers, etc. We'll have Toxic Avenger cups and we might bring shot glasses too. And I will sign any Tromabilia for free.

You'd be surprised where people have asked me to put my signature on. I've seen many people with Toxic Avenger tattoos and my face . . . but they usually put my face on their ass. My wife is not so fond of that.

ES: Are there any other films or presentations?

LK: We could also show Volume 1 of *Return to Nuke 'Em High*, which hasn't had any screenings in BC that I know of. And we can have the focus group for the rough cut of Volume 2. I did one at the University of Southern California and we handed out questionnaires. We had one hundred and fifty people giving us very good feedback in how to improve the film.

I will be presenting a two-hour version of my *Make Your Own Damn Movie!* master class. I got examples of how we raise money, how we do special effects, how we squash a head, open a movie. I've taught this course worldwide.

ES: Prior to dedicating yourself as a filmmaker at postsecondary, did any of your coursework in college influence your filmmaking style? That is, as most readers know, you majored in Chinese studies.

LK: When I was in high school, I thought it heavily emphasized Western culture. I studied Latin and French. When it was time for Yale, I decided to devote my time to studying Asia and Africa. In fact, I stayed a year in Chad—central Africa—in the bush, no electricity, no phones, no running water.... It was difficult.

But afterwards, since coming home, I've led my life according to Daoism (the *Tao Te Ching* and Zhuangzi), and I believe in the yin and yang. They certainly govern the universe. You can't have the good without the evil, comedy without the tragedy ... they're all together. I believe going with the flow of nature than against it. I'd say Chinese philosophy has become very much a part of my life, and as part of my Asian studies, what I learned certainly had an influence when filming *Toxic Avenger Part II* in Tokyo. And it was also prominent in the creation of *Sgt. Kabukiman N.Y.P.D.*

When you look at *Tromeo & Juliet*, you will see Daoist signs. Where I put it is subtle, but it's everywhere.

ES: And as I've heard, that's also influenced how you run your business.

LK: In our Troma building in New York, yes. We have one big room just like in Japan when I visited in 1967. Here, all the people can talk to each other openly. They don't have private offices. Maybe the executives do, but it seemed to me that most of the people in the corporations have a huge room to talk in. I liked that idea and that's how we've run Troma all these years.

Back then, I didn't get to visit China to see how they operate because Nixon had not yet visited. It's different now. Nobody expected China to open up so quickly.

When we were making *Return to Nuke 'Em High*, we lived in a vacant funeral home. Most of the people slept on the floor, they had air mattresses, and only the two stars had their own room. We had about eighty people living together in that space for three weeks!

ES: Wasn't that really creepy?

LK: Yes. It was haunted, too. Some of the cast and crew said that they saw ghosts. According to the *New York Times*, the Mafia owned the place and they did kill people downstairs in the basement. They were brought down to the basement, killed, and incinerated.... Now how cool is that? I mean, you can work for Spielberg and, yet, you will not get to see the real thing. You can work for Ching Siu-tung (*A Chinese Ghost Story*) and might be making movies about spirits but won't see them. If you go on our YouTube channel, you can see some documentaries that we have made about the places we've been. It's mostly about the movies we made; but, there you can see what we've done.

ES: I imagine that these reels are more about showing the community spirit that's developed in the crew instead of the ghost stories, eh?

LK: Yes, you can see what we've done. Some of them become very close friends. A few even married. Of course, there will be some fights. In our film, *Poultry in Motion: The Truth Is Stranger Than Chicken*, you can really see what goes on behind the scenes. It's about ninety minutes long.

ES: What's the one thing you've noticed from all the people that's become part of the Troma cooperative?

LK: You'll see that people will make lifelong friendships while working here. In fact, Asta Paredes and Clay Von Carlowitz (*Return to Nuke 'Em High*) are getting married. Even Robert Prichard and Jennifer Babtist (Slug and Wanda in *Toxic Avenger*) got married, had children, and divorced. Oh, the cycle!

ES: Which is pretty much what yin and yang is about.

LK: That's just the nature of the game. It's very intense. For the most part, it happens. I can tell you James Gunn made a lifelong friend when we were making *Tromeo & Juliet*.

I say the Tromic experience is pretty interesting. We're here for making art. It's not about making money or getting the glamor. We're not Paris Hilton or Kim Kardashian. We want to make a film that people will really be impressed with. Plenty of famous people got their start with us, like Samuel L. Jackson, Eli Roth, Kevin Costner, and Oliver Stone.

When you go to California, I think almost every film company there will have had someone who got their start with Troma.

Even Mark Torgl is doing well. I think he specializes in editing trailers now. He's working on putting the finishing touches to a mockumentary called *Toxic Tutu*, which is an homage about him and his life after playing Melvin. You may be able to find clips online.

ES: When did you discover him?

LK: He appeared in *The First Turn-On!*, originally as part of the crew as a scriptwriter, and this was the movie we made before *Toxic Avenger*. It's a very funny raunchy comedy and it's Vincent D'Onofrio's first movie. He's a big star these days and appears in *Law & Order: Criminal Intent*.

I immediately knew Torgl was funny, and I had him appear in the dinner scene. What he did cracked me up! From there, I asked and he agreed to play Melvin; the rest is history.

ES: With such a huge fan base of your products, where do you see the growth happening? That is, there is TromaDance.

LK: We are still a very small company and our emphasis is in making movies, which is what we are more about. People come along and they can easily license

T-shirts from us, toys, and etc. In fact, I believe there are Toxic Avenger energy drinks and beer.

It's possible that if somebody wanted to do a proper convention, they can talk to us and get the rights to do it. But I think for us, we have too many things in our plate. Like we're still working on *Return to Nuke 'Em High Volume 2*. It's taking us three to four years now, since we started to try to finish it up.

ES: When do you hope to have Volume 2 out?

LK: It should be completed by the end of the year, Volume 2. But we are victims of the international conglomerates that control all the theaters. We have to find a venue to show this product.

I want to make it really, really good so fans will be happy. We don't have the big money, so we can't go fast. We have a small staff in the office and lot of the work is stuff we have to do ourselves. We can't bring in specialists to create the effects and do color correcting of the negative. There's also the sound work and that takes a long time.

ES: What can you reveal about the story?

LK: Volume 1 left off on a cliffhanger and Volume 2 continues the story where you will see the evil Herzkauf, owner of the Troma Organic Foodstuffs business, developing his nefarious plan, and you'll see how the beautiful romantic lesbian lovers will have to fight him. But I don't want to be a spoiler.

ES: What do you know about the *Toxic Avenger* musical?

LK: The New York Broadway production played for one year, and I loved it. I heard it cost six million dollars to produce. They invited me to go to Hawaii for a show, and we even went to Toronto where I was brought in to host. It's played in fifteen cities now. I think they are booking it as a road show or something. I'm happy to hear it's coming to Vancouver. I know that MTI[2] agency just licenses the rights to local groups, universities and the like so they can put on the production. I wish them, the Vancouver group [Last Chance Productions], the best.

ES: Will there be more Toxic Avenger from you?

LK: Yes, we've written the fifth *Toxic Avenger*, but unfortunately we don't have any money to produce it. Other than that, everything's great. But other than that, full steam ahead. I'm being ironic. So, we've got to somehow find someone who'll give us enough.

ES: Well you can always move your base to Canada where you can get more support.

LK: Maybe, maybe but I have to finish Volume 2 of *Return to Nuke 'Em High*. Once I finish that, I can turn my attention to trying to find some money and to get the *Toxic Avenger Part V* organized. We want to make it in Chernobyl. That's the setting we're going to use.

We actually had a billionaire from Ukraine who was going to give us about half the money but then the civil war in the Ukraine broke out and the Russians came in.... The daughter is a big fan of our works and she wanted to break into the movie industry. She got her father to agree to pay for half of the movie but unfortunately they've disappeared now. So, we're up a river without a paddle.

ES: What's in the future for Uncle Lloyd?

LK: Fernando Alle, the special effects person for *Return to Nuke 'Em High Volume 1* and *Volume 2*, wrote a script called *Mutant Blast* that we are financing. He will direct it and he asked me to play a small part, so we'll go to Portugal in December to hang out a bit and I'll make a cameo.

He also made a made a forty-five-minute movie called *Banana Motherf**** that we're also going to distribute. You gotta look for it!

ES: How does it feel for you to see your crew move onto making their own independent work or making ways into the Hollywood system, or elsewhere in the entertainment industry?

LK: It's a great honor, its wonderful! They remember me and keep Troma alive at the same time.

I feel that it's very difficult for us to be a 100 percent independent movie studio. We have no help from the mainstream, so we really depend on you, James Gunn, Eli Roth, and those folks to keep us going.

ES: Do you have anything to say in closing?

LK: Thank you to all our Troma fans that have supported us for over forty years. To those who want to make movies, I believe Shakespeare said it best: "To thine own self be true." Do what you believe in. Express your soul.

Notes

1. Previous, attenuated version of story ran in the same year via *Absolute Underground Magazine*.
2. Via Music Theatre Internationals website: "One of the worlds largest leading theatrical licensing agencies, granting theaters from around the world the rights to perform the greatest selection of musicals from Broadway and beyond."

Deep in the Bowels of Tromaville with Lloyd Kaufman

Drew Fortune / 2017

From *Paste Magazine*, May 11, 2017, https://www.pastemagazine.com/movies/lloyd-kaufman /deep-in-the-bowels-of-tromaville-with-lloyd-kaufma/. Reprinted with permission.

Spending an afternoon with Troma cofounder Lloyd Kaufman, deep in the bowels of Tromaville (in actuality, a modest two-story in Queens, NY), is akin to stepping into Pee-wee's Playhouse on acid. Props, posters, and hundreds of film canisters and DVDs from Troma's forty-three-year history haphazardly "decorate" the office. There's order to the chaos, albeit in typically ramshackle Troma fashion.

Across from Lloyd's desk sits the much tidier bunker of Troma's better half, the reserved and rarely seen cohead Michael Herz. The two met at Yale University and balance each other nicely: While Kaufman is the P. T. Barnum and face of Troma, Herz is the man behind the curtain. Herz shakes his head in disbelief at Kaufman's antics throughout my visit, and you can almost hear him thinking, "Jesus, Lloyd . . ."

A proud proponent of free speech and anticensorship, the seventy-one-year-old Kaufman injects his directorial efforts, amid the vomit, gratuitous gore, and nudity, with sharp social commentary. The studio's latest, *Return to Return to Nuke 'Em High AKA Volume 2* takes on greedy corporations, toxic processed foods, and LGBTQ rights. The world premiere screenings for the film will be at the Cannes film festival this May 23–25 at Arcades Cinema. After crashing Cannes, Troma fans are encouraged to call their local cinemas and request they play the movie.

I spoke to Kaufman about the film, working with the dearly departed Lemmy, and how Troma is the herpes of the movie industry.

Paste Magazine: What's a typical day for Lloyd Kaufman?

Lloyd Kaufman: I don't want to talk about it, because if I did, I'd have to kill you. All I can say is that Michael Herz and I are the hardest-working men—well, he's a man; I'm kind of half and half. But, we're the hardest-working men in show business. We're the James Brown of the underground. Forty-three years of disrupting entertainment. No independent movie studio in history has lasted forty-three fucking years.

Paste: We all love how good you are to your fans.

Kaufman: I'm not just good to my fans. I'm good to my air conditioners.

Paste: How was the *Return to Return to Nuke 'Em High Volume 2* shoot? Was it crazier or smoother than previous Troma outings?

Kaufman: This has been seven years in the making. My cowriter Travis Campbell and I have been working on this project for seven years exclusively. It's a big deal. We don't take ourselves at Troma seriously, but we take our movies very seriously. I think we have the best cast we've ever had.

Paste: Your personal politics play into your films. *Volume 2* takes on greedy corporations and GMOs.

Kaufman: That's true. It's also antibullying. It makes the point that the LGBT community ought to have some rights. This was before Bruce became Caitlyn, so we're usually a little ahead of the game when it comes to politics. We're more visionary than the mainstream. We got into environmental issues in 1983 with *The Toxic Avenger*, long before Fatso Gore discovered the internet and stole the Nobel Peace Prize from two deserving scientists. [In 1983, h]e and his fat wife were trying to censor music and tell adults what we should listen to. He was busy trying to censor Dee Snider and Frank Zappa.

Paste: Tell me about growing up. Were you born into a liberal, creative family?

Kaufman: Did you say "throwing up"? People have thrown up during our movies. Sometimes I'll have a big burrito and throw up. Why are you interested in that? Vomit! Farting! Diarrhea! We pioneered that! Now you see movies like *Deadpool*, and Terrence Malick has diarrhea scenes in all his movies.

Paste: Troma has the lockdown on bodily fluids?

Kaufman: We certainly pioneered it. We definitely pioneered the fart. You can ask Trey Parker and Matt Stone about that. [They're] big fans. Their first film, *Cannibal! The Musical*, is a Troma movie. They will tell you that the first couple seasons of *South Park* are Tromaville. They had a character named Kaufman. They wanted a character named Herz, but Michael is very private. He does not like to be in public. If we were still directing together, I'd be talking to the *New York Times*, not to *Paste*.

Paste: Have you always been drawn to the rude, crude, and over-the-top?

Kaufman: No! I'm the ultimate bourgeois. I went to Trinity School in New York and Yale University. I'm extremely well educated and speak French fluently, but it's a useless language.

Paste: When did the switch happen, when you were suddenly obsessed with gore and bodily fluids?

Kaufman: There's nothing new about what we're doing. Grand Guignol has been on theater stages for two hundred years. We're just following in that particular tradition. Satire, politics, and social issues are really what we're getting at. We're trying to make a difference and appeal to young people. Old people know about *Fast Food Nation* but they don't do anything. The rich, old liberal bullshitters in the mainstream opposition read that book but didn't give a shit. The young people saw *Poultrygeist: Night of the Chicken Dead*, which was against fast food, and did something. McDonald's changed their menu, and now all they have to do is give their workers a decent wage and not torture their animals. If we focus on healthy food, it might eventually be a decent industry.

Paste: Is this a particularly scary time in terms of censorship?

Kaufman: This is a horrible era we're living in! We have a First Amendment, but we can't say anything. We have Freedom of Speech, but you can say nothing. Steve Martin is older than I am—he must be one hundred years old—but he said something about finding Carrie Fisher beautiful and then finding her very smart,[1] and he was publicly shamed for it. I tweeted the same thing about Betty White, who wasn't even dead yet. This is the era we live in. It's an age of public shaming, trigger warnings, and safe spaces. It's an age of socially conscious warriors who are constantly whining but doing nothing.

Paste: Do you consider yourself a libertarian?

Kaufman: I don't consider myself anything really. I think I'm pretty left-wing for the most part. I don't believe anybody should be making twenty million dollars a year. The quasiliberal George Soros should be allowed to make two million a year maximum. Why should Tom Hanks be making that kind of money? Why should these stupid, scum-filled celebrities, who are telling people how to live their lives, be making so much? It's obscene! The people in Yemen are dying every second of the day, thanks to our bombs and our allies. CNN sits back with their asses in a tub of butter. It's bullshit.

Paste: When I interviewed Roger Corman, he said Lloyd Kaufman makes the most insane films he's ever seen. Is that the ultimate badge of honor?

Kaufman: When I was at Yale, the reason I thought we could start our own damn movie studio was because I saw his movies. He put it in my head that you could make movies on no budget, with good acting and compelling storytelling. I also grew up on masterpieces by Howard Hawks, John Ford, Renoir, Brakhage, and all those guys. Corman was making movies that were entertaining, provocative, well acted, and socially relevant. He was doing it in a way where people would actually show up to watch. I make movies where no one shows up. I've refined his model.

Paste: Troma regulars Joe Fleishaker and Lemmy passed last year. What was your experience like working with Lemmy?

Kaufman: He was great! He had this facade of being grouchy and irritable, and occasionally he'd have temper tantrums. We had a huge fight during *Terror Firmer* and he walked off the set. He was generous, sweet, and never turned us down for anything. He never charged a dime, other than a bottle of Jack Daniels. Later, when he saw we were doing better, he moved up to Maker's Mark and two Tromettes by his side.

Paste: How do you think Hollywood views you? Do fat cats turn their nose up at you?

Kaufman: As far as I'm concerned, Hollywood doesn't even know we exist. Akiva Goldsman, an Oscar-winning writer, is remaking *The Toxic Avenger* into a two-million-dollar epic. I guess we have some kind of footprint, in that all these people, like James Gunn, Eli Roth, Oliver Stone, Samuel L. Jackson, and tons of others started with us and have gone up the food chain. If you look at *Deadpool*, that basically is a Troma movie. Those guys are big Troma fans. *South Park* is very informed by Troma, and we helped them with their first movie. I don't know how great it is, because when Matt and Trey were on *60 Minutes*, they dismissed *Cannibal! The Musical*. They said something like, "I don't think you could even call that distribution." They didn't say, "Gee, thanks Troma for discovering us and giving us a shot." It kinda pissed me off.

Paste: Can you pinpoint a scene or a Troma film that you're the most proud?

Kaufman: Maybe this can be a lesson to the social warrior bullshitters, but I'm most proud of the fact that I've been married to the same woman for forty-three years. I don't think there's anybody in the history of the movie business who has had the same partner or studio for forty-three years. That's something to be proud of.

Paste: Who do you envision turning over the Troma reins to when you retire?

Kaufman: Troma has a life of its own. It's the herpes of the movie industry. It's not going away.

Note

1. A tweet posted by Steve Martin in late 2016 at the time of the passing of his longtime, dear friend Fisher; Martin ultimately deleted the tweet after a firestorm of backlash sparked by the fact that he blasphemistically dared to mention Fisher's "beauty" before her "smarts."

I'm Lloyd Kaufman, President of Troma Entertainment and Creator of *The Toxic Avenger*!

Lloyd Kaufman / 2017

From *Reddit AMA*,[1] May 10, 2017. Reprinted with permission. (*Excerpted; all original spelling/grammar retained*)

Greetings from Tromaville!

The Troma Team and I are preparing for screenings of "Return to Return to Nuke 'Em High aka Vol. 2" at the Cannes Film Festival! May 23–25 at the Arcades 3 (77 Rue Felix Faure 06400)!

NSFW trailer: https://youtu.be/Tee33q5nZMU Family Friendly trailer: https://youtu.be/gTFqy_GCEdI

www.watch.troma.com

2017 Marks my 50th year making feature length movies! Ask me anything!

Let's discuss . . .

Mightydein:
Troma was the first American company to distribute hayao miyazaki movies. Any plans on distributing more animated movies in the future?

LloydKaufman:
Yes! If something one of a kind and brilliant, such as My Neighbor Totoro or A Very Troma Christmas, comes along we'll certainly be happy to introduce it to the American public, as we did with Miyazaki's film.

[deleted]:
In 50 years, what's changed the most for you in making films? What's stayed the same?

LloydKaufman:
What is different: The media industry has become a cartel of a small number of conglomerates which has economically blacklisted the genuinely independent artist. What has remained the same: The media industry has become a cartel of a small number of conglomerates which has economically blacklisted the genuinely independent artist.

retrovertigo23:
Best. Response. Ever.

Nox_Stripes:
Shooting the truth.

LloydKaufman:
Hi Everyone! See you in 20 min! Until then I'll be on the toilet, anyone have a good cure for a bad burrito?

[deleted]:
The real question is why are you stopping? This is Reddit, most of these posts are from people sitting on the throne.

Namagem:
It was a really bad burrito.

fundudeonacracker:
Dude—half the people on this AMA are pooping.

dejus:
I know which half I'm in.

greymalken:
Only half?

Ultravioletgray:
I've always heard ice cream helps sooth your stomach with Mexican food.

GodOfAllAtheists:
I heard a pound of sugar-free gummy bears does the trick!

delfino319:
How do you feel about James Gunn's success/Guardian's of the Galaxy?

LloydKaufman:
I love James Gunn. The minute he started working for Troma I knew he was a great talent, and after he masturbated on my desk I was forever indebted to him.

JohnnyLightning42:
I always love seeing your cameo in GotG.

MattBaster:
Are you amazed at the cult sensation that The Toxic Avenger has become?

LloydKaufman:
After Toxie's sex tape went viral, I'm not suprised!

suaveitguy:
If you were 25, with $5000 in the bank—how would you go about building the modern equivalent to Troma for the internet?

LloydKaufman:
For 5000 dollars you can make a movie. You can start your own damn company and your own damn career. Look at the guys who did "Father's Day." They are now making movies for 100 times the amount we gave them.

skilledwarman:
That was actually the first Troma movie I ever saw (Thanks Achievement Hunter and Theater Mode). I think I've shown it to all my friends at this point.

oglafa:
I wish I had people in my circle that'd appreciate Father's Day. Film is glorious.

[deleted]:
Amazing movie and legendary Theater Mode.

[deleted]:
Any chance of some Troma TV shows? We need a weekly does of depravity on the streaming box in our living room where we can hide our shame.

LloydKaufman:
Troma would love to do a "Class of Nuke 'Em High" TV series. It would be "Ash vs Evil Dead" meets "Twin Peaks" meets "Saved By the Bell"! Everyone write to Netflix and demand it! And be sure to watch "Kabukiman's Cocktail Corner" on The Troma Movies YouTube Channel! It has just been renewed for a second season! YAY!!!

JoeyHollywood:
OOH ooh can you call it SAVED BY THE HELL.

[deleted]:
This absolutely needs to happen.

suaveitguy:
You went to school with George W. Bush? Ever have quality time with him?

LloydKaufman:
George W. Bush was in my class at Yale. We took a bath once a week together. But his habit of going around campus looking for weapons of mass destruction was very annoying.

suitcase88:
Do you think Mike Pence ever munched on a dick?

LloydKaufman:
Yes, yours.

6DollarCoffee:
Like you need Lloyd to answer this one.

xulevi:
Hey Lloyd, can you be my grandpa? I'd be a dope grandson straight up.

LloydKaufman:
You can be a dope grandson but I want to be a woke grandmother.

xulevi:
Deal, Grandma!

[deleted]:
Oh I want in on this, both sets of grandparents have passed. Be my Grandma Lloyd too!

Redanditchy:
You are seriously one of the best people ever. Thanks for all the great entertainment.

davecampfield:
You can't! I'm already his grandson.

coryrenton:
if you had the funding, what would be the largest budget for a movie that you'd be comfortable with?

LloydKaufman:
There are no reasons for a movie to cost more than half a million dollars. It is obscene that people are spending 2 million dollars on a piece of fluff. This age of Kim Kardashian and conspicuous consumption will be looked upon in 50 years in disgrace.

Pakliuvom:
Hi Uncle Lloydie, this is Marcus Whitlow from Twitter. My question is, John Brennan is being gracious enough to allow my brother in law and I to make a weekly Troma comic that will go on the websites, but I'm torn between two ideas, one set in the Tromaville Hospital and one that's like The Muppet Babies, but Troma Babies instead. Which do you like better?

LloydKaufman:
Try both! Thanks for your TROMAtic art!

postfish:
Why not both? Hospital has a pediatric ward, right?

Pakliuvom:
One more question Uncle Lloydie, one of importance. I tweet many anti-Ajit Pai rants and cartoons on Twitter but it seems like the majority of people aren't as outraged by the possible destruction of net neutrality as they should be. What can be done to get others behind the cause and realize what a major, major topic this is?

LloydKaufman:
We need the fake PC phonies like Will Smith and Meryl Streep to speak out on behalf of Net Neutrality, but like the other elites, such as Hillary Clinton and the Trump gang, they'd rather close their gates, enjoy their

riches, and stay behind their YUGE wall. Read my Huffington Post article about Net Neutrality here: http://www.huffingtonpost.com/entry/innovation-and-our-better-future-depend-on-preserving_us_5848ac6fe4b08f092ddd9926

[deleted]:
Im a mega low budget director, and huge troma fan. Ive always wanted to have a movie released by troma (which is a dream of mine) Is there any advice on what steps to take to make that possible? Thanks for everything you have done.

LloydKaufman:
Make a movie that's entertaining and one of a kid then send it to The Troma Team! www.troma.com. Also, watch my Make Your Own Damn movie lessons for FREE on The Troma Movies YouTube Channel!

[deleted]:
Thanks! And send kabuki man my love.

suaveitguy:
How was New Line Cinema so sleazy?

LloydKaufman:
New Line Cinema put together an amazing team of scumbags. They also produced A Nightmare on Elm Street by Wes Craven, which is great, so fuck me.

suaveitguy:
What do you think of Roger Corman's work/legacy?

LloydKaufman:
When I was a Yale student I was inspired by Roger Corman's movies, The Man with the Xray Eyes, The Poe Trilogy, etc proved that independent movies could be excellent. Roger Corman is a great guy, an excellent talent.

RetroDave:
I was wondering this too, thanks for asking.

fanboyz:
When are you putting Terror Firmer and Surf Nazis on Blu Ray?

LloydKaufman:
We have no money for blu rays right now, but Terror Firmer and Surf Nazis are in the queue

fanboyz:
License out your catalogue, people love them some classic Grade A Troma.

Heiminator:
I love Surf Nazis, and I gotta say it has a ridiculously well done soundtrack for a low budget movie. I listen to "Blood on the Water" all the time.

good_myth:
Do you have any projects for people that don't like gross stuff?

LloydKaufman:
Good Question! Go to Troma Movies on YouTube and you'll see Toxic Crusaders, Doggie Tales, Monster in the Closet, and at least 100 other movies that are family friendly.

Blebbb:
Yeah, I know you're excited for an R remake of Toxic Avenger, but as a little kid I was always disappointed the cartoon and comic for Toxic Crusaders didn't launch in to more kid shows. Toxic Crusaders, The Tick, Bucky O'hare, etc all ended rather quickly.

SUBHUMAN_RESOURCES:
"Stuck on you" falls into this category and is hilarious!

dissenter_the_dragon:
Can I pay you to be in y'alls next flick? I want to leave my daughter a legacy of her dreadlocked daddy in a Troma film, can we make that happen or nah?

LloydKaufman:
We're writing The Tempest/Shitstorm. Watch my Twitter and Troma Social, when you see we're casting be very aggressive. We cast anyone that's very aggressive for the part. We'll give you an Arm and a Legacy.

dissenter_the_dragon:
I'll do whatever it takes to come out ahead in a neck and neck competition, except for puns. Thanks for the info though, will definitely be keeping watch!

spinachcakes:
Will we ever see another Tromeo & Juliet? How do you cast perfect Tromaville citizens and how do I become one?

LloydKaufman:
We're writing The Tempest, my favorite Shakespeare play. It'll be called Troma's Shitstorm. Be aggressive when we post that we're casting. We always cast the most aggressive people.

Eorily:
This is fantastic news. I hope it has a gender-swapping beast person too. Thanks for doing what you do.

spinachcakes:
Yes! That is amazing. Thanks you!!

liamquane:
What films do you love that you don't think people would expect?

LloydKaufman:
All the movies by John Ford, Mizoguchi, Robert Bresson, Eric Rohmer, and of course, the great cinema poets and interpretive dancers The Mitchell Brothers. Stan Brakhage in my opinion was the greatest visual artist of my lifetime.

Jimmy_Melnarik:
Uncle Lloyd loves Brakhage! Oh my heart!

HonkeyDong:
Brakhage makes a brief cameo in the Troma distributed Cannibal! The Musical.

liamquane:
Do you have any directorial advice?

LloydKaufman:
Make art that comes from your heart, brain, and soul. Otherwise it aint worth it. One of the richest directors in the world jumped off a bridge a year ago.

MightyDein:
How do Troma movies get onto television? I watched Cannibal the musical on IFC Canada.

LloydKaufman:
We had a little mouse that would go into the TV sets all over Canada and it was trained to show our movies. Unfortunately that mouse was eaten by Rupert Murdoch, so no more movies on TV from Troma.

MightyDein:
That poor mouse didn't stand a chance.

[deleted]:
Hey Lloyd! I've been getting into your work and Troma in general over the past few months. Inspiring stuff. Nobody likes cancelling projects, but I'm assuming that's especially true for you, given your work ethic of trying make as much shit as possible. That said, there are a few cancelled Troma movies that I've seen mentioned, like Schlock and Schlockability, and Lenge: Legends of Troma. What are the stories behind these two (and any others that you care to bring up)? What would you say the "point of no return" is on making a movie, where you're far enough into the process that you have to finish it even if you can tell it's a disaster? EDIT: Also, know anything about this movie[1] or where one could find it?

LloydKaufman:
I personally must finish every movie I start. But, if you watch Tales from the Crapper, which I spent 4 years on, you'll see that that's very stupid.

ace_vagrant:
Tales from the Crapper was on the Netflix dvd list of mine, many years ago. The bastards never sent it. I did get to see Sugarcookies though, so there's that. I've had "Sally Go 'Round the Roses" stuck in my head ever since.

liamquane:
Hi Mr. Kaufman! May I ask, do you have any advice on getting a film actually together and made?

LloydKaufman:
Get out of bed and do it! You don't need money anymore. Thanks to the miracle of digital technology, and armies of film nerds who are willing to work for nothing to support you, you can make your own damn movie. I've written six books about it!!

liamquane:
What do you think of Digital film-making becoming the general way of doing things?

LloydKaufman:
Thats a great question. It's yin and yang, thousands of excluded people can now enter the walls of filmmaking thanks to the miracle of digital filmmaking. It has democratized a heretofore artform that has been controlled by money. You don't need money to make a digital film. On the other hand its almost impossible to live off your art unless your digital film is produced by one of the massive media conglomerates.

[deleted]:
In the time of youtube and a hordes of directors trying to have a shot, how would the young Lloyd Kaufman would stay alive and do well if he had started making films just last year?

LloydKaufman:
Great question. First, I'd have to decide do I want the Oscar and riches. In which case it would be imperative that I blow somebody in California. If teenage Lloydie wants to be an independent filmmaker and doesn't mind living in a refrigerator carton with the bath salts crowd, then teenage Lloydie would stay in NY, take a day job and make 5000 movies.

LloydKaufman:
We have time for a few more questions, 10 more minutes! I must go back to planning for "Return to Return to Nuke 'Em High" at the Cannes Film Festival! We are taking 15 people! We will have parades and street theater! It's like a circus. Watch "All the Love You Cannes" on the Troma Movies YouTube Channel to get an idea of what Troma's experience at Cannes is like!

Kiylyou:
In planet terror, one of the actors had his face on a bunch of balls. Don't you wish this was your part?

LloydKaufman:
Over my 50 years of making movies, my face has been on more balls then you'll ever meet. Remember I have lips like a woman, and I know how to use them.

the_dork_avenger:
I've been a huge Troma fan for most of my life and have had the privilege to meet you on a few occasions. I've always has a soft spot for the older movies such as Squeeze Play, First Turn On and such, do you think you

would ever make another movie along the lines of the older comedies such as those?

LloydKaufman:
I am happy to hear you have a soft spot for soft core. Stuck on You is one of the greatest raunchy comedies of all time. I love those movies, but I have moved on, as you will see when you experience "Return to Return to Nuke 'Em High aka Vol. 2." Picasso had his blue period, I have my blue balls period. I am now into something more Cubist.

AntoniaPantoja:
What would it take for Troma to distribute a finished film? Is there a specific process or guideline to follow?

LloydKaufman:
Send to The Troma Team when it's complete via www.troma.com

boardgamejoe:
The scene in the first film, where the assholes from the gym hit the kid and knock him off his bike, and then as he is struggling to get off the road, they purposefully back over his head. Well that scene kinda messed me up for a long time. Do you feel any guilt about that?

LloydKaufman:
Same thing happened to Donald Trump and look where he is.

TorchGoblin:
Greeting Lloyd! I've been trying to get in contact with you for the last 3 years. I sent you a personal letter and your assistants have confirmed that they have given you this letter on at least two occasions but I still haven't gotten that sweet tromatic reply. Should I give up or should I continue pestering your assistants? Thanks! CRETINS RULE!

LloydKaufman:
I answer every letter, every tweet and every email I get. All you have to do is send an email to oliverstone@gmail.com

gusmoreno15:
I wrote a book where a little girl gets lost and finds her way back home. Am I the little girl?

LloydKaufman:
Yes, you are that little girl and you need help.

[deleted]:
Just want to say thanks for everything, I'm forever influenced and indebted to you. Also what does Trey Parker smell like?

LloydKaufman:
Thanks! Trey smells like success!

AntonioPantoja:
Besides Fernando Alle and Kansas Bowling, who are some of your favorite up-and-coming filmmakers? Who's the next big thing?

LloydKaufman:
Brandon Bassham is TROMAzing! He wrote and directed "Fear Town USA" and "The Slashening" available on our streaming service Troma Now www.watch.troma.com. Bassham is writing a draft of my next feature "William Shakespeare's The Tempest Presents Troma's Shitstorm"!

suaveitguy:
Any memories of working with Oliver Stone in The Battle of Love's Return?

LloydKaufman:
Oliver and I were best friends from 2nd grade through college. He was always a psycho. He got into movies because I was making movies. Obviously he was very much influenced by his time on Battle of Love's Return and Sugar Cookies

suaveitguy:
Did you know Herschell Gordon Lewis?

LloydKaufman:
Yes, I knew Herschell Gordon Lewis, I've written about him in my books. He was a lovely man. And although he always stressed marketing strategy over art, he was a real artists. In spite of his business acumen.

sectorfour:
I have so many good memories of watching Toxie, the subhumanoids, Sgt Kabukiman, etc during high school and my early college days. Back then, we relied on the neighborhood video store and their limited selection for entertainment.

Do you think the expanded choices we have today with streaming entertainment help or hurt studios like Troma?

LloydKaufman:
It can only help. The more competition and variety we have in our lives the better we will all be. By the way, subscribe to Troma Now and help support independent art, and make the world a better place. www.watch.troma.com

liamquane:
Why do you make the types of films you do? Do you think you will try a different, more mainstream style anytime soon? Not that you need to, just curious. :~P

LloydKaufman:
Great question. But, the kinds of movies Michael Herz and I make reflect what's in our minds and hearts. We're not interested in making sausages or trying to ride the wave of what's popular now. Class of Nuke Em High has become a classic because it's entertaining and has a universal message and love story that will resound through the ages.

liamquane:
What is it like running an entertainment company? How did it all come together?

LloydKaufman:
It's a wonderful life. Everyday is different. And I want to blow my fuckin' brains out 24/7.

PandaEatsRage:
I just wanted to say your work is what made up a lot of my high school years and my future humor. Thank you for all you've done That said. What's the most memorable project you've turned down?

LloydKaufman:
She's not a project, but we turned down Madonna for The First Turn On. Not just the most memorable but the most stupid. Thank you Michael Herz.

kitsune1011:
I am a current film/multimedia/video student. I'm about ready to finish my degree and would love to work for a company like yours. How can I score a sweet/raunchy/awesome job at Tromaville? Or at the very least how can I get a good word doing the thing I love (which is making things look awesome)?

LloydKaufman:
You have to live in the New York area. Right now we have an opening for a graphic designer, 400/week plus free lunch on Friday. We also have 2 positions for unpaid enterprise observers that just opened up!

stevencastle:
People can live in New York on $400/week?!?!?!

TimmyPacker:
Where will I be able to check out this Troma Now Podcast I'm hearing about?

LloydKaufman:
It'll be on Troma Movies on YouTube in a few days! Brilliant!

ShaneSullivan:
Me and my friends from high school love Troma and you inspired us to make a short for YouTube. No one in our school really gets it but maybe you'll say it has some Tromatic merit to it? https://www.youtube.com/watch?v=2qLnZJoOqWk

LloydKaufman:
Tweet it at me and I will retweet! Congratulations on making your own damn movie!

6Dollarcoffee:
Hey Lloyd I bought rabid grannies off you personally at dragon Con but haven't watched it yet. Do you get to see any granny titties in it?

LloydKaufman:
Yes. There are many granny breasts and there is an amazing scene where one of the grannies fucks Kim Kardashian. I'll never forget it as long as I live. Buy another copy!

davecampfield:
What's all this I hear about THE TROMA NOW PODCAST? :)

LloydKaufman:
Go to Troma Movies on YouTube where we have given away about 400 movies free as a thank you to our devoted fans. In the next few days we'll be putting up an amazing new podcast called The Troma Now Podcast which is pure genius.

kwzombi:
Why is Troma now the greatest streaming service ever?!

LloydKaufman:
Because we have TROMAzing world premiere movies, curated selections from the Troma library, and wonderful short content. Watch "Dolphinman Battles the Sex Lobsters" starring Sgt. Kabukiman NYPD! It will blowhole you out the back wall of the theater!

liamquane:
How did you first get your work into festivals? Did you start off small and then build?

LloydKaufman:
For the most part festivals have come to us. We don't think it's right to be paying to submit a movie to a festival, so we don't have a lot of contact with festivals. That is why we established the all FREE Tromadance Film Festival 18 years ago. Submissions are still open for this year! Deadline is June 1st! www.tromadance.com

PJ_Griff88:
Is there any personal favorite film of yours that you would ever want to do any Tromatized version of, so to speak?

LloydKaufman:
The musical Pal Joey by Rodgers and Hart. There is a very bad version with Frank Sinatra. Pal Joey is a very dark story that would make a great Tromusical!!!

6Dollarcoffee:
You're a Yale man. We're you in skull and bones or did you just bone a few skulls?

LloydKaufman:
I was invited to skull and bones but I turned them down. Boy was I stupid. I joined the Elihu Society instead cause I though it was more open.

diosmuerteborracho:
What's your favorite porn title?

LloydKaufman:
I would have to say Behind the Green Door and Forrest Gump. My favorite pornographic food is Raw Chocolate Chip Cookie Dough. If you go to my Instagram you'll see a pic I put up a few days ago.

ShaneSullivan:
Which do you prefer Gore Gazette or Fangoria?

LloydKaufman:
Toxie and I love them both.

LloydKaufman:
Thanks everyone for a great AMA! Troma has the best fans in the world! "Return to Return to Nuke 'Em High aka Vol. 2" is the greatest movie we've made in 43 years. Please contact your local cinema to book it. If there's enough advanced notice I will attend in person and create a great independent, idealistic, art event! Also, subscribe to Troma Now! www.watch.troma.com. Any questions unanswered here, please Tweet them to me @lloydkaufman and I will answer!

Notes

1. "Ask Me Anything" is a routine posting thread on the social/discussion network Reddit in which a high-profile personality welcomes questions from public users who quite literally ask said personality/poster "anything," which he or she hopefully answers truthfully. Essentially a public forum Q&A format online.
2. Hyperlinked to the Lost Media wiki page for *White Elephant: The Battle of the African Ghosts* (1984).

Troma: A Love Story

Leslie Pariseau / 2018

From *The Ringer*, October 17, 2018, https://www.theringer.com/movies/2018/10/17/17979564/troma-movie-studio-lloyd-kaufman-toxic-avenger-independent-film. Reprinted with permission.

In 2018, it's harder than ever to be independent in the world of movies. With Thanos and T. rexes and computer-animated superfamilies descending upon our multiplexes, the do-it-yourself spirit of film history is being crowded out, one IP blockbuster release at a time. But there are still some fearless, indie-minded artists fighting the fight. This week on The Ringer, *we'll look at some veterans of the field and some exciting new entrants, and try to understand where independent cinema will go from here.*

There are no fewer than forty people scurrying around the set of *#Shakespeares-Shitstorm*. More than two-thirds look as if they've wandered in from a strip club or a Coney Island freak show or a high school Halloween dance. There's a platinum-blond woman in a slinky string bikini and platform shoes, a half-naked girl in a wheelchair with a lipstick joker mouth, several other women in fishnet stockings and lingerie, a bevy of people in ill-fitting suits, a guy wearing a dashiki and wig of gray dreads, and a four-piece band dressed in old-timey black tie as if for a Roaring Twenties party.

And then there's Lloyd Kaufman. At seventy-two years old, Kaufman is the cofounder of Troma Entertainment, the world's longest continually running independent film company. A small, gray-haired man with skinny arms, he's dressed in drag—a strapless red number with a little ruffle at the bust and an auburn wig. By the end of the day, it will be drooping to expose a bustier. Dark glasses are perched on his nose, and his phone is on a string around his neck. He's wearing kitten heels and a touch of lipstick. Kaufman is watching a scene live on the monitors. Against a ship-deck background, the band plays "Nearer My God to Thee," the song that accompanied the *Titanic*'s sinking. People are drunkenly wobbling across the deck, waving to something in the distance.

"Cut! Fuck! Goddamn it! No, no, no!" yells Kaufman, waving those skinny arms. The band stops playing. Everybody slumps a little. "I'm sorry, I'm sorry, I don't mean to yell," he says quickly. "You just can't turn your back to the camera. Do it like this." In his kitten heels, he struts before the lens.

Known to his fans as "Uncle Lloyd," Kaufman is an unlikely hero, beloved by hundreds of thousands of followers who call themselves the Troma Army. When he's not in drag, he's usually dressed neatly in a blazer with a pocket square and a bowtie. And though he has a penchant for euphemisms and winking, naughty humor, his manners are impeccable. With a flexible, stretchy face that often lifts into an expression of wide-eyed surprise, mouth slightly agape, as if someone had just goosed him or pinched his nipple, Kaufman is the Mister Rogers of the punk-nerd film underground. He's been making movies for fifty years, and is best known for raising a middle finger to Hollywood while specializing in a genre so specific—a combination of comedy-satire and surrealist shock-horror—it's simply called "Troma." Back when video stores still existed, so did sections devoted solely to Troma movies.

Kaufman's latest film, *#ShakespearesShitstorm*, is a reimagining of the Bard's *The Tempest*. Of course, his interpretation takes the story to new heights—or depths, depending on your point of view. In it, Kaufman plays Prospero as well as Prospero's evil sister, Antoinette; hence the drag. *Shitstorm*—if you can imagine a literal shitstorm—opens with whale fecal blooms, a blind, masturbating Miranda, an orgy on a yacht, a stripper-Stephen-Hawking-like Ariel, and so much more. But, like all Troma films, the absurdity is couched in a scathing societal critique. *Shitstorm* takes on the pharmaceutical industry, social justice warriors, social media, and political correctness.

Like most Troma productions, the cast and crew is a mixed bag of amateur and professional, sex worker and slam poet. There's Pat Kaufman, Lloyd's wife and the former New York state film commissioner (she recently retired and is producing *Shitstorm*), all the way down to an eighteen-year-old woman who has never acted. There's Nadia White, an adult fetish model, and Adam Zaretsky, an artist who works in transgenics.[1] Nobody really gets paid on Troma films—the labor force is provided by volunteers who just really love Lloyd Kaufman and his work. Even so, everybody is happy, buzzing, excited to be in this weird nightclub in Astoria dancing around naked, covered in fake blood, being yelled at by Kaufman. "I love being supported and loved!" someone yells when everyone breaks for lunch. It's one big, happy, fucked-up family.

Kaufman has just arrived back with some of the cast and crew from Albania. Arranged by one of the producers, Justin Martell, who has a side hustle as a film production fixer in Eastern Europe, the shoot was one of the first by an American film company there. It's still cheap in Albania, and Kaufman will tell you they've got to save money. "It's not easy to make a $20 million movie for $500,000," he likes to announce every so often.

Troma sometimes gets its locations at a discount, thanks to the generosity of fans. *Shitstorm*'s set looks handmade, extras' costumes are likely self-sourced, and the props include toy money, flour-cocaine, and—eventually—gallons and gallons of oat-based fake feces, plus a few liters of Troma's signature green toxic goo. That day, the special-effects team was mixing a batch of tapioca-starch-based semen for an orgy scene.

Despite the studio's forty-four-year history of disruption and provocation, *Shitstorm* may be the company's most outrageous film yet. It may also be Kaufman's last.

Or at least that's what he's telling people. After five decades of directing thirty-some features and more than a hundred shorts, after cowriting and coproducing a hundred more, after distributing five-hundred-plus films, it's over. Final act. Curtain call. Lloyd Kaufman and Troma, out. And without Troma's perpetual stick-it-to-the-man shit stirring, without its David-to-the-Goliath-of-Hollywood crusade, the *truly* independent film industry will never quite be the same again.

But hold up—you've never heard of Lloyd Kaufman? You've never seen a Troma movie?

To be completely honest, before I began reporting this story, I hadn't either. It's because Troma is the inverse of the mainstream. The give-zero-fucks, *MAD-Magazine*-meets-dada-nonsense agitator. Troma is the proverbial rabblerousing Puck so far outside of the Hollywood system, it's unclear whether Hollywood is even aware that Troma exists. Best known for its 1984 cult classic *The Toxic Avenger*, Troma champions the misfits and weirdoes and outsiders and freaks and everything fringe. If you're a Troma fan, if you're one of those misfits or weirdoes, you already know.

For everyone else, welcome to Tromaville.

Be forewarned: Troma movies are graphic, violent, and full of gross-out humor. Heads crushed by cars, hands reaching out of graves into buttholes, bodies falling into meat grinders, bellies splitting open with popcorn and rodents, up-close nipple piercings, radiation-induced seizures, sex on fast-food restaurant floors, and earthworm-eating kabuki masters. There are brains spilling out of skulls, jingoistic babies, and teeth-torn umbilical cords. But they're also strangely feel-good. They have a message and a vision. They're not scary, but they are an outrageous, phantasmagorical, primordial soup populated with gallons of Karo-laced blood, dozens of dismemberments, more T&A than an issue of *Hustler*, and some of the sweetest antihero monsters ever to grace celluloid.

The point is that Troma movies are specific, and they possess a meaningful legacy. Kaufman argues that Troma has advanced the art of American film. That it's introduced the world to a whole new way of seeing genre, and to a generation of once-unknown actors and moviemakers, including James Gunn, Trey Parker, Matt Stone, Eli Roth, Marisa Tomei, Samuel L. Jackson, Billy Bob Thornton, J. J. Abrams, and Oliver Stone.

The story of Troma is the story of the little guy against the machine. It's also the story of Michael Herz, Kaufman's unsung cofounder, and Pat Kaufman, the love of Lloyd's life. And ultimately, the story of Troma is the story of Lloyd; the two are indivisible.

A fifth-generation New Yorker, Kaufman grew up on the city's Upper East Side. "It was about as bourgeois as you can get," he says. His mother was obsessed with the theater and occasionally worked on or invested in productions. He recalls being awoken in the middle of the night by parties with "lots of theatrical laughing." Elaine Stritch and Bobby Short hung around. Montgomery Clift once knocked on their door. Kaufman saw all the Broadway flops, all the hits, and has an encyclopedic memory for who starred in what, as well as the scores to each. Many of his film's soundtracks are inspired by operas or riff on classical scores.

His paternal grandfather worked for a stint in vaudeville, and Kaufman's father was a lawyer who pioneered derivative shareholder law (the proto class-action lawsuit). Charles, his younger brother, says their father had a fantastic sense of humor, and was always trying to make them laugh. Lloyd is the eldest of three. Charles directed films, including the cult classic *Mother's Day* (1980), and now has a successful baking business in San Diego. Susan, the youngest, is a set designer for television and films, and is currently working on *The Marvelous Mrs. Maisel*. Kaufman's three daughters all work in film as well. They describe being influenced or inspired by Kaufman's own fearless, unexpected dive into the film industry.

"My parents taught me that you could have a beautiful life without a lot of money," says Kaufman. "They were pretty free range. Very decent people, but wild socially. Much wilder than I am." His grandmother, a socialist widow who initiated correspondence with the leftist intelligentsia, introduced him to the work of I. F. Stone, the radical leftist journalist, and C. Wright Mills, author of *The Power Elite*, an analysis of the average American citizen as helpless against the manipulation of dominant power structures.

Kaufman was deeply affected by these philosophies, and remains indebted to their messages. "Tromaville is abused by the bureaucratic elite, the labor elite, and the corporate elite," says Kaufman. Whenever Troma makes a movie, it's always in reaction to the dominant powers.

Kaufman thought he might be a social worker or a teacher, but when he arrived at Yale, his confidence was shaken. He realized he knew nothing about the world outside the United States, so he took a year off and moved to Chad to teach English. "There was no electricity, no telephones. I got every disease you can imagine. It was the opposite of living in Manhattan and watching *My Fair Lady*."

When he returned to Yale, he majored in Chinese studies in hopes of broadening his worldview. ("China was one of the biggest disappointments of my life," he says. He's been asked to speak at the Chinese American Film Festival where he has castigated the Chinese government for its censorship practices and atrocities against humanity.) Kaufman roomed with a film nerd who ran the university's film society. He began reading *Cahiers du Cinéma*, learning about auteur theory, and watching films by Samuel Fuller, Tay Garnett, John Ford, Orson Welles, and Kenji Mizoguchi. By then, he'd caught the bug. Around the same time, he met Michael Herz, another film buff and his future partner in Troma. In the summer before his final year, while studying at Stanford, Kaufman directed his first feature, *The Girl Who Returned*.

The story of Troma as we know it begins in 1974, when Kaufman and Herz formalized Troma Entertainment. It's a word that actually means nothing, but evokes "trauma." ("Tromatized" is an adjective that gets thrown around when referencing the experience of watching a Troma movie.) Their first works were "sexy comedies" and included *Waitress!* and *Squeeze Play!*, the latter of which was inspired by the Equal Rights Amendment and women's lib. It preceded *Porky's*, perhaps even inspired it. "The [*Porky's*] director Bob Clark, great guy, visited us and interviewed us, trying to figure out what we did," says Kaufman. "The only thing that wasn't fair about it was he used great actors and had a big budget and a great script."

When the college-humor-meets-erotica category got crowded, Kaufman and Herz began to cast around for the next thing. Herz saw a headline in *Variety* declaring horror dead. So they decided to make horror. But preferring to make people laugh rather than scare them, they combined the genres to form what some today call "schlock horror." More accurately, they could be described as low-budget, surrealist horror-comedy with lots of nudity thrown in.

This is where *The Toxic Avenger* was born. And the green goo. And the blood and guts. And the breasts and the butts and the head crushings. This is what Troma fans think of when they think of Troma.

The Toxic Avenger centers on Melvin, a nerdy janitor at a health club in Tromaville, New Jersey. Gyms were just becoming a popular aspect of American life, and its working title was *Health Club Horror*. One day, while being bullied by the gym's violent meathead/bimbo members, Melvin is exposed to toxic waste and transforms into a massive, mop-carrying, tutu-wearing beast with superhuman strength. Offended by the evil that Toxie sees in the world, he seeks to destroy its perpetrators. In the process, he rescues a blind woman, who falls in love with him. In the end, Tromaville is saved and Toxie becomes its heralded hero.

When *The Toxic Avenger* debuted in 1984, it got some good reviews, but wasn't paid much attention by the mainstream. And as tale of the cult classic goes, fans rallied and traction followed. It spawned three sequels; a television cartoon series, *Toxic Crusaders*; and a musical that had a successful off-Broadway run in 2009 and toured internationally. Conversation about a remake has been circulating for years, but has yet to come to fruition.

The Toxic Avenger provided the classic structure and message of many Troma movies to come. The bad guys are always avenged. The monsters or outcasts ascend to heroes. It's a tale of the underdog heralded, and the monster living happily ever after. "I always felt terrible about Frankenstein's monster. Poor monster," says Kaufman.

Most of Troma's films are set in Tromaville, New Jersey, an American village tormented by violence and crime perpetrated by greedy overlords. "The people of Tromaville are innocent and have their spiritual and economic capital sucked out and controlled," says Kaufman. Generations of fans have been introduced to Tromaville through *The Toxic Avenger*, and for many of those fans, the movies have had a profound effect on their lives.

"There is nothing else like a Troma film," says Gabriel Friedman, a former longtime Troma employee. "They look like nothing else." Friedman cowrote *Poultrygeist: Night of the Chicken Dead* and the first outline of *Shitstorm*, among other works.

"I grew up in Kentucky, and in the early eighties," says Trent Haaga, another former employee and actor. "It was a cultural wasteland. I was always a weirdo and a freak, interested in punk and skateboarding when these were not things that you did." When he saw his first Troma film, it was like someone crawled into his preadolescent brain and made the movies of his dreams. Haaga, a former IT guy at CompuServe, took a major pay cut to work for Troma in the nineties. When he went broke, he went back to his IT job for six months, saved up money, and quit again to work for Troma. He went on to write *Citizen Toxie* and his own recent feature, *68 Kill*.

Many Troma employees grew up dreaming of working on a Troma movie. On the set of *Shitstorm*, I met no fewer than a dozen people who had left jobs or come to New York on their own dime to work on the production. One guy was from London. Another from California. And another from Missouri. And they were all working for free.

When Kaufman shows up to conventions like Comic-Con, hundreds of fans line up to talk to him. "People come up to me and tell me very personal things," says Kaufman. "Many times I've had kids stand up and say they were being bullied at school or that they were going to commit suicide, but they saw *Troma's War* or something else, and they decided not to." (Kaufman gave one of these fans a part in *Citizen Toxie*. For the most part, Kaufman shoots his films linearly, beginning to end—extremely uncommon in mainstream productions—so that he can write in guest actors who show up in the middle of filming; one day on *Shitstorm's* set, a couple of dads from his daughters' high school showed up because they wanted to appear in a Troma film.)

In so many ways, *The Toxic Avenger* saved Troma, too. Toxie is the outfit's mascot. He goes to every convention and every engagement. Wherever Lloyd goes, so goes Toxie. Lily Hayes, Kaufman's eldest daughter, recalls family vacations in Tunisia and Cameroon, where her father would pull out the Toxie mask on the side of a highway or in front of a banana plantation so he could take a picture or a mini movie with him. Where Frankenstein was misunderstood, feared, and ultimately cast out, Toxie is beloved by the masses—and by the mad scientist who brought him to life.

"Here's this character who loves his mother, is loyal to his wife," says Pat Kaufman. "He cares about the underdog and supports the little people. He's enraged by evil and must stop evil wherever it is. Who do you think that character is? It's Lloyd! Lloyd was the ninety-pound weakling. Lloyd is like the superhero fighting for the rights of little people," she says proudly. "I have always contended that Toxie is Lloyd."

The Troma studios are housed on a desolate street in a modest brick building in Long Island City. The roll-up door is covered with a mural that says "Welcome to Tromaville" above a jolly spray-painted Toxie with his mop. Where many East Coast film companies are often shiny boutiques in loftlike spaces, Troma is a homespun living room. The ground floor contains a garage full of props, a room of merchandise and DVDs (Troma still direct-mails all its own orders), and a library stocked wall-to-wall with masters.

Upstairs, Kaufman's and Herz's desks face each other in a brightly lit office. Where Herz's area is Spartan and neat, Kaufman's looks like a Coney Island funhouse garage sale. There's a toxic-waste prop barrel, miniature Toxie busts, a giant foam Toxie head, Tromaville bumper stickers and posters, a broken-down mannequin in a tropical shirt, and dozens of pieces of fan art. There are piles and piles of papers and Post-it notes and scripts and books and fan mail. There's a coded John Nash–like aura about the mess.

Herz, seventy this month, a golf-tanned, fit man, has both feet kicked up on his desk. Kaufman is dressed in a hoodie and running shoes. They both insist I take a tour, and send me out the door with an editor, who proceeds to explain in almost parodic detail each nook and cranny of the Troma office, down to the shower stall tiles used in *Return to Nuke 'Em High* Volumes 1 and 2. It's difficult to tell whether he's a superfan or he's just fucking with me. Maybe it's both. The Troma universe is like that. Everyone is a superfan, and everyone treats life like one big piece of subversive performance art.

Herz has preferred to stay out of the spotlight, and focuses on the business aspect of the studio. Even though he proclaims to be shy, he's charismatic and self-possessed, turning a brilliant sound bite when pressed: "I always felt a company should be represented by one iconic individual. There's Bill Gates, Steve Jobs, Warren Buffett, Louis B. Mayer, and Lloyd Kaufman. There should be one visionary. [Lloyd] is like the Grandma Moses of cinema. Lloyd is the icon."

On another visit, Herz proclaims a fervent love for President Donald Trump—which feels like he's trolling everyone, though he never breaks character—while Kaufman makes Rodgers and Hammerstein references and decries a Sloan Kettering doctor who accepted money from drug companies. Every so often, Herz lets out a couple of belches, and whenever I address him, he declares he wants no part of the interview. The Troma universe is so bizarre, so outside of normal reality with its monster heads and superfan tour guides and political dichotomies, I can't tell what's a joke and what isn't. For years Kaufman cast a five-hundred-pound actor named Joe Fleishaker as the character Michael Herz to needle him. It's one of Troma's key inside jokes.

Troma movies are full of them, self-referential in the way that *South Park* or *Family Guy* or *The Simpsons* is, but amped up with the feeling that each succeeding gag—and film—is trying to outdo itself. Throughout the years, the films have become more meta, more postmodern, more fragmented in a way that is a bit dizzying to dissect unless you've started at the beginning.

After *The Toxic Avenger* came *Class of Nuke 'Em High*, about a Tromaville high school next to a nuclear power plant. Then came *Troma's War*. Then came *Toxic Avenger* and *Class of Nuke 'Em High* sequels. They were mostly ignored or poorly reviewed. *Sgt. Kabukiman N.Y.P.D.* got two thumbs down from Siskel and Ebert, but the *New York Times* kind of liked it. Around the same time, Troma became more distanced from the studios. When video stores started to fail, the company began to market and distribute their own VHS tapes.

Over the years, Troma continued to acquire libraries and distribute films for up-and-coming talents, many in the horror genre, all of them wildly fringe, with budgets that ranged from $10,000 to just under $1 million. Then in 1996, they had a breakout. *Tromeo & Juliet* was a modern reimagining of Shakespeare's classic love story written by *Guardians of the Galaxy* director James Gunn, who was just starting to work in film. Truly a product of the nineties, it features Lemmy from Motörhead as the narrator, music by Superchunk and Sublime, and a surfeit of piercings, flannel, and tattoos. Critics liked it. The *Times* called it "goofily exhilarating" with "poetry to match its sex and gore." Anne Morra, the assistant curator of film at MoMA, who included it in her "Breaking Bard" series, says it has "dreamscapes which remind me of surrealism. This is *Romeo and Juliet* as if Salvador Dalí had a hand in it." *Tromeo & Juliet* went to Cannes, James Gunn went to Hollywood, and love conquered all.

In 1999, Troma followed up with *Terror Firmer*, a postmodernist metastory about a narcissistic blind director (played by Kaufman) making a horror film whose set is plagued by a serial killer. The *Times* called it "artless," but also "a piñata of in-jokes," which, depending on who you are, renders the film brilliant or pointless. Then came *Citizen Toxie* and *Poultrygeist: Night the Living Chicken Dead*. At the time of the latter's writing, Kaufman was horrified about a McDonald's that had opened next to the then-Troma building on Ninth Avenue in Hell's Kitchen. He'd also read *Fast Food Nation* and, in solidarity with his daughter Charlotte, became a vegetarian. (He remains a vegetarian today, though he professes to hate vegetables.) *Poultrygeist* was shot in an abandoned McDonald's in Buffalo, and is about a burial ground where the souls of dead chickens unite with the spirits of Native Americans to seize revenge upon the restaurant built atop it.

During release, in true Troma fashion, the company picketed the Tribeca Film Festival, which forced one of its venues to take down *Poultrygeist* posters and stop playing its trailers. The film went on to play in international festivals. The *Los Angeles Times* called it "a heaping helping of political incorrectness gleefully spiced to offend just about every sentient being," and the [*New York*] *Times* declared it "as perfect as a film predicated on the joys of projectile vomiting and explosive diarrhea can be." So, all in all, for Troma, it did pretty well.

The last few years in Tromaville have been focused on *Return to Nuke 'Em High* Volumes 1 and 2, which were filmed in an abandoned funeral parlor in Niagara Falls. Volume 1 was released to fair reviews—MoMA included it in its prestigious "Contenders" series alongside *Blue Jasmine* and *Blue Is the Warmest Color*—while Volume 2 has yet to be fully released. (It has shown in Los Angeles, and will show sometime in the next year in Oregon and Texas.)

In the meantime, Kaufman has been making and starring[2] in *Shitstorm*, which he seems to be enjoying immensely. Whenever I dropped by the set, he was either calmly directing—an anomaly[3] for most Troma productions, as veteran crew members and several behind-the-scenes documentaries will attest—sitting through makeup, or acting comfortably, characteristically as Uncle Lloydie, eyes wide, mouth thrown open, his neck working in a sort of bobblehead circuitry.

According to IMDb, he has three hundred and forty-three acting credits, which include a drunk in *Rocky*, a drunk in *Rocky V*, and a doctor in Parker and Stone's *Orgazmo*. Many of these roles have been cameos in which people ask him to play the Uncle Lloyd they know and love. (He has played Rabbi Lloyd, Llord Lloyd, Lloyd the Coffee Cart Guy, President Kaufman, Floyd Faukman, and

Father Lloyd, among others.) In his own movies, he's often playing the same part over and over again—a version of Lloyd, the director who just wants to make art.

Kaufman and Pat live in a brownstone on a sleepy street on the Upper East Side. Out front, dead center, above the door, is a mottled bust of Toxie, looking innocently gruesome, one eye melting down a cheek. "Many women have a strange sexual reaction to Toxie," says Kaufman in his memoir and movie-making guide *All I Need to Know about Filmmaking I Learned from the Toxic Avenger* (the book, which documents Troma's work up to 1998, was cowritten by James Gunn). "Perhaps it's because it was a woman who originally molded his face." It's tough to say Toxie is sexy, but even from this gargoyle perch he's more adorable than sinister.

Inside, Kaufman is making a cheese plate. His daughter Charlotte, thirty, is setting up her camera to film our conversation. She's been making a documentary about Troma and her dad for several years. Charlotte is a director of photography for documentaries, including *Divide and Conquer*, a forthcoming doc on Roger Ailes,[4] and has appeared in Troma movies since 1989, when she played a blind baby in *The Toxic Avenger Part II*. The Kaufman house is filled with Japanese and Chinese art, china cabinets full of curios from travels abroad, and fan art that Lloyd just can't bear to part with.

Pat, a tiny, slim woman with blond hair in a scrunchie and purple tortoiseshell glasses, sits down with us, too. After forty-four years of marriage, it's clear they are devoted to each other. Without exception they sit next to each other at dinner, and she travels with him to all of his appearances. "Pattie Pie," as Kaufman calls her, is a force. While film commissioner, she was appointed by Republicans and Democrats alike (unheard of in this position) and created the incentive for New York–based film crews, which allowed productions to receive 30 percent of costs back. To avoid any conflict of interest, Troma never once took advantage of the incentive even though, arguably, the company needed it more than anyone else in the film world.

When I ask Pat whether she's ever objected to anything in Troma movies, she tells me she reads every script before anything else happens. She makes notes about what she would tone down or cut out. In *Shitstorm*, she attempted to contain what she could. "I always tell Lloyd that he's like Dumbo, and the blood and the guts and the boobs are his feather. He thinks he needs them to be successful." Pat thinks that he could make a movie without them, that he could make something cleaner with a more straightforward message—all he has to do is spread his elephant ears and fly.

But Kaufman says he likes all that stuff. He shrugs and chalks it up to fun. Charlotte says she's worried that people will construe things the wrong way when *Shitstorm* comes out, that they may conflate Kaufman's views with that of Breitbart or the alt-right, because he comments derisively on the current climate of ultrasensitivity. He's always hated political correctness, he says. For a moment, she was also worried when Gunn was fired from Disney. Because of Gunn's association with Troma, right-wing trolls stalked Charlotte's social media. Kaufman put out a statement in support of Gunn, separate from the Hollywood mainstream.

Kaufman, obviously, has a complicated relationship with the mainstream. He never misses a chance to criticize its elitism, money-grubbing, or narrow-minded perception of what a movie should be. He denounces its constant censorship and rejection of art. All of his books are about democratizing filmmaking, sharing secrets with the masses about lens tricks, special effects, marketing, and selling "your own damn movies" as the series is called. A large part of his oeuvre is available for free on Troma NOW, the company's streaming service, and YouTube.

But there's also a feeling that he would like to be seen by the mainstream, to be recognized for his advancement of the boundaries of film. And some people do cite their influence. Quentin Tarantino's current editor, Fred Raskin, once interned at Troma, and Tarantino himself has cited his admiration of Troma. Trey Parker and Matt Stone owe their breakout to Troma. No matter how fringe Troma is, it's undeniably prolific, and has shaped a generation of film nerds who have endured the boot camp of its production. A parallel between Kaufman and Roger Corman, the prolific director and producer who gave breaks to Coppola, Scorsese, Jonathan Demme, and more, could be made. "We've been compared to Corman," says Kaufman, who has known the B-movie director for years, "but he's infinitely more mainstream and infinitely more profitable."

Back in the early days of Troma, Kaufman used to take his films to Cannes, and other film festivals, but pulled back when they became corporatized. "When they made *Cannibal! The Musical*, Trey Parker and Matt Stone were obsessed with getting into Sundance. But they didn't even get a fuck-you letter," says Kaufman of the duo's first film, which Troma distributed. "They decided that they didn't not get invited, so they rented a place and screened the movie." Parker and Stone basically crashed Sundance with *Cannibal!* And today we have *South Park* and *The Book of Mormon*.

A few years later, Kaufman held the inaugural TromaDance festival concurrent to Sundance in Park City. There were no entry fees, no ticket fees, and no VIP sections. "I recall Mickey Rourke waiting in line to get in," says Kaufman. "I recall quite a few celebrities coming to TromaDance." One year a couple of employees were arrested for handing out flyers, and the next year they handed out flyers with the First Amendment printed on them. Another year, the cops took away Toxie's mop, deeming it "a weapon." Which, technically in the movie, it was. But if there was ever a symbol of the underdog being battered down by the man, this was it. TromaDance ran for ten years in Park City, then Asbury Park for several years, and is now based in New York City.

To Kaufman, Sundance is not representative of truly independent films, but of mainstream Hollywood. "They're flying business class or first class and eating at fancy restaurants because that's all they talk about. They don't talk about movies very much." Kaufman argues that these are films with huge budgets, films where boundaries aren't pushed. Just like Hollywood, it's exclusive. "For years before anyone else, we had Black people and women working for us. Trans people, too." Is that a good thing? "Not really, because they weren't getting paid working for us, and couldn't get jobs in Hollywood."

The issue, the real reason Troma stands in such stark opposition to the mainstream, will always be its outrageous content. At some point, they stopped paying MPAA to rate its films, which Kaufman calls "disembowelment," meaning they were forced to remove violent or sexual content, which he believes is less offensive than the mainstream because it's cartoonish rather than hyperrealistic. "There is no more theatrical distribution for us. When *Waitress!* came out, it was shown in ninety-two theaters in the New York metro area," says Kaufman. Now, if he wants a screening in New York, he'll have to pay a theater. "The IFC told us to stop contacting them," he says. Over the years, each film has become more absurd, more convoluted, and more limit-pushing than the next.

Anne Morra, the MoMA curator, sees past the shocking surface matter. "The films are deceptively complicated in terms of their narrative," she says. "On the surface you think you're watching a monster movie or a high school movie, but what he's really getting at is a much deeper story." Furthermore, she sees it as important that people know how intelligent Kaufman is, that they understand what an intense vision he has.

Troma's tagline is "Movies of the Future." The company has always been ahead of the curve, even if it is a bloodstained, toxic-goo-drenched, titty-shaking curve.

"Today's *New York Times* was slobbering all over themselves to praise *MAD Magazine*, a division of Warner Bros." says Kaufman, referring to an article in which the paper considers a recent comic strip satirizing school shootings. "I have a satire in my 2000 movie *Citizen Toxie* making fun of those shitty kids at Columbine in the long coats. We called them the Diaper Mafia. No pat on the back for that in 2000." He is a fan of *MAD Magazine*, but he laments the sentiment that it requires having an umbilical cord to the mainstream to get recognized. Kaufman just wants you to know that he's been pushing boundaries and satirizing the evil he sees in the world for way longer than those sellouts up in their cushy Hollywood studios have been—all for the sake of making art.

"He is so serious about his work, that it was never even a question that it was art," says Lisbeth, Kaufman and Pat's middle daughter, who founded KitSplit, a film-gear-sharing service. "He's so fanatical about his vision of the world and that he's trying to change the world, to help people tell stories. Surprise people with a voice that's different."

Shitstorm producer Justin Martell grew up dreaming of working with Kaufman because of what he identified as vision. "He's an auteur. He creates chaos, but believes that from the chaos art emerges. He always follows his artistic intuition and never compromises."

If this is true, what does it mean to make a Troma movie in the era of #MeToo and Trump and social media and the death of traditional media forms? What does it mean to film a satire that blasts social justice warriors, the liberal elite, the slimy corporate aristocracy, and fascist right-wingers in the same breath?

"Troma films are a maximalist vision wagered in response to a society that operates in maximalist terms," says Dylan Mars Greenberg, who started working with Troma when she was in high school and now, at twenty-one, directs her own features.

In these terms, it's as if Kaufman and his troops have co-opted the language with which the world speaks—a brash, ugly, abrasive language—and reimagined it with latex monsters, toxic goo, whale shit, and penis monsters, and volleyed it back with a serious message. Sometimes that message is about the environment (*The Toxic Avenger*), sometimes it's about loving who you want to love (*Tromeo & Juliet*), sometimes it's about boycotting industrial agriculture (*Poultrygeist*). But there is *always* a message.

The oddity of Troma is that all this weirdness, all this fantastical stretching of reality comes from bourgeois, Ivy League–educated, bowtie-wearing Kaufman. Lloyd Kaufman who is munching on candy corn in his classic brownstone. Lloyd Kaufman who is doddering around refilling a dish full of tortilla chips. Lloyd Kaufman who wants me to see the crazy, ten-foot weed in his neighbor's backyard because he knows it's evidence of climate change. Lloyd Kaufman whose daughters attended debutante balls and worked as bankers and went to business school and weren't allowed to watch R-rated movies until they were fifteen. All this came from Kaufman, a straight white Jewish man who says he doesn't give a fuck what you think.

And whatever you think about his movies, whatever you perceive them to mean, you cannot argue that Kaufman is, if nothing else, uncompromising in his vision. "I've been preaching 'to thine own self be true' for a long time. I think I was brainwashed by the Godards and the Chabrols," he says, referencing the French auteurs. And despite his single-minded drive to create the movies that he wants to create, he is softened by his appreciation for the people who have "eaten cheese sandwiches, slept on floors, and defecated in paper bags" for him—all the hands and hearts it takes to make movies when there is no money in the till. Ask anyone—he remembers everybody's name, writes thank-you notes after every film, and will champion anyone who says they are making art for art's sake. So, what does it mean that *#ShakespearesShitstorm* is Troma's final work, and Kaufman's exit from the world of truly independent film?

Wait, who told you that? That's just a rumor. Lloyd Kaufman still has stories to tell, money to raise, meetings to take, hands to shake, babies to kiss, monsters to make. "I don't think he's going anywhere," half a dozen confidantes tell me when I ask what will happen to Troma without Kaufman. Even Herz tells me he's confident Kaufman will direct another feature.[5] They don't think he'd give up the dream or the art as long as he's alive. Kaufman isn't sure he'll make another movie, "unless he wins the lottery," but Troma certainly isn't going anywhere. At least not until he and Herz make a sound like a frog.

Like a demented, upside-down Marvel Cinematic Universe, Troma will hold on by the skin of its teeth, championing its horrifying heroes, its social pariahs, loser rejects, and hopelessly pathetic, pure-hearted nerds. As long as Lloyd Kaufman is around, the good guys will always be avenged, and the little people of Tromaville will always live happily ever after.

Notes

1. Appropriately enough, basically the science of mutations.
2. "Starring" is slightly generous; Kaufman is more of (one of many) a featured player.
3. The "calmly" part, *not* the "directing" part.
4. Featuring Troma regular Babette Bombshell as Ailes during stylized dramatization segments.
5. At the time of this book's production, Kaufman is engaged in directing his (loose and "Tromatic," as always) adaptation of Fyodor Dostoevsky's *Crime and Punishment* (1866), currently titled *The Power of Positive Murder!* and written by award-winning playwright Martin Murray, whose previous film work includes codirecting *Sleepaway Slasher* (2020).

Lloyd Kaufman's Top Five Troma Films of All Time

Chris Gore / 2020

From *Film Threat*, October 29, 2020, https://www.youtube.com/watch?v=F-nIPVxNxzE. Transcribed from video/audio with permission.

[*Lloyd Kaufman playing the clarinet*]
Chris Gore: Let's talk to Lloyd Kaufman about Troma Entertainment. Let's talk to Lloyd.
[*More Kaufman playing the clarinet*]
CG: Welcome. Welcome, Lloyd Kaufman
[*Kaufman continues playing the clarinet*]
Lloyd Kaufman: Hi, Chris.
CG: Hey, how you doing? Lloyd Kaufman, also known to people who know him affectionately as "Uncle Lloyd" from Troma Entertainment, the creator of so many amazing independent film franchises, I would say. *The Toxic Avenger* being probably one of the most famous. *Sgt. Kabukiman* and so many others. And Lloyd, I reached out to you for two reasons. One, I want to have you on the show. Look: there's Toxie right there.
LK: Oh, he's here. He loves you, Chris. He loves *Film Threat*.
CG: Is that one of the original masks?
LK: No, it's a publicity mask.
CG: Ah, there you go.
LK: There are pieces, they're appliances.
CG: But I've seen . . . I think I've seen that one at like events like San Diego Comic-Con and other things.
LK: Yeah, we have. . . . This is kind of our. . . . It was made by a fan actually in Texas. Matt in Austin.
CG: Wow, *anybody* can be Toxie in that mask. But—

LK: That's the beautiful thing, yeah. You create your own damn movie stars, right, Chris?

CG: Well, I love your book *Make Your Own Damn Movie!* It's a brilliant book. I recommend it to a lot of filmmakers getting started. It's incredibly inspirational. It has really real world practical advice. So, *Make Your Own Damn Movie!* In addition to enjoying all the Troma entertainment, get that book!

I wanted to bring you on because one, it's the Halloween season, which is my favorite time of year. I mean, this is to me the best holiday, right? And it's a time I think we're reminded to watch a lot of great horror films. And I want to talk about some of the great horror films from Troma. But there was something that happened recently. We did a story on *Film Threat* about the Troma channel getting banned from YouTube. What happened? I want to hear in your words what happened.

LK: Well, we woke up one morning. One of. . . . Lily Hayes Salzberg, our eldest daughter, noticed that the six or seven hundred thousand subscribers. . . . Our free Troma movie channel on YouTube was gone. It disappeared. And we got a notice that the community standards. . . . So, and then. . . . Luckily you, being a path-finding member of the Fourth Estate, immediately wrote up something about it, and then our fans created a hashtag: #FreeTromasFreeChannel. And first YouTube immediately. . . . We tried to appeal and we got a robot thing back immediately saying, "No, get lost." And then two days later, I assume because of you and the fans, suddenly our channel was restored.

So, I've made a documentary, Chris, called "Independent Artists vs. Corrupt Cartels,"[1] where I lay out how YouTube and Prime, Amazon, are screwing with the independent artists because we take eyeballs away from them. They don't demonetize CNN with the body parts from wars. They don't demonetize Netflix's clips from the pedophilia movie *Cuties*. And you see plenty of bestiality and people getting their heads chopped off, and there's all sorts of stuff on YouTube. But for some reason, forty-seven-year-old Troma—after our channel's been up for as long as YouTube's been around—somehow our movies suddenly become against community standards.

Movies, which the Museum of Modern Art have premiered. Movies where the American Film Institute and the Cinémathèque Française and the Russian St. Petersburg Film Academy . . . I mean I can go on and on and on talking about communities, not to mention the six hundred thousand subscribers to our free channel on YouTube. So, what community they're talking about—except the oligopoly, the cartel, the near monopoly of the big guys—don't want the public looking at any kind of entertainment other than what they determine?

CG: Well—

LK: Something like *Iron Man Part 53*, which is [*cuts out briefly*] with it.

CG: I'm sure that's coming, *Iron Man*—

LK: —democracy. *Not* democracy.

CG: Right, well, it's, I've seen just as, you know . . . I haven't been in the business as long as you have, but I have noticed that the amount of money that independents are able to generate has. . . . It's just decreased and decreased and decreased. I mean, I remember we had a company called Film Threat Video in the nineties, and I remember the size of the checks that we were sending to filmmakers from all over the world. It was amazing. And now, like, it's, you know, if you've got an indie film on Amazon, it's pennies. You know, it's—

LK: —like nothing. Yeah, using us to subsidize their billions of dollars of new, what they call "content." We prefer to call it *art*. My little documentary, it's only ten minutes, "Independent Artists vs. Corrupt Cartels." And I lay it out. We've got a movie, a typical movie on the Troma channel, it did a million views, you know, or a little bit over, and we got about a thousand bucks. The next year, we did better with that same movie. I think it's called *Vegas . . . Vegas* something-or-other.[2] I can't remember. We didn't make it. It's one we bought. And the next year, we got a dollar eight from. . . . So, one year it went from a thousand, even though we had more viewers the next year, and went back down to a. . . . Went down to a dollar and eight. And then there's all sorts of other horseshit. So, thank you for paying attention and putting out that article, because that got our fans active and the fans saved us as they always do.

CG: Yeah, YouTube's a tricky game. I mean, frankly, I haven't figured it out. We're not allowed to monetize our channel. Our *Film Threat* channel's not monetized here, which is why if you're watching this on YouTube, you'll see we've got like little things running on the bottom that helps support us. So, you know, in fact, you can—

LK: —they now push you into, like, branding. I think Twitter does the same. Even if it's not branding, they stick you. . . . You know, I say, "Toxie says, 'Vote!'" Oh, that's branding. That goes all over the world. We're gonna. . . . You know, goddamn it. So [*cuts out briefly*] cruel world. Cruel world. Well, luckily, *Film Threat* is here to lead us and to help independent thought and commerce.

CG: Well, and luckily, Troma is here to entertain us. You've got a new film that I have to admit I haven't seen. But just . . . it's one of those things where it's like: *Troma movies*! When you see the poster, you're like, "That's it, I'm sold!" It's . . . is it *Shakespeare's Shitstorm*?

LK: Well, actually it's *#ShakespearesShitstorm*.

CG: Hashtag, all right, okay.

LK: The hashtag is a very important part of the title.

CG: Can you tell us about that movie?

LK: Well, *#ShakespearesShitstorm* is inspired or based on Shakespeare's *The Tempest*, which is my favorite Shakespearean play, and I'd be happy . . . I would have done it back when we did *Tromeo & Juliet*, but I wanted to wait until I was old and could feel Prospero's angst and his loss of power and his continuation with magic; movies being magical, that kind of stuff. So, I think it's my best film, certainly my most personal and very reflective. Rather, a little bit melancholy, but full of sex and violence and all the things that Troma and I and our fans enjoy. I'd be happy to send you a private link. We've got a few festivals playing it, and if Covid ever goes away, we'll put it in Laemmle Cinemas and the New York one. Maybe we'll get a couple of hundred theaters. Not all at once, but one by one by one and blah, blah, blah.

CG: Well, it's interesting now with movie theaters being kind of off the table for, I think, at least the next eighteen months. I feel like movie theaters—because mass vaccinations are not gonna be in play until 2021—I don't think movie theaters are coming back. But what's, I mean . . . indie film is always used to struggling, right? Like the deck is stacked against indie film anyway. I think this is gonna dramatically change the Hollywood model. I think Hollywood is going . . . will be making smaller films. I think it's actually gonna be a boon to independents, because independents are now going to provide an alternative, right?

Like, you're not going to have movies making a billion at the box office probably for the next five years. I just think that that's just not going to happen, because movie theaters are not going to be around. So, in a way, this is an opportunity for independents to step up, because that model's always been there, right? Like, that's sort of, like, "Hey, we're in movie theaters just to kind of advertise, but it's mostly revenue from VOD[3] and streaming." And I have to. . . . But, you have, you can get your movies at Troma.com, right? You can just go to the Troma—

LK: No, we have a streaming service, Troma NOW. You go to watch.troma.com and the first month is free. We got about a thousand movies, music videos, shorts, and comic books, and a few Tromette photographs available. And it's a good deal. It's a month for free, only $4.99 a month. But we took down all the movies from YouTube, because we hate them now.

CG: Yeah, well, yeah.

LK: But, our fans at least have a month to cruise Troma NOW for free and they can probably see an awful lot of stuff. And if they want to help us, if they want to keep forty-seven-year-old Troma and old Uncle Lloydie alive . . . the word of mouth is very good. We're getting subscribers every week, and it's a good system; but it's our only source of revenue right now.

CG: Well, for $4.99 . . . I mean, that's less than the cost of one rental for, as you pointed out, thousands of movies. So, with the first month free, so. . . . There'll be a link in the description of this YouTube video if you're watching this on YouTube. If you're listening: Troma NOW.

LK: Thanks, Chris.

CG: But, yeah, because it is the Halloween season, and we were talking before we started recording, Troma films: I mean, you can categorize some of them as horror films, I guess. Maybe that's a simple way. But Troma movies, to me, have never just been about what the surface level elements are. I mean, you can see a poster for a film like, say, *Poultrygeist*, right? And it's not a horror film involving a fast food chain, necessarily. I mean, that's part of it. I feel like the Troma films that.... And the reason Troma has continued and continues to be relevant is because the movies are not just about what the poster reveals.

There are elements underneath the surface for all the Troma movies, at least from *The Toxic Avenger*, to *Poultrygeist*, to, I haven't seen *#ShakespearesShitstorm* yet, but I am assuming there's elements in that. *Tromeo & Juliet* for sure. There's always some, you know, and it's not beat-you-over-the-head, right? Like what happens in a lot of your Hollywood Oscar movies, right? Like, there's a message, but it's sort of woven in kind of a fun way. Not in a sort of dogmatic, you know, pushing-it-on-you way. Can you talk about that a little bit? Because I feel like that's been a thread that's run from the time I discovered Troma, like in the eighties.

LK: My paternal grandmother, Grammy Kaufman, was a very left-wing person. And she infused in me a lot of her sort of countermainstream views, things when I was growing up, like Castro in Cuba is actually a hero. He has thrown out the corrupt dictators and the parasites at the casinos and the hookers, and he's giving everybody education and food. And she was against the Vietnam War. And, when I was in sixth grade, I remember coming to school and saying, you know, I don't think the Vietnam War such a good deal.

And, so, she was a big influence, and she used to send me subscriptions to *I.F. Stone's Weekly*, which was a socialist journal. Very entertaining, very good weekly stuff like that, and I believed it. And I, to this day, I, pretty much.... All the movies I've made, number one is to be entertaining, and then usually there are themes within that I've become obsessed with. In the case of *Poultrygeist*, we had a McDonald's that moved in next to the Troma building and they were very bad neighbors. And Gabe Friedman, who was working for us as editor, who you have met at TromaDance—

CG: I know Gabe.

LK: You were the moderator at, I think, the second or third TromaDance, thank you very much, which was in Park City, Utah, during Sundance. Not to.... The Sundance people weren't so happy. And we still do that, by the way. We still have TromaDance in New York City now. It's moved back, because it's sort of a serious film festival, but all free, still free. And, at any rate, we. . . . What was I talking about?

CG: Gabe Friedman.

LK: Yeah, Friedman gave me the book. I would never have read it. *Fast Food Nation*. And, wow! Wow! So, based on that and the fact that McDonald's was so nasty, and we had rats the size of raccoons weekending in our basement, we decided, "Let's make *Poultrygeist: Night of the Chicken Dead*!" Make it a kind of a. . . . I always liked musicals. I'd always wanted to do a musical, which *Poultrygeist* is not really; it's not a classical musical like *Oklahoma!*. But, it's great. It's all about the evils of the fast food industry, about the fact that we've exterminated millions of what are called "Indigenous Americans" or Native Americans. I call them Indians, of course, being uneducated, as you can see. And it's a great film. It's terrific.

And a lot of people think they only get . . . a lot of people only see the sex and violence. But, you see the underlying theme. *Toxic Avenger* was all about the environment long before Al Gore discovered the internet or *created* the internet or whatever he did and stole the Nobel Peace Prize from the deserving scientists who should have gotten it. Then, he'd never heard of "the environment." I think the first time he heard about the environment is when he kissed his big fat wife on national TV during the inauguration and everybody almost puked. That was the only environmental contamination he ever thought of. And he dumped her very soon. She was the one who wanted to tell us adults what kind of music we were supposed to listen to.[4] She [*cuts out briefly*] the whole big censoring. "Let's censor the music, because the American people aren't smart enough to choose music for themselves." And she didn't succeed, of course, thanks to Frank Zappa and Dee Snider and John Denver, who went down to Washington and bravely went against the McCarthyism of the Gores.

So, anyway, all our movies—the most recent *#ShakespearesShitstorm*—have two major themes but lots of smaller ones. One is that for the whole fifty years of my marriage to the commissioner, every morning we wake up and there are commercials for pills, Big Pharma, brainwashing. For three generations, that pills is the answer to everything. You've got a hangnail, take a pill. You've got a pimple, take a pill. You've got the rickets, take eight pills. And little children have been watching these commercials while they eat their Fruit Loops and become fat.

And we have a national problem. Both the problem of addiction with the opioids, because once the doctors stop giving you the little purple pill or whatever it is, then you go and get the opioids. And now we have a generation of . . . we have three generations of people who are obese and your children, my grandchildren are going to be paying for the diabetes pills. You know, more pills.

CG: Well, it's interesting. Like, you know, with Toxic Avenger, I mean, I noticed —

LK: Well, hold it, wait a minute. The other theme of *#ShakespearesShitstorm* probably is the more controversial: Is the "snowflakes," the social justice warriors who make their bones by destroying people online, that "Twitter hate." I'm not going to name any names, but we've all suffered. I've been almost canceled at least once and luckily James Gunn kind of helped me and the fans got me out of it. The fans went after these little shits.

CG: I do think, it's just . . . I find that strange, because people have tried to cancel me or *Film Threat* or whatever. I mean, we're pretty . . . I mean, we have a really diverse group of people who write for *Film Threat*. And by that I mean diverse in terms of opinion as well, you know? Right? Like, it's, I think it's important to represent all sorts of news. But yeah, I don't . . . I don't mind, like, people saying, "Hey," like, like, for example, "I don't like country music, but I'm not trying to shut country music down."

What's new that I've noticed is that people are trying to stop other people from doing things when it's just like, well, you can live and let live. And. . . . But what I've always loved about the Troma films is, while there is an environmental thread through the Toxic Avenger's movies, there's also, you know, it's also just a super-fun movie. It's a super . . . it's kind of a parody of a superhero movie. It also has that messaging. But the way that you weave in messaging is: there will be blood, guts, um, comedy, nudity—all, to me, healthy ingredients—along with a little political messaging. But not so much that if you're not, you know . . . you can just enjoy the movie.

It's entertaining first. I feel like there's one big box that's checked when you watch a Troma movie, and that is entertainment. There's other things that are there if you seek them out, but you don't even need to notice them because you'll have a good time. I'm just thinking of things like *Sgt. Kabukiman*, among others. And, also, I will say, I'm hoping through your website, you're still . . . I know you're still selling DVDs. You have some of the best DVD commentaries. One of my favorites was *Citizen Toxie*, when you just completely bullshit and lie, and you're just off the top of your head riffing, and you're saying like, you know, "Oh, that's Brad Pitt in that scene." And, like, I just . . . I feel like you're doing a commentary, like you think no one listens to them. I listen to your DVD commentary.

LK: Yeah.

CG: And they're hysterical. So, I would recommend, you know . . . look, sign up for the [*cuts out briefly*], but also get those DVDs, because the commentaries are hysterical. You weave in like really good film advice, and then you're just fucking with people in a way that, like, "Are they paying attention? I'm just going to check if they're paying attention."

LK: Good point. And we have full-length documentaries, for example, on *Return to Nuke 'Em High* and *Return to Return to Nuke 'Em High*, a two-disc

Blu-ray. Oh no, they're each separate Blu-rays, I'm sorry, but the documentary is called *2 Girls, 1 Duck*.[5] It's terrific. It's worth a year of film school. And *Poultrygeist*, the best one of those [BTS] documentaries is *Poultry in Motion: Truth Is Stranger Than Chicken*.

These documentaries, they're all on Troma NOW. And if you're a film student, watch them, because $80,000 a year for film school.... You can watch four or five of our ... I think we have six feature-length "making of" documentaries. And I don't, you know ... that, plus *Film Threat* the book[6] and, you know, [auto]biography of Charlie Chaplin and some of the great filmmakers: I think you got it. I don't know that you need film school.

CG: No, I agree. I think these days, really, if you're a voracious reader, I think the best education is: experience life and travel and get just some life experience under your belt, and then additionally just listen to DVD commentaries and read your book *Make Your Own Damn Movie!* I do want to, because I have you on now ... I do want to kind of corner you and ask you about *The Suicide Squad*. James Gunn ... you were in *Guardians of the Galaxy*. I hear that you might be in *The Suicide Squad*. Is this—

LK: Well, if, uh, Mr. Gunn doesn't cut me out like he did with *Seizure!* and, and he told me.... No, no! Not *Seizure!* That's Oliver Stone's movie.[7] He wanted me to be in the, put me in the trunk with Michael Caine, though, but I refused to get in the car trunk.[8] No, Oliver Stone started with me. No, Gunn cut me out of—

CG: *Slither*?

LK: *Slither*. If you look real hard, you'll see me in the police station. But I did a great improv, and the crew and the actors all laughed hysterically. But, it didn't really fit. So, that was that. But, wait till you see me in—assuming Mr. Gunn keeps it in—and Fred Raskin, who is his editor, also started with Troma[9] and was on *Tromeo & Juliet*.... So, hopefully Raskin will make sure that, you know, I stay in there. But, I ... I pledged by signature I wouldn't give any more information now. I think it's one of my best cameos. Let's put it that way.[10]

CG: Well, I hope ... I know that James Gunn ... I saw the panel he did on DC FanDome ... it was really cool to see him talk about it. It sounds like a lot of characters are going to die. If you get offed, I hope it's in a very interesting way. But don't [*cuts out briefly*].

LK: [*Laughing*] I want to get offed for real. I'm ready to go. I'm wondering: COVID is.... I learned this ... I didn't learn it, but I took lessons in third grade, sixth grade and I found this thing [*Lloyd presents the clarinet he was playing earlier*]. I haven't looked at for sixty years.

CG: Wow.

LK: So, I've been fooling around with it, but that's it. I'm totally depressed, miserable. Except for movies.

CG: Yeah.

LK: And reading and enjoying *Film Threat*.

CG: Oh, well, thank you. Thank you. It's . . . I will say this to add to your. . . . You know, we were saying about film school, if you go to storyblocks.com/filmthreat, they are the sponsor of the *Film Threat Podcast*, makes it possible for us to interview filmmakers and indie film legends like Lloyd Kaufman. Go to storyblocks.com/filmthreat. There's a million-plus pieces of—

LK: —Storyblocks—

CG: Storyblocks.com/filmthreat. It's like a stock footage company, but they also have other tools like music and special effects tools. It's, like, if you're a filmmaker, it's indispensable to use Storyblocks. We started using it, and then I approached them, like, "Hey, do you wanna sponsor this podcast?" So, I wanna make sure to get that in, because I try to weave in tips for indie filmmakers and people starting out, and they're a great sponsor of ours.

LK: That's a great idea. And we've got about a thousand movies we own or control, and most of them are nonunion. So, if they need explosions or things like that, we got a lot of them.

CG: Well, you might want to see, like, Storyblocks. You probably could license some of your footage to them. They have, like, this, you know . . . it's sort of—

LK: That's great. Sounds great.

CG: I will pass along the contact info I have at Storyblocks. But, Lloyd Kaufman, it's Halloween. And what are your top five Troma horror films that you should see that are on your Troma NOW platform. What do you think are your top five?

LK: Well, first of all, October is Tromaween. Tromaween. #Tromaween at Troma-Queens[11] in New York and the world famous Bel Aire Diner, which has installed a beautiful drive-in cinema in their parking lot. They're going to be showing Troma movies all month of October. Tromaween at the Bel Aire Diner in Queens. In terms of the movies that we have. . . . As I say, our movies are more like a Cuisinart, a mixture of genres.

CG: Right.

LK: I suppose, I think the best one, honestly, I wouldn't have picked it, but Eli Roth says that *Mother's Day*, which is my brother's movie, Charles Kaufman, is the best horror film he's seen. And I agree, it's beautifully written, it's perfectly . . . it's a masterpiece. It's just a rather . . . in its day, in 1980, a little bit ahead of its time. But, when it opened in New York: a full-page ad in the *New York Times*, which was pretty amazing. That's how times have changed.

So, I would put *Mother's Day* way at the top. And my brother, by the way, if you're in San Diego, he has a bakery and a bread factory that manufactures high-end bread, French bread, olive loaf, rye bread, and the best raw chocolate chip cookie dough. He has a cafe in San Diego on University Avenue.[12] Stop in, because also he keeps the negative to *Jakarta*,[13] a movie we made together, that he wrote and directed. Shot in Indonesia. It's terrific. He keeps the negative in with the cookie dough. So, if you go in there and order, "Give me an olive loaf with a six inches of *Jakarta* on the side," he'll get a kick out of it. He's got about four hundred people working there.

Mother's Day is going to be shown at the Bel Aire Diner in October. I think . . . I'm not sure what day it is, but I think it's the eighth. And it'll be shown with Troma's *Father's Day*, which is a wonderful film. But I would say *Mother's Day* first. *Def by Temptation*. I don't know if it was [*cuts out briefly*], but it's Samuel Jackson's first movie.[14] Again, I didn't direct it, but we financed it. I think those two are terrific.

Toxic Avenger, you know, was the, I guess, an obvious one. Again, it's not scary. It's more shocking and, you know, it stretches you in different directions. As a side, as a footnote, of the *Toxic Avengers*, I would prefer *Citizen Toxie*. I think that's the very, very best. Our friend-cousin Macon Blair has written a big-budget *Toxic Avenger*, a reimagining of *Toxic Avenger*, which is, I think the script is much better than the original *Toxic Avenger*. Legendary is hopefully producing it right now. They're on hiatus with a force majeure situation because of COVID. So, they sort of put it . . . they're not really doing much until COVID's over. But, hopefully they'll make a beautiful, Macon Blair–directed big, big, big-budget *Toxic Avenger*, and Uncle Lloydie will have plenty of cat tranquilizers to make him happy in his old age.

I also think that—again, these are only my own opinions—but I would say *Sgt. Kabukiman N.Y.P.D.* is probably our most—and tell me what you think, Chris—but, I think it's our most accessible. It's got the least amount of graphic sex and violence, and relies more on the . . . well, I don't know . . . it's got women's rights in it, where Lotus beats the crap out of Kabukiman before he becomes Kabukiman. It's got a lot of interesting themes in it; especially the fact that, in its day, Japan was buying a lot of American assets and there was a great hostility in this country to Japan, even in Congress. A congressman said that when Japan bought Rockefeller Center, one of the congressman said this is Pearl Harbor all over again. So, that got me thinking, and that's kind of where Kabukiman originated even though we had a Kabuki Boy in *Toxic Avenger Part II*.

Let's see. How many was that? Four?

CG: Yeah, we got *Mother's Day*, *Father's Day*, *Toxic Avenger*, *Citizen Toxie*, *Sgt. Kabukiman*. One more. I would say *Poultrygeist* is probably one of my favorite more recent—

LK: Recently, reviewers have said that *Poultrygeist* . . . I've seen more reviewers saying *Poultrygeist* is their favorite. But, what happens is very often the reviewers will say, you know, "*Poultrygeist*: very good movie, but didn't come close to *Terror Firmer* or close to *Class of Nuke 'Em High*," you know, "but it's good Troma." Anyone who's into Troma, they always say that. Although, recently I think *#ShakespearesShitstorm* is a bigger, better looking production, and I think it will emerge as what is considered my best, even though again we combine all the genres in each of our movies. At least the ones from *Toxic Avenger* on.

CG: Right, but it's almost like—

LK: [*Cuts out briefly*] movies were more slapstick raunchy like *Porky's*. We got ahead of, we came out ahead of *Porky's*, and so we did very well with *Squeeze Play!*, *Stuck On You!*, *First Turn-On!*, *Waitress!*, and we're making the Blu-rays now for them, and they're wonderful movies from the seventies and early eighties. They're great. They did very well until the major studios started to do the same thing, like *Porky's*.

CG: Right.

LK: So we'd [*cuts out briefly*].

CG: Yeah, I mean, there are just so many good ones. You know, I would add *Tromeo & Juliet* to that also. But, when you've got a thousand movies on your platform . . . I mean, it's hard to pick five. But, it's what I've always loved. It's like, you're right. It's not. . . . We were talking before about horror. It's like, yeah, there are horror elements in some Troma films, but Troma films are kind of like, in a way. . . . This is why I think you've used the word "Troma" in so many of the movies. It's just like, are they happening in Tromaville? "Troma" is like a thing like, you know, like Marvel has even said it; Kevin Feige[15] would speak about, like, they don't really make "superhero movies."

They include all the entertaining elements of a movie, you know: comedy, horror, drama, you know, action. It's, like. . . . And that's the thing, you know. I'm just realizing this now as I'm talking to you. Like, Troma movies have all those elements, especially I think *The Toxic Avenger* was kind of the first one that landed, at least . . .

I was in high school, and I saw it and just loved it, because it was funny and tragic and weird, and it was about a nerd that becomes a superhero and gets a hot girlfriend, and it sort of had all that stuff going on. But it's also got, like, this, you know, messaging in it. But not in a way that's, you know, hit-you-over-the-head. Like, Troma movies kind of like . . . they check all these boxes of basically one giant box, which is fun and entertainment.

LK: That's the formula we enjoy and even movies like *Nightbeast*, which we didn't make but it was made by Don Dohler in the good old days in the eighties. But, we're putting it out on Blu-ray. He deals with rape in a time when, you know . . . and he deals intelligently with it within a movie for which J. J. Abrams wrote the music,[16] and it's got some minor stars. But, it's a good movie and it's got some thought-provoking stuff in it. *Terror Firmer*, it reminds me, is one of our better ones. We've got a theme in there about the "self-affirming rape," which was a satire of NPR trying to teach us adults what to do. You know, like we don't know what to do.

CG: Wait, J. J. Abrams wrote the music for that movie?

LK: What's that?

CG: J. J. Abrams wrote the music for that one movie?

LK: Yes, yes he did.

CG: *Nightbeast*. Oh, wow.

LK: And if you look at *Lost*,[17] many people think that *Lost* was very much inspired by *Troma's War*, because of the set's mise en scène. *Troma's War* is a great one. Joe Bob [Briggs] had a big deal with it on, uh, his show *Last Drive-In*. It's great.

CG: I highly recommend that one, too. Uh, Lloyd Kaufman, I want to thank you for being on the *Film Threat Podcast*. You're a legend. You're a hero of mine, and I love that you still talk to me. And, so, I can't wait to see. . . . Also, I want to thank our sponsor Storyblocks. Go to storyblocks.com/filmthreat. I know we talked about earlier. But, Lloyd, I can't wait till this lockdown is over. I can't wait till there's a vaccine and we can walk amongst each other. And I'm looking forward to seeing you at a convention, hopefully San Diego in 2021. I'm just . . . Fingers crossed we'll be there. And, I just, I love you, Uncle Lloyd. Just thank you for being on the *Film Threat Podcast*.

LK: Well, thank you, Chris. You are the son I never had, but also always wanted. And, here: I can perhaps play you off with—

CG: Play me off!

LK: See if you can recognize what the song is.

CG: Okay.

[*Kaufman once again plays his clarinet*]

LK: Did you tell what that was supposed to—

CG: I can't. I'm—

LK: A very old song. You know, kind of Sinatra, Nelson Riddle, although that was more like Nelson Fiddle. "Birth of the Blues." "Birth of the Blues."

CG: "Birth of the Blues."

LK: We have the blues in 2020 with everything that's going on. Oh, my God: the debates, the fires, the guy in the White House who allegedly rapes people. Oh, my God. What a crazy period. Forced hysterectomies on the immigrants. It's not a Troma movie. It's real.

CG: I know. Like 2020 is a Troma movie. It's become stuff that's so ridiculous. You just, like, you know: murder hornets and just, like, what is this? What has this year become? It's crazy.

LK: It's a watershed year. But, we've.... If you go to my Instagram @LloydKaufman and my Twitter, we produced some PSAs to get you voting. We think this election could be very, very close. And your fans, my fans, independent underground artists, underdogs, you know, one hundred votes, one thousand votes could make the difference. So, my daughters said I should make some PSAs to get people to vote. And please check them out, and please, you know, retweet them or share them or whatever. They're... one is Troma-style with a beautiful Tromette, and the other one is with a little baby, a little three-year-old baby.

CG: Cool. Well, Lloyd, thank you so much for talking to us on the *Film Threat Podcast*.

Notes

1. A short, ten-minute documentary made in 2019 and still available on, ironically enough, YouTube.
2. Likely *Vegas in Space* (1991).
3. Pay-per-view Video On Demand.
4. He's of course speaking here of Tipper Gore and her cofounding of the PMRC (Parents Music Resource Center) in 1985, which, among other things, was responsible for the "Parental Advisory" labels on albums.
5. 2019 BTS (Behind-the-Scenes) documentary on the making of the final two *Nuke 'Em High* films.
6. Kaufman is being cheeky here; there is no "*Film Threat* book," per se; although Gore has published a number of film books and there have been compendiums of *Film Threat* published in book form, so to speak.
7. Stone's 1974 directorial debut; interesting to note that, as with early Troma sex comedies, the title is punctuated with an exclamation mark.
8. Kaufman may be speaking here, whether kidding or not, of Stone's 1981 *The Hand*, which stars Michael Caine; *Seizure!* (1974) does not feature Caine in any capacity.
9. Once again, Kaufman may be flubbing it up here a bit: Although Raskin, who went on to work with some of the biggest indie and mainstream directors in Hollywood, was indeed an apprentice editor on *Tromeo & Juliet* (1996), he had already worked on a few other films in the same role, most notably Paul Thomas Anderson's debut feature *Hard Eight* (1996).
10. Gunn and Raskin did end up keeping in a very brief, wordless cameo (of sorts) with Kaufman in *The Suicide Squad* (2021) in which Kaufman appears momentarily in the Corto Maltesian club where Task Force X encounters the Thinker.
11. "Regular" Queens, NY, but, you know, "Troma-fied."
12. Bread & Cie (350 University Ave).
13. 1988 film starring *Sex and the City* (1998–2004)'s Chris "Mr. Big" Noth.
14. As mentioned earlier in this book, though Kaufman frequently affirms this as truth, it very much is not.
15. Longtime president of Marvel Studios.
16. This is true, and more incredibly still, Abrams was a mere fifteen-year-old high school student at the time.
17. Cocreated by Abrams.

Troma Cofounder Lloyd Kaufman Tells Us What Disgusts Him in Movies

Danny Gallagher / 2022

From *Dallas Observer*, March 17, 2022, https://www.dallasobserver.com/arts/lloyd-kaufman-doesnt-hang-with-people-his-age-because-theyre-boring-as-fuck-13609191. Reprinted with permission.

It's hard to imagine a guy like Lloyd Kaufman being disgusted by anything. His Troma Films production company bathes in bodily fluids, cartoonish gore, and unapologetic humor.

Your view probably gets skewed when you've been a totally independent studio for forty-five years in the shadow of the Hollywood media machine.

"If you're going to go into the arts and even if you're a narcissist, and maybe I am a narcissist, you shouldn't be looking to make money," Kaufman says from his studio headquarters in New York. "I really believe that, fifty years from now, we're gonna look back on this era of the eighties, nineties, and two thousands as conspicuous consumption."

Every Troma movie follows the pathos of its founders Kaufman and Michael Herz, who make films on their own terms without marketing schemes or input from people who've never made a movie. There's no formula to Kaufman's filmmaking. He knows his audience and what they want to see on the screen. As a result, Troma has produced underground cinema classics such as: *Sgt. Kabukiman N.Y.P.D.*, *Class of Nuke 'Em High*, *Cannibal! The Musical*, and *The Toxic Avenger*—which is currently being rebooted with stars Peter Dinklage, Elijah Wood, and Kevin Bacon.

Kaufman's latest film *#ShakespearesShitstorm* marks his fifty years in filmmaking and calling out his industry and the world's bullshit by flinging as much of it as he can at his cast and the screen. In this instance, that's not just a metaphor.

"When I'm dead, the world will get it," Kaufman says. "For the time being, we're the last of the independent movie studios, the genuine cult movie studio whose fans are rabid. They totally make us look like a big corporation."

#ShakespearesShitstorm is a musical retelling of William Shakespeare's *The Tempest* in which Kaufman plays a modernized Prospero who's banished to the storied land of Tromaville for daring to challenge the greedy, Big Pharma executives for raking in millions over opioid addiction. However, instead of conjuring a storm of seawater, Kaufman's Prospero conjures a storm of whale shit to smite his shipwrecked enemies.

Kaufman is taking the movie on tour across Texas starting with The Texas Theatre this Saturday, followed by a live Q&A.

Kaufman says he's been wanting to tackle *The Tempest* since *Tromeo & Juliet*, the 1996 Troma black comedy hit he wrote with future filmmaking star James Gunn.

"I wanted to feel Prospero at his age, and I think I was seventy-four and I could feel Prospero," Kaufman says. "Of course, he was dead by the time he was seventy-four, but I understood what he was going through, that loss of power for one."

The title alone makes it hard for *#ShakespearesShitstorm* to get any festival play, except for an anchor screening at the Fantasia International Film Festival in Montreal and an upcoming screening at the Museum of the Moving Image in Queens. So, naturally, Kaufman is taking his latest epic comedy horror musical to Texas.

"It's unbelievable," he says. "Texas has a huge art community. I've been to places like the Deep Ellum Film Festival. I've hung out there at galleries. More people know me in the streets of Texas than New York City, to be honest."

Kaufman is the very definition of a showman with his trademark bowtie and boundless enthusiasm. His energy bleeds into every film he's made and produced.

"It's just to get people's attention and entertain them," Kaufman says. "I tend to gravitate towards younger people because older people my age are boring as fuck and the famous older people, they won't answer my calls. So, what are you gonna do? I painted myself into a corner with a lot of talented young people for fifty years."

Kaufman's contribution to cinema extends beyond the classic cult films that fans devour on VHS, DVD, and streaming services like Troma NOW. He and Herz also gave some of the film and TV industry's biggest names their first jobs: Samuel L. Jackson, J. J. Abrams, Oliver Stone, Marisa Tomei, and *South Park* creators Trey Parker and Matt Stone.

"The guy who runs The Texas Theatre [founder Barak Epstein] worked for us as an intern," Kaufman says. "He probably doesn't want people to know that, but he worked on *Citizen Toxie: The Toxic Avenger IV*."

The Clown and the Auteur

Mathew Klickstein / 2023

The following interview was conducted via phone between author Mathew Klickstein and Lloyd Kaufman on June 11, 2023, exclusively for this publication.

He knew now
Man, he really knew now!
But it was too late
And all he wanted was to make this crowd laugh
Well, they were laughing
But now he knew
— CHARLES MINGUS, "THE CLOWN"

Mathew Klickstein: Let's start with a simple one. This book is a series of past interviews with you. I've been going through them all, and it's clear you're always very available for these people who want to talk to you and pick your brain for as long as they need. Sometimes longer. You even talk about how available you are in your books in which you often give out your email for those who might want to contact you. Which begs the question: Do you enjoy being interviewed? Is this fun for you?

Lloyd Kaufman: Certainly. Being a professional narcissist, there's nothing I like better than talking about myself. But also, we don't have money for advertisements at Troma. And my partner Michael Herz refuses to go public personally with anything. He doesn't interact with the public. He doesn't want publicity for himself. So, as ugly as I am, I have to be the face of Troma.

MK: Despite Michael's aversion to being personally public, you keep purposely talking about him in your books, while mentioning how much he doesn't want you to do that.

LK: [*Laughs*] That's right. I do.

MK: I have to ask, in *All I Need to Know about Filmmaking I Learned from the Toxic Avenger*, you also keep talking about your editor on that project, Barry

Neville. How much of that was true? Is Barry Neville even a real person, or was that more of a narrative device or a way to seem extra irreverent—you essentially mocking your editor the whole time, while, Troma-style, breaking the fourth wall throughout?

LK: No, he was real! And every time he'd say something, I'd write it down or [coauthor] James [Gunn] would write it down, and we'd put it in the book. Like the paper shortage issue. Barry didn't want to use up too much paper on our book. "It has to be 353 pages," he kept saying, "because we don't want to use up too much paper on this." The paper was worth more than the book! We made it all sound funnier than it was, but anything we talked about with Barry Neville in the book probably really happened. Really good guy. In fact, we ended up putting him in *Terror Firmer*.

MK: I find in your interviews a fascinating dichotomy in that you make these movies involving so much graphic violence and sex, and you can of course be extremely vulgar in what you talk about with all these reporters speaking with you.... Yet, you also drop in so many references to extremely high-brow, sophisticated art filmmakers or European cinema—Stan Brakhage, Bergman, and their ilk. You're obviously a very educated, knowledgeable, and articulate person. How much would you say Troma—and you, by proxy, in these interviews—focuses on the "sex and violence" because it's provocative, compelling, and in many regards commercially viable, and how much is it because you personally really enjoy this kind of smutty, gallows humor posturing?

LK: I have to say that I like all of that stuff. A lot of it is aimed at younger, cutting-edge minds and audiences, too. At the same time, I enjoy interweaving political statements that may get our viewers and the readers of these articles to think a little bit outside of just the naked men and women in my movies or some of the shit talk I'm spouting out in these pieces you're talking about.

MK: "A spoonful of sugar helps the medicine go down"?

LK: Right. I can make some important points about how fucked up everything is in our world on a very important level through saying a lot of the crazy things I say in these interviews. Just as we do the same thing in our movies filled with people getting their heads getting chopped off. Meanwhile, yes, all of our Troma movies are informed by all the top directors. Take Toxie and [love interest] Sarah, the blind girl. That's Chaplin's *City Lights*. Tromaville is also very much Preston Sturges's fond satire of American villages. In *Troma's War*, there's quite a bit of Sam Fuller and Robert Aldritch. The opening of *Terror Firmer* is supposed to be a tribute to Fritz Lang's Glen Ford movie *The Big Heat*. I could go on and on.

MK: Would you say you're parodying these films, or are you actually trying to emulate them?

LK: They really are tributes. For example again, I use the song "Shall We Gather at the River" quite a bit, because that was a big theme in many John Ford movies. I do that because I love John Ford and I love that hymn. Truly.

MK: What would you say to those who would think you're totally fully of shit right now? You're talking about John Ford and Charlie Chaplin, and meanwhile you're making films where people's heads aren't just getting chopped off—they're getting smashed by car tires and pulverized by slime-covered mutants.

LK: All I can tell you is that the Museum of Modern Art showed *Tromeo & Juliet* in their Shakespeare series. It took them thirty years, but they did it. And they also played the world premiere of *Return to Nuke 'Em High Volume 1*, which is an LGBT movie . . . that is also filled with the head crushings and all that. And then the Museum of Moving Image played the world premiere of *#ShakespearesShitstorm*. How do you judge art? It seems our fans like us, and so do museums. In fact, most of the theaters we do get into these days are art house theaters.

MK: A lot of this makes sense, actually, considering many of the filmmakers you talk about having so much admiration for in your interviews tended to have much more acclaim in artistic circles in Europe than in mainstream audiences back here in the States.

LK: Take Jerry Lewis who was in the pantheon of the underground the way that we've been decades later. We all know how much he was beloved in France, and that's true for us, too. They've really understood our movies, and the Cinéma Français has done several "seasons of Troma." So, they get it. Japan gets it. But, we still don't have distribution in many countries, even though we have a lot of fans thanks to bootlegging and people passing around our films all over the world. We also had so many festivals around Europe selecting and promoting our movies. Spain, Italy, as well as Portugal and all over Scandinavia.

That was a while ago, though, back when they would get government subsidies so they could select movies like ours that were truly independent. Now, unfortunately, the economics are not so good, so they have to rely on advertising from the studios who now subsidize what they're doing instead. It becomes sponsorship from the big studios, and that impacts what movies these festivals are showing now. They're more likely now to play so-called independent movies from Fox Searchlight and HBO. That's not really independent. Even Tribeca now plays these $200 million films as their opening features.

MK: That's definitely been going on for years now, where you have these festivals like Sundance that have basically become marketing posts for films that are already ready to go and don't really need the publicity the way true indie pictures need who don't have that same studio, network, or streaming support the way true indies like you guys truly need.

LK: Yes, my daughter is now finishing a documentary called *Occupy Cannes* all about how Troma was policed out of the festival after supporting the Cannes Film Festival for fifty years. It'll be a great film but doesn't exactly show Cannes in a nice light.

MK: Yeah, what the hell is the new Indiana Jones movie doing there right now?

LK: Well, nobody knows about it, so they need the publicity. [*Laughs*] The filmmakers really need some more exposure.

MK: All joking aside, here you go again—Going back through all of your interviews over the years, you've never pulled back from being brutally, balls-out honest in what you're talking about, even when it comes to naming names and speaking very specifically about those you deem as heroes and villains of the film, media, and political communities.

This hasn't just been recent for you, is what blows my mind. Even in the beginning before Troma and you had something of a cachet, you spoke your mind without any filter at all. You just came right out of the gate talking about "the system" and Hollywood and what you always call "the elites" as soon as you started being interviewed, going all the way back to your earliest, earliest days. That was really shocking to me to see in print. These weren't simply words of a long-time, jaded filmmaker who had been in it for decades. You were like that in the very beginning, back when you were still in your twenties!

LK: [*Laughs*] I think a lot of that was because of Grammy Kaufman. My grandma wasn't a Communist, but she was pretty close to it. And she gave me stuff to read from the time I was very young about people like Castro and anti-Vietnam [War] literature. She supported [activist] David Dellinger and Scott Neering who was a professor at the University of Pennsylvania who got kicked out and blacklisted; many of the kind of agitators of the fifties and sixties. She'd get me to read *I. F. Stone's Weekly*. She'd explain why the war was bullshit. And she gave me a book to read, *Brave New World*, which was not the book you're thinking of—It was about how great China and Mao were, entering a "brave new world." Anticapitalist and all of that. [*Laughs*] I was so young! Probably read it before I read the "real" *Brave New World*.

MK: Let's move on to some of the more entertaining aspects of how you position yourself and Troma. You have this very carnival barker type of strategy, with the bowties and the brightly colored striped suits. It's so clear what a great performer you are in the interviews you do. You do it very well. But I can't help but feel that many of the people talking with you are kind of goading you on a little bit, and you react in kind by playing the part, so to speak, of the "wacky Troma president and filmmaker." Can you talk about that and how, for instance, your wife Pat has said in the past that you're not really like that in your everyday, domestic life?

LK: Dressing up as a clown is an act to get attention. Wearing a tie, jacket, suit or whatever, I want to respect the film festival or interviewer, too. In the old days, the director would often wear a jacket and suit on set. I never did that, but I thought about it quite a bit. Show respect for the crew, too.

MK: Your typical outfit almost has a kind of Henny Youngman meets used car salesman quality. Like an old vaudevillian or Borscht Belt comic. When I watch some of the videos of your interviews or when I've seen you at signings and other promotional events, I almost feel like you're going to break out with an accordion and a monkey at some point. How did you develop this uniform of a sort over the years?

LK: A lot of it comes from my father. He had a great sense of humor, was genuinely funny. I don't know that I'm genuinely funny myself. Really, though, it can be an Achilles heel for me, because all of my movies are comedies, and comedies don't work universally. They're the most difficult medium. My father used to tell me that a lot, how ill-advised I was to keep making comedies. What's funny in Ohio is not always funny in Rome. Also, it's very hard to make people laugh. You can even watch some of the great classic comedies of the twenties and thirties, and some of them are hilarious, but others are too timely and don't really work anymore, if they ever did.

But, I have been very proud of the fact that our movies have a certain timelessness. Look at something like *Squeeze Play!*, which people are really only now starting to rediscover. It's a very funny film and has a very good theme to it, namely the underdog quality of women and the ERA, even though it was a raunchy movie about softball with balls getting hit in people's butts and sex and goofy slapstick. Very entertaining, yet still making an important point. I mean, women still are the underdogs today, almost fifty years after that movie came out.

I guess everything we do is about underdogs, though. Take *Return to Nuke 'Em High*, with the two lesbians who are underdogs in that movie—and yet it's still a funny movie today. And I imagine it'll be funny in twenty years. So, who knows. I guess maybe it really does come down to the old Frank Capra quote of him saying that the best causes worth fighting for are the hopeless causes.

MK: Similarly, you in your interviews and certainly in your films are always especially agnostic about the way you attack and mock all sides—the soi-disant right, left, and in between—of so many political angles and issues. You're exceptionally even-handed in how you dole out the satiric jabs, very much like *South Park*, created by one of your protégés, Trey Parker.

LK: That was why I loved *Cannibal! The Musical* right away when I first saw it. It still needed to be finished—they had to shoot a more "Troma-esque" opening before we could really take it on, but they did that and we've loved everything Trey and Matt have done ever since, always seeing a bit of Troma in their future projects, too. They're able to get away with a lot more than we do, though, because *South Park* is animated, and our projects are live-action. Even though you may see [*South Park* regular] Kenny getting his arms ripped off the way you might in some of our films.

MK: Even as a kid, when I was growing up with Troma movies on the USA Network and TNT evening programming—*Up All Night with Rhonda Shear*, and Joe Bob Briggs's show, etc.—I could tell that you guys were doing something that was very forward-thinking. And nowadays, these many years later, it does indeed seem Troma's motto, "Movies of the Future," has been vindicated. So many of the films you've made are not only timeless but have proven to be extremely prescient in content, style, and agenda. This includes your pioneering takes on environmentalism in films, vegetarianism, and the fact you guys really were the first to kick off the "sex comedy" craze of the eighties, well before *Porky's* and *Revenge of the Nerds*.

LK: It's amazing, isn't it? Take the guys who made the *Deadpool* movies: There's no question they were greatly inspired by *The Toxic Avenger*. They've talked about it quite a bit in the past. And of course we've got our own James Gunn out there continuing to make movies that are very "Troma-ish." There's that new movie that just came out, *Renfield*, and they have two scenes that are exact copies from *Citizen Toxie*. The *New York Times* way-back-when said the filmmakers behind *RoboCop* clearly looked at *The Toxic Avenger*, too.

MK: What do you think changed for Troma? There was a point, as you've said numerous times before, when you guys were making some decent money, or at least would get your investors paid back or could get enough money to make more films more quickly. When did that change to how it's become for you over the past few years where it's nearly impossible to get funding for a Troma film?

LK: Well, I think it really started up right as we began breaking out, ironically enough. When Reagan became president in the eighties, he got rid of the consent decree of 1948.[1] This meant, among other things, that studios could now own theaters again the way they did before 1948. This also led to the theaters all merging into an extremely small handful of chains. Which was not, in the long run, very smart. Because, today, they're all going bankrupt. Oligopoly doesn't work. You need competition to create innovation. And the Powers That Be don't want competition.

We've always seen this whenever there's any new technology. The oligopolies want to screw it all up unless or until they can take it over. Which is what they've always done and which is what they're doing now with AI. What they've done with the internet. Look what happened with Blockbuster—they took over the video market, they got rid of all competition, there was no longer any innovation, and the people running it couldn't keep it going, and it went out of business. And it took down the entire video market, which independents like us—real independents—needed to keep us afloat. We lost the independent theaters, we lost the video market, and now we can barely even play in the online world.

Streaming? Forget about it. They don't want us, but they're in charge, so they can do whatever they want. Which makes life very difficult for Troma and all the other true independents like us. Look at airlines: no competition, so there's no amenities and no innovation. The experience has become horrible. No one likes to fly anymore. But then you look at hotels, and there's plenty of competition there, so they have to innovate with better and better comforts and amenities and innovation to get people to come to their locations over all the other ones that exist. There it is right there.

MK: What you've said here about streaming services and the internet is interesting, I think, because a lot of people would believe these online portals and opportunities would be a big help to companies like Troma.

LK: Well, without a doubt, streaming has been helpful to us in some ways, actually. We have our own streaming service, of course—Troma NOW—which is small but is working. It's probably the only profitable streaming service on the face of the globe. And it's great, too! No advertising aside from me being a clown. Lots and lots of great movies, too. Even movies we've been acquiring like Robert Downey Sr.'s *Putney Swope*, and *Dynamite Chicken* with the guy who burned himself up—

MK: Richard Pryor?

LK: Yes! Hilarious guy. It's a terrific film. And also all these films by new people, all the James Gunn's of the future. Like Mercedes [The] Muse's very feminist, experimental, and crazy movie *Divide & Conquer*. Men will be shocked, but women will understand. It's a wonderful film. There's all sorts of great stuff we've been getting, not to mention all of our own classics. All of this without any advertising aside from me doing my little videos and live events, and word-of-mouth through our fans. So, yes, the streaming has helped us, without a doubt. It's helped us to connect and reconnect with those people who may not know who we are or watched us maybe when they were younger and are now coming back to remembering all of our great movies that have also influenced, as you've been saying and as we know, so many of the current generations of filmmakers, too.

MK: This is actually something I was talking with your assistant Garrett about when we were all together at our book signing[2] a few weeks ago: It's the idea that John Cassavetes used to say that everyone wanted to make movies like him, but nobody wanted to help him make more movies. You had something similar going on with Kubrick, too. Everyone respected him and wanted to emulate him, and yet he had so much trouble toward the end making the movies he wanted to make.

With you, we have now an entire generation—or maybe two or even three at this point—of extremely successful filmmakers who say they got their start with Troma or were greatly inspired by Troma films . . . and yet, if we're being honest, a lot of the general public would have no idea who you are or even what Troma is. How do you reconcile this dichotomy?

LK: That's a very good point. [*Laughs*] I don't really know what to say. The problem is we've never been able to advertise, so we just end up getting steamrolled. It's very unfair. Especially when it comes to certain filmmakers who go so far as to trade on our name or who are blatantly ripping us off. They know they can get away with it, because people know who they are and don't know who we are. And the other problem too is that our movies don't make any money anyway, because we're economically blacklisted. There's no way for us to get deals on Amazon and those kinds of places. Those streaming services are worse than terrible. Or they want to censor us. So, there's no money to be made there. Netflix and all that stuff.

If I direct a movie and I go there with a suitcase full of merch like Willy Loman, they'll play the movie maybe. But only for one or two nights. In New York, maybe we get a couple of weeks. In LA, maybe a couple of weeks. But the rest of the country? Maybe one or two nights or a midnight screening or something. I enjoy meeting the fans and all that, but I'm seventy-seven years old and it's getting to be a bit much. I can't keep carrying everything all over the place anymore!

We're just not making any money, which means I can't tell people that if they put their money into Troma you'll make money. Twenty years ago, our movies would make money—quite a bit of money, or the worst that would happen would be that after two years, there'd be a small profit at least. Today, though, you invest in Troma, and you'll lose money. As good as they are—and they're even better today than ever! Take *#ShakespearesShitstorm*.

My wife and I had to put up all the money for it ourselves—with a little help from a company called Bad Dragon, which I suppose you could call the "General Motors of dildos." They paid for about 15 percent of the film, really as patrons, as fans. But we haven't been able to make any money off of it yet. Nothing. Nobody wants it. We only got it in one film festival, but they weren't able to get any media traction on it namely because of the title. And the Museum of Modern Art didn't want it due to the content, which was too much for them this time around. And it's a shame, because it really is my best movie yet, and my most personal. People will get it in twenty-five or thirty years. But, I won't be around by then!

MK: Dour! Can't you leave us with some light at the end of the tunnel here for what may very well be your last interview ever since you're edging so very close to, as you often say, making a sound like a frog?

LK: Look, Troma has a life of its own. And Michael Herz is younger, too. As I become more infirm and demented, he's in great physical and mental shape. So, I think it has a fair amount of time ahead under his leadership. But the company has got some very valuable properties that in the right hands could make quite a bit of money. *Sgt. Kabukiman* has already been optioned twice by Legendary to become a series; people all over the place want to do things with *Poultrygeist*.

With some money behind it, the Troma brand name could be very, very successful. It's worldwide known. You can look at my Twitter feed, and people think we're doing great! Troma does have a life of its own. And then there's the fact that, though I've urged her not to, my oldest daughter has been considering taking the reins once my two grand-monsters get past high school. Which won't be too long.

Notes

1. As ruled by the landmark Supreme Court case *United States v. Paramount Pictures Inc.*, the consent decree essentially broke up the monopolies major studies had over the entirety of the Hollywood film system, disallowing ownership of theaters by studios (for example) and creating other crucial policies that would allow not only more independent fare but foreign films to be exhibited and marketed more easily in the United States. Indeed, the ruling is also known as "Hollywood Antitrust Case of 1948." This was systematically reversed by President Ronald Reagan and, later, by President Bill Clinton during their respective tenures, particularly via Clinton's Telecommunications Act of 1996.
2. Kaufman took part in Klickstein's 2022 book *See You at San Diego: An Oral History of Comic-Con, Fandom, and the Triumph of Geek Culture*.

Index

Abrams, Simon, "Troma's Lloyd Kaufman: 'I Hope the MPAA Burns in Hell,'" 115–19

Academy Awards, xxxv, 6, 10, 46, 54, 57, 63, 79, 91, 102, 108, 139, 164; Oscar winners, 16, 86, 91, 102, 114, 129

Accomando, Beth, "Produce Your Own Damn Movie!," 86–94

AFMA. *See* American Film Market Association (AFMA)

All I Need to Know about Filmmaking I Learned from the Toxic Avenger, 36, 101, 155

American Film Market (AFM), 31, 86–87, 91–92

American Film Market Association (AFMA), xxi, xxxv–xxxvi, 30–31, 87; "Lloyd Kaufman Chides AFMA on Press Freedom," 30–31

Angry Video Game Nerd, The. *See* Rolfe, James

Battle of Love's Return, The (1971), xxviii, xli, 33, 78, 90, 141

Bell, Aaron, "Kaufman Brings His Mutants to Life in Tromaville," 32–34

Bush, George W., 53, 56, 73–74, 79, 133

Cannes Film Festival, xxv, xxviii, xxxv, xxxvi, xxxixn4, 10–11, 14–15, 32, 44, 106, 126, 130, 139, 154, 156, 178

Cannibal! The Musical, xxxiii, 33, 68, 74, 89, 90, 96, 97, 109, 137, 156, 173, 179

Carli, Vitorrio, "Lloyd Kaufman Interview," 55–58

Carroll, David, "Holy Shit! What Is All This Green Stuff?," 20–29

Chaplin, Charlie, xvi, xix, 20, 37, 49, 56, 80, 117, 167, 176, 177

Citizen Toxie: The Toxic Avenger Part IV (2000), xvi, xxxixn2, xlviii, 36, 39, 41–42, 44, 57, 71, 97, 115, 117, 121, 151–52, 154, 157, 166, 169, 174, 180; working title *The Toxic Avenger Part IV: Mr. Toxie Goes to Washington*, 28

Class of Nuke 'Em High (1986), xxxii, xliv, 12, 14–15, 17, 21–22, 24, 41, 55, 61, 71, 74, 86, 104, 115–16, 153, 170, 173

Class of Nuke 'Em High Part 2: Subhumanoid Meltdown, 24

Class of Nuke 'Em High Part 3: The Good, the Bad and the Subhumanoid (1994), xxxiii, 21, 23–24, 63

Corman, Roger, xxiv–xxv, xxxii, 22, 42, 52, 55–56; New World Cinema, 59, 70, 91, 128, 135, 156

Costner, Kevin, 18, 19n1, 26, 28, 32, 33, 57, 90, 100, 123

COVID, 163, 167, 169; COVID-time, xii

Dinklage, Peter, xxxi, xxxviii, 173

Direct Your Own Damn Movie! (2008), xxxv, 87, 92, 100

INDEX

Disney, xxxi, xxxviii, 49–50, 68, 97–98, 116, 156; Disneyland, 44; Euro Disney/Disneyland Paris, 31n3

Dobbs, Sarah, "The Den of Geek Interview: Lloyd Kaufman," 66–73

Dowling, Neil, "A Tale of Two Toxies!," 51–54

Fat Guy Goes Nutzoid (1986), 15–16, 32

First Turn-On!, The (1983), xliii, 6, 8, 33, 35, 38, 60, 90, 123, 170

Ford, John, xxiii, 20, 37, 59, 80, 117, 128, 137, 150, 177

Fortune, Drew, "Deep in the Bowels of Tromaville with Lloyd Kaufman," 126–29

Friedman, Gabriel, xlviii, xlix, li, 151, 164–65

Gallagher, Danny, "Troma Cofounder Lloyd Kaufman Tells Us What Disgusts Him in Movies," 173–74

Girl Who Returned, The (1969), xxvii, xxxv, xli, 37, 41, 79, 150

Gore, Chris, "Lloyd Kaufman's Top Five Troma Films of All Time," xii, 160–72

Gunn, James, xxxiv, xxxv, xxxviii, xlvii, 58, 62, 66, 69, 71, 75, 92, 101, 115–16, 118, 120, 123, 125, 129, 132, 149, 153, 155–56, 166–67, 174, 176, 180–81

Haanen, Roel, "Anything I So Desire," xxvin10, 41–50

Herz, Michael, xvi, xviii, xxvii, xxix, xxx, xxxv, xlii, xliii, xliv, xlv, xlvi, xlvii, xlviii, xlix, l, li, 3–5, 10–13, 18, 20, 23–26, 28, 33, 35–36, 47–48, 51–52, 56–57, 90, 93, 100–101, 105, 109, 111, 113, 115–16, 121, 124, 126–27, 142, 149–50, 152–53, 173–75, 183

Jackson, Peter, 56, 61, 74–75, 78, 105

Jackson, Samuel L., 33, 90, 123, 129, 149, 169, 174

Jeremy, Ron, xlviii, xlix, l, 57, 75, 83–84

Kaufman, Lloyd: chronology and filmography, ix–xl, xli–li, 3–10, 12, 14–28, 30–33, 35–93; "Lloyd Kaufman Chides AFMA on Press Freedom," 30–31; "Lloyd Kaufman on *Squeeze Play!*," 113–14; "Lloyd Kaufman's San Diego Comic-Con 2009 Roast Retort," 82–85; quoted, 20–29, 30–33, 35–93

Kaufman, Patricia Swinney, xvi–xvii, xix, xxxi, xxxiii, xlix, li, 35, 121, 147, 149, 152, 155, 157, 178

Kleinfield, N. R., "Filmmakers: Cecil B. in a West Side Walk Up," 3–5

Klickstein, Mathew, "The Clown and the Auteur," 175–83

Lanford, Jill J., "TROMA Films: They're Not Art, but They Make Money," 6–9

Lloyd, Uncle, xix, 125, 137, 147, 154, 160, 171. *See also* Lloydie, Uncle

Lloydie, Uncle, 134, 154, 163, 169. *See also* Kaufman, Lloyd; Lloyd, Uncle

MacDonald, James W., xxiii; "The Art of Trash: Evaluating Troma Entertainment as Paracinema," xxvni, 59–65

Make Your Own Damn Movie! (2003), xxxv, xxxixn11, 71, 75, 87, 92, 96, 98, 100, 121, 135, 161, 167

Mathews, Jack, xxi; "Cannes 87: Mayhem, Toxic Waste—The Fun Side of Cannes," 14–16

Miramax, xxxi, 49, 68, 72, 98

Motion Picture Association of America (MPAA), 25, 72, 97, 103–4, 107, 114–16, 157

MPAA. *See* Motion Picture Association of America

net neutrality, 68, 72, 73n3, 97, 107, 134, 135

New York Times, xxx, 10, 17, 78, 98, 111, 118, 122, 127, 153, 157, 168, 180

INDEX

O'Neal, Sean, "Lloyd Kaufman," 74–81
Oscars. *See* Academy Awards

Pariseau, Leslie, xix; "Troma: A Love Story," 146–59
Peary, Gerald, xxiii
Poultrygeist: Night of the Chicken Dead (2006), x, xxv, xxxvii, xlix, 55, 58, 62, 67, 69, 74–77, 79, 86, 89, 96, 104–5, 111, 115, 117, 128, 151, 154, 158, 164–65, 169, 170, 183
Produce Your Own Damn Movie! (2009), xxxv, 86–93, 100

Raskin, Fred, 156, 167, 172nn9–10
Reilly, Patrick, "Savage Movies Don't Bloody Investors in Troma's Schlock," 10–13
Return to Nuke 'Em High Volume 1 (2013), xxxvii, l, 101, 104–6, 115, 121, 122–25, 152, 166, 177
Return to Return to Nuke 'Em High AKA Volume 2 (2017), xxxviii, l, 125–27, 130, 140, 152, 166
Rolfe, James, xviii–xxi; "Lloyd Kaufman Interview with James Rolfe," 100–112
Romeo and Juliet, xxxiv, 76, 154
Roth, Eli, 62, 66, 69, 71, 92, 123, 125, 129, 149, 168

Sakmann, Doug, xxiii, xxv, xlviii, l–li; "Troma Entertainment: Movies of the Future!," 35–40
Schlosser, Eric, ix, xxxvi, 75
Sell Your Own Damn Movie! (2011), xxxv, 100
Sgt. Kabukiman N.Y.P.D. (1990), xxv, xxxii, xxxiii, xxxixn10, xlvi, xlvii, xlix, 20–24, 28, 32, 39, 55, 57, 60–61, 64, 71, 74, 110, 117, 122, 144, 153, 160, 166, 169, 183
Shakespeare, William, x, xxxvii, li, 22, 43–44, 53, 75–76, 86, 137, 141, 153, 163,

174, 177; "To thine own self be true" (*Hamlet* 1.3.78–80), x, 22, 40, 62, 80–81, 93, 108, 125, 158
#ShakespearesShitstorm (2020), x, xii, xxv, li, 137, 141, 146–47, 159, 162–66, 170, 173–74, 177, 182
Smith, Andrew, "Green on the Screen," 17–19
Snider, Dee, 127, 165
South Park, x, xii, xxxiii, xxxixn11, 33, 55, 68, 74, 75, 89, 90, 102, 109, 115, 127, 129, 153, 156, 174, 180
Spielberg, Steven, 91, 122
Squeeze Play! (1979), xxx, xlii, 3–6, 11, 27, 29n10, 35, 41, 44, 53, 60–61, 78–79, 101, 109, 112, 113, 114, 139, 150, 170, 179
Stone, Matt, x, xxxiii, 55, 66, 75, 90, 95, 109, 115, 127, 149, 156, 174; *Orgazmo*, 154
Stone, Oliver, xv, xxviii, xli, 17, 28, 33, 55, 74, 78, 86, 90, 123, 129, 141, 149, 167, 174
Stuck On You! (1982), xliii, 6, 35, 41, 56, 60, 79, 109, 136, 140, 170
Sugar Cookies (1973), xxviii, 14, 35, 109, 138, 141
Sum, Ed, "Getting Tromatized with Lloyd Kaufman, an Interview," 120–25
Surf Nazis Must Die, 14, 16–17, 27, 32
Sundance Film Festival, xxxiii, xxxiv, 49–50, 53, 69, 95, 156–57, 164, 177

Terror Firmer (1999), xiv, xvi, xvii, xviii, xxxv, xlvii, 37–39, 42, 45–47, 53, 55, 63–64, 90, 115, 117, 135–36, 154, 170–71, 176
Trump, Donald, 134, 140, 153, 158
Toxic Avenger (character): creation of, 18, 36–37, 150; description of, 15, 36, 101, 150, 152; in Marvel, 70; mask, 72, 82; mentions of, xii, xxxv, 14, 46, 50, 53, 56, 61, 71, 92, 132, 166

Toxic Avenger (franchise), 74, 120; merchandise, 121, 124

Toxic Avenger, The (1984), xv, xxv, xxix, xxxi, xliv, 10, 15, 17, 21–23, 26, 33–34, 36, 38, 41–42, 53, 55–57, 60–61, 70–71, 75, 79, 98, 102–3, 114–15, 116–17, 123, 127, 150–53, 158, 160, 164–66, 169–70; influence of, 180; reception of, 44, 78, 151; remake, 129, 136, 169

Toxic Avenger and Other Tromatic Tales, The (2007), xxxvi, 69

Toxic Avenger Part II, The (1989), xlv, 36, 57, 110, 117, 122, 155, 169,

Toxic Avenger Part III: The Last Temptation of Toxie, The (1989), xlvi, 36, 63; live action film, xxxiv; NES game, 103

Toxic Avenger Part IV, The. See *Citizen Toxie: The Toxic Avenger Part IV* (2000)

Toxic Avenger Part V, The, xvi, 92, 98, 124

Toxic Avenger: The Musical (2008), xxxi, xxxvi, 76, 102–3, 124, 151

Toxic Avenger: The Novel, The (2006), xxxi, xxxv

Toxic Crusaders, The (1990), xxxii, 70, 102–3, 136; Time Warner, 51, 58, 72, 76–77

Tomei, Marissa, 22, 149, 174

TromaDance Film Festival, xxxiv, xxxvi, xxxvii, 49, 53, 69, 95–96, 98, 144, 156–57, 164

Tromaville, xx, 15, 32, 39, 46, 56, 61, 86, 92, 100, 113, 126, 130, 137, 143, 148–49, 151–52, 154, 159, 170, 174, 176; Battle for Tromaville, xxxii; reference to *South Park* as part of, 127; *The Tromaville Café* (1997), xxxiv, xln18; Troma Central, 120; Tromaville Health Club, 36; Tromaville high school, 153; Tromaville Hospital, 134

Troma's War (1988), xxxi, xliv, 17, 25, 42, 45, 61, 115, 116–17, 152–53, 171, 176

Tromaween, 168

Tromeo & Juliet (1996), x, xxx, xxxiv, xxxvii, xln18, xlvii, 28, 32–33, 42–44, 56, 58, 60, 62, 75, 105, 115–16, 122–23, 137, 153–54, 163–64, 167, 170

Tromette, 129, 163, 172

van Gogh, Vincent, xviii, 49, 88, 110

Waitress! (1982), xlii, 4, 7, 56, 111, 150, 157

Warhol, Andy, xxi, xxviii, 59, 64, 74, 79–80, 107, 117; Warholesque, xxvii

Warner Bros., 21, 68, 116, 157

Yale University, xv, xxvii, 18, 20, 100, 126, 127; Yale Film Society, xxviii, 79–80

YouTube, xxxvii, 68, 100, 108–9, 117, 120, 122, 133, 135, 136, 139, 143–44, 156, 160–61, 162–64

Zappa, Frank, 127, 165

Ziegler, Robert, "Lloyd Kaufman Interview," 95–99

About the Editor

Mathew Klickstein is a longtime multiplatform storyteller who typically traffics in book publishing, reportage, filmmaking, playwriting, comic book/graphic novel creation, ghostwriting, guest lecturing, and podcasting. His work tends to focus on nonfiction, primary-source pop culture histories including those chronicling such high-profile institutions as the Nickelodeon network, *The Simpsons*, and Comic-Con. His work, credits, and clips can be seen at www.mathewklickstein.com.